Transnational Penal Cultures

Focusing on three key stages of the criminal justice process, discipline, punishment and desistance, and incorporating case studies from Asia, the Americas, Europe, Africa and Australia, the thirteen chapters in this collection are based on exciting new research that explores the evolution and adaptation of criminal justice and penal systems, largely from the early nineteenth century to the present. They range across the disciplinary boundaries of History, Criminology, Law and Penology.

Journeying into and unlocking different national and international penal archives, and drawing on diverse analytical approaches, the chapters forge new connections between historical and contemporary issues in crime, prisons, policing and penal cultures, and challenge traditional Western democratic historiographies of crime and punishment and categorisations of offenders, police and ex-offenders.

The individual chapters provide new perspectives on race, gender, class, urban space, surveillance, policing, prisonisation and defiance, and will be essential reading for academics and students engaged in the study of criminal justice, law, police, transportation, slavery, offenders and desistance from crime.

Vivien Miller is Associate Professor of American and Canadian Studies at the University of Nottingham. She is the author of *Hard Labor and Hard Time: Florida's 'Sunshine Prison' and Chain Gangs* (2012) and *Crime, Violence and Sexual Clemency: Florida's Pardon Board and Penal System in the Progressive Era* (2000), and co-editor of *Cross-Cultural Connections in Crime Fictions* (2012). She is currently working on capital punishment in the pre-1972 United States.

James Campbell is Lecturer in American History at the University of Leicester. He is the author of *Slavery on Trial: Race, Class and Criminal Justice in Antebellum Richmond, Virginia* (2007) and *Crime and Punishment in African American History* (2012). He is currently working on a study of the death penalty in twentieth-century Jamaica.

Routledge SOLON Explorations in Crime and Criminal Justice Histories
Edited by Kim Stevenson, University of Plymouth, Judith Rowbotham, Nottingham Trent University and David Nash, Oxford Brookes University

This series is a collaboration between Routledge and the SOLON consortium (promoting studies in law, crime and history), to present cutting edge interdisciplinary research in crime and criminal justice history, through monographs and thematic collected editions which reflect on key issues and dilemmas in criminology and socio-legal studies by locating them within a historical dimension. The emphasis here is on inspiring use of historical and historiographical methodological approaches to the contextualising and understanding of current priorities and problems. This series aims to highlight the best, most innovative interdisciplinary work from both new and established scholars in the field, through focusing on the enduring historical resonances to current core criminological and socio-legal issues.

1. Shame, Blame and Culpability
Crime and violence in the modern state
Edited by Judith Rowbotham, Marianna Muravyeva and David Nash

2. Policing Twentieth Century Ireland
A history of An Garda Síochána
Vicky Conway

3. Capital Punishment in Twentieth-Century Britain
Audience, justice, memory
Lizzie Seal

4. The Origins of Modern Financial Crime
Historical foundations and current problems in Britain
Sarah Wilson

5. Transnational Penal Cultures
New perspectives on discipline, punishment and desistance
Edited by Vivien Miller and James Campbell

General series introduction

The volumes in this series contribute to the unashamedly interdisciplinary exercise in which SOLON has engaged since its inception in 2000: something now enhanced by the collaboration with Routledge to present cutting edge interdisciplinary research in crime and criminal justice history. The focus is on issues which, while rooted in the past, have also a crucial current resonance and so the volumes reflect on key issues and dilemmas which persist in terms of contemporary priorities.

This is the second edited collection in the series which, amongst other things, demonstrates the maturity of comparative transnational studies, and the importance of historically contextualised approaches to criminological issues. In light of current concerns with high prison populations, this collection presents a diverse range of histories of penal cultures and international penal perspectives across all five continents, which are harmonised and advance, significantly, a lexicon of transnational penology. It also advances consideration of the problems of crime and punishment in comparative, interdisciplinary and global terms. Edited by Vivien Miller and James Campbell, who are both well respected experts in the field, the volume is part of a UK Arts and Humanities Research Council funded project, Translating Penal Cultures. We are therefore delighted and honoured to include it in the series, believing that it represents truly cutting edge, research-inspired analysis and challenging conclusions. The three key themes, discipline, punishment and desistance, offer new perspectives on race, gender, class, urban space, prisonisation and defiance, and advance understandings of how 'state' power was and is used, shaped and challenged. We are sure that readers will agree that this text will stimulate the interdisciplinary study of criminal justice and its historical contexts in fresh directions.

Kim Stevenson, Judith Rowbotham and David Nash

'This is a stimulating and timely collection which brings together wide-ranging contributions on historical penal cultures. What makes it particularly distinct is its interdisciplinarity; with contributors drawing on the social sciences, demography, post-colonialism and transnationalism to complement the historical evidence. The circulation of ideas about crime, criminal justice theory, and the practices and transfer of domestic and colonial regimes are key themes. I have no doubt that this collection is a major addition to the field of comparative history and to criminal justice history too.'

Heather Shore, Reader in History,
Leeds Metropolitan University, UK

'Over the past three centuries, the prison has emerged as one of the most enduring and pervasive institutions of European imperial expansion. Transnational Penal Cultures describes how the global experience of imprisonment has connected different cultures, but challenges any complacent view that this experience has been uniform. The cases gathered here, based on new research and drawing upon a fascinating range of archival sources, take us from the penal colonies of Austria and Russia, to the faith-based prisons of Brazil.

Along the way, the penal reform theories of Foucault and Elias are found wanting. And while the prison is everywhere seen as a potent symbol of state authority and power, it is not reform but the practice of state violence that marks the penal cultures described in this volume. This book stands as an invigorating and significant contribution to the literature of histories of punishment.'

David M. Anderson, Professor of African History,
University of Warwick, UK

Transnational Penal Cultures

New perspectives on discipline, punishment and desistance

Edited by
Vivien Miller and James Campbell

Routledge
Taylor & Francis Group

LONDON AND NEW YORK

First published 2015
by Routledge
2 Park Square, Milton Park, Abingdon, Oxon, OX14 4RN

and by Routledge
711 Third Avenue, New York, NY 10017

Routledge is an imprint of the Taylor & Francis Group, an informa business

British Library Cataloguing in Publication Data
A catalogue record for this book is available from the British Library

Library of Congress Cataloguing in Publication data
Transnational penal cultures : new perspectives on discipline, punishment, and desistance / edited by Vivien Miller, James Campbell.
   pages   cm – (Routledge solon explorations in crime and criminal justice histories)
   1. Criminal justice, Administration of.   2. Punishment.   3. Prisons.
   4. Criminal justice, Administration of–Case studes.   5. Punishment–Case studies.   6. Prisons–Case studies.   I. Miller, Vivien M. L.
   II. Campbell, James M.
   HV7231.T73   2014
   365–dc23
   2014016219

ISBN: 978-0-415-74131-6 (hbk)
ISBN: 978-1-315-81531-2 (ebk)

Typeset in Times New Roman
by Out of House Publishing

Contents

Figures

Maps

Tables

Contributors

Sascha Auerbach is currently a lecturer in the History Department at the University of Nottingham. He specialises in metropolitan legal culture and the history of race and imperialism in the late nineteenth and early twentieth century. His first monograph, *Race, Law, and 'the Chinese Puzzle' in Imperial Britain*, was published in 2009. His contribution to this volume is drawn from a larger study of 'courtroom culture' in modern London. The research for it was made possible by generous support from the US–UK Fulbright Commission, the Canadian Social Sciences and Humanities Research Council and the University of Northern British Columbia.

W.J. Berridge has recently taken up a three-year post at Northampton after completing a PhD in Sudanese History at Durham in 2011. Her PhD research focused on the history of policing, prisons and homicide trials in colonial and early post-colonial Sudan, and this has been complemented by recent research on Sudan's 'morality police'. She has published material on political violence in the Egyptian Revolution of 1919, and will soon be publishing a monograph on the history of Sudan's two civilian uprisings of 1964 and 1985. Her work deals with topics such as post-colonialism, Islamic radicalism and 'post-Islamism'. She has travelled to Sudan on a number of occasions, and engaged in volunteering there.

James Campbell is Lecturer in American History at the University of Leicester. He is the author of *Slavery on Trial: Race, Class and Criminal Justice in Antebellum Richmond, Virginia* (Florida, 2007) and *Crime and Punishment in African American History* (Palgrave, 2012). He is currently working on a study of the death penalty in nineteenth- and twentieth-century Jamaica.

David Cox currently lectures in criminology and criminal justice history at the University of Wolverhampton. He has published widely in the field of criminal justice history, with recent books including *Crime in England 1688–1815* (Routledge, 2014), *Policing the Factory: Theft, Private Policing and the Law in Modern England* [co-authored with Prof. Barry Godfrey] (Bloomsbury, 2013) and *'A Certain Share of Low Cunning': A History* *of the Bow Street Runners 1792–1839* (Routledge, 2012). He has also authored numerous journal articles, the most recent being '"Trying to get a good one": Bigamy Offences in England and Wales 1850–1950', *Plymouth Law & Criminal Justice Review* vol. 4 (Autumn 2011): 1–32.

Sacha Darke lectures in Criminology in the Department of Social and Historical Studies, University of Westminster. His research interests are in comparative and transnational criminology, convict criminology, prisons and urban security. He is co-director of British Convict Criminology, www. convictcriminology.org/bcc.htm, and also an active member of the Global Prisons Research Network, https://sites.google.com/site/gprnnetwork. He is currently involved in research projects on inmate collaboration and self-governance in Brazilian prisons, higher education in prisons and prisoner mentoring.

Barry Godfrey is Professor of Social Justice in the School of Law and Social Justice, and Research Lead for the Faculty of Humanities and Social Science at Liverpool University. He researches the history of crime, criminal justice policy in the realm of sentencing, and the management of habitual and serious offenders, and has an interest in longitudinal studies of offenders and offending. His latest books, written with colleagues, include two volumes in the Clarendon Series in Criminology (*Criminal Lives*, 2007; *Serious Offenders*, 2010); *Policing the Factory* (2013); and *Crime in England, 1880–1945* (2013).

Daniel J.R. Grey is Lecturer in World History at Plymouth University. He has published several journal articles on the history of infanticide, child abuse and gendered approaches to criminal justice in both colonial India and Britain. Currently, he is working on two book projects: *Degrees of Guilt: Infanticide in England 1860–1960* (contracted to Liverpool University Press) and *Feminist Campaigns Against Child Sexual Abuse: Britain and India 1860–1947* (contracted to Continuum).

Lawrence Ka-Ki Ho is a Lecturer in the Department of Social Sciences at the Hong Kong Institute of Education, Hong Kong. He is also an Honorary Fellow of the Centre for Criminology at the University of Hong Kong. His research interest includes comparative policing practices and criminal justice in the decolonised region and Greater China. Lawrence is currently engaged in several research projects on Hong Kong and Macau policing practices, including protest management, private policing, knowledge transfer and social media in policing. His latest academic publications include *Policing Hong Kong, 1842–1969: Insiders' Stories* (2012); 'Transformation of Macau Policing: From Portuguese Colony to China's SAR', *Crime, Law and Social Change* (2013) and 'Women Police Officers in Hong Kong: Feminity & Policing in a Gendered Organization', *Journal of Comparative Asian Development* (2013).

Stacey Hynd gained her D.Phil in History from the University of Oxford in 2008. She lectured at the University of Cambridge before joining the University of Exeter as Lecturer in African History. She is currently preparing her monograph on capital punishment in British colonial Africa, c.1890–1968. She has conducted research in Ghana, Kenya, Malawi and Tanzania, and published on African legal and criminal history, capital punishment, state violence, prison labour, gender and juvenile delinquency. Her current research focuses on histories of human rights in Ghana, criminal law in the British Empire and the history of child soldiering in twentieth-century Africa.

Helen Johnston is Senior Lecturer in Criminology at the University of Hull. Her research interests lie in the experience and administration of imprisonment in local and convict prisons in the nineteenth and early twentieth centuries and in offenders' lives after release. She has written a number of journal articles and is author of *Crime in England, 1815–1880: Experiencing the Criminal Justice System* (Routledge, forthcoming). She is editor of *Punishment and Control in Historical Perspective* (Palgrave Macmillan, 2008) and with Yvonne Jewkes of *Prison Readings* (Willan, 2006). Her current project (with Heather Shore) is an AHRC funded research network entitled 'Our Criminal Past'.

Rebecca Kippen graduated with a PhD in Demography from the Australian National University in 2002. She is currently a Senior Research Fellow in the School of Population and Global Health at the University of Melbourne. Her research interests include historical causes of death, early-life influences on later-life mortality, the life courses of convicts transported to Australia and their descendants, and modelling future population trends for Australia.

Fiona Macaulay is Senior Lecturer in Development in the Department of Peace Studies, University of Bradford. Her research interests and publications concentrate on gender, politics and policy, human rights, and criminal justice system reform issues in Brazil and Latin America. She started researching the prison system in 1997 while she was Brazil Researcher at Amnesty International, and developed her work on justice sector reform as Ford Foundation fellow at the Centre for Brazilian Studies, University of Oxford. She is on the boards of the *Journal of Latin American Studies* (of which she was also editor), the Brazilian Forum on Public Security and Conectas, a human rights network in the global south.

Hamish Maxwell-Stewart is an associate professor in the School of Humanities, University of Tasmania. He has authored several books on convict transportation to Australia including *Closing Hell's Gates: The Death of a Convict Station* (2008) and *American Citizens, British Slaves: Yankee Political Prisoners in an Australian Penal Colony* (2002) as well as being a co-editor and contributor to *Chain Letters: Narrating Convict Lives* (2001).

Vivien Miller is Associate Professor of American and Canadian Studies at the University of Nottingham. She is the author of *Hard Labor and Hard Time: Florida's 'Sunshine Prison' and Chain Gangs* (2012) and *Crime, Violence and Sexual Clemency: Florida's Pardon Board and Penal System in the Progressive Era* (2000), and co-editor of *Cross-Cultural Connections in Crime Fictions* (2012). She is currently working on capital punishment in the pre-1972 United States.

Laura Piacentini is Professor of Criminology at the Law School, Strathclyde University. She is a prison sociologist who, for nearly twenty years, has been researching the contemporary Russian prison system. She has researched penal labour, penal geography, human rights, women's imprisonment and children's incarceration in numerous penal colonies, employing Russian language, ethnographic techniques and deep cultural immersion. Her books on the subject have won major awards and been nominated for numerous others. A new phase of prison research, funded by Leverhulme, will begin in 2015 when she will carry out the first sociological study of rights consciousness amongst Russian prisoners.

Stephan Steiner is an Austrian historian teaching at Sigmund Freud University Vienna. He has published several books and a wide range of articles on questions of extreme violence in early and late modernity. His work includes a study on the persecution of Carinthian Protestants, 1734–36, and one on deportations in the Habsburg monarchy of the early modern period. He is editor of the political writings of the philosopher Jean Améry and has worked on the Shoah and the genocide in Rwanda.

Joanne Turner is a lecturer in Criminology at the University of Chester. Joanne's doctoral research centred on the criminal justice experiences of female offenders at the end of the nineteenth century. Her initial publications arose from her doctoral research, but have more recently come from postdoctoral research within similar fields, in particular her involvement in the *Costs of Imprisonment* project. As well as teaching the history of crime and punishment to undergraduates, Joanne's research interests remain in the broad field of the history of crime and punishment. Presently, Joanne is researching the experiences of convict women when discharged from prison.

Acknowledgements

This book originated from a two-day symposium on 'Translating Penal Cultures', that was held at the University of Nottingham, UK, in July 2012. The editors would like to thank the Arts and Humanities Research Council for funding this event and all the participants who made it such a success and have contributed to the present volume. Thanks also to Judith Rowbotham and Kim Stevenson, who encouraged us to submit the manuscript to the SOLON series and to Heidi Lee and the rest of the editorial team at Routledge, who have guided us through the production process with great professionalism and no little patience.

A substantial portion of Chapter 5 was originally published in *Policing Hong Kong 1842–1969: Insiders' Stories*, ©2012 City University of Hong Kong Press, while part of the analysis on the evolution of Macau policing appeared in Lawrence K.K. Ho and Agnes I.F. Lam, 'Transformation of Macau Policing: From Portuguese Colony to China's SAR,' in Springer's *Crime, Law and Social Change* (On-line First article), 17 November 2013: http://link.springer.com/article/10.1007%2Fs10611-013-9493-3.

Introduction

Vivien Miller and James Campbell

Ideas about crime, policing, punishment and offenders have circulated within and between nations, throughout colonial empires and across post-colonial societies for centuries. Travellers' accounts, newspaper reports, pamphlets, journals, memoirs, official government records and the meetings of national and international prison congresses have provided spaces in which penal cultures have been interpreted, challenged, adapted, transformed and translated. Understandings and practices of criminality, policing and punishment have also travelled with and evolved through the work of law enforcement officers, lawyers, judges, prison wardens and administrators as they moved between different judicial and penal regimes, particularly in colonial contexts. They have been further shaped by defendants, offenders and convicts, whose encounters with criminal justice systems and penal institutions have often had global dimensions. For example, in their chapter in this volume Hamish Maxwell-Stewart and Rebecca Kippen note that the British government oversaw the transportation of over 160,000 convicts to its penal colonies in New South Wales, Van Diemen's Land and Western Australia between 1787 and 1868, and a report that up to 13,000 persons journeyed from European Russia into Siberian exile every year in the 1880s is noted in Vivien Miller's chapter. Criminal operators and illegal activities also span often complex transnational and transcontinental networks. For example, the distribution network underpinning the opium trade uncovered by police in Liverpool during the First World War – and described in Sascha Auerbach's chapter – mirrored that of legal products as raw opium was smuggled to Britain from Hong Kong, processed into the finished product for smoking or ingesting in the UK, then re-exported back to the colonies through the same merchant shipping network that formed the backbone of imperial trade, and which was reliant on a multi-ethnic and multi-racial maritime labour force.

Several chapters in this collection also highlight the existence of a transnational penal lexicon, particularly from the nineteenth century onwards, as terms such as 'ticket-of-leave' – identified here in specific UK, Australian and Siberian contexts – circulated, adapted and were appropriated to give recognition and meaning to different national audiences and readerships. 'Prisons' could refer to a range of different institutional forms, including separate and congregate systems in panoptical stone fortresses, as well as penal styles of operation in workhouses and labour camps that were punitive rather than panoptic, but was understood to conform to certain punitive, coercive and disciplinary mechanisms, including the involuntary removal of an offender from his or her community to another specific place of detention or confinement. Further, the ubiquitous shaven heads, chains and leg fetters, and distinctive clothing that accompanied the processing and symbolic othering of offenders were found in many penal locations.

While the histories of policing and punishment are well-established fields of enquiry, it is only in recent years that scholars have begun to recognise the subjects' global dynamics and the potential for comparative and transnational studies to provide new critical insights. Yet, comparative and transnational projects can often be daunting as individual researchers as well as research teams negotiate multiple linguistic, archival and methodological challenges. Several chapters in this collection were originally presented at an Arts and Humanities Research Council (AHRC)-funded symposium on 'Translating Penal Cultures' at the University of Nottingham in July 2012; others resulted from the interdisciplinary and intercultural discourses and connections established through the Translating Penal Cultures research network. The aim of the AHRC project was to develop an intercultural, interdisciplinary and international dialogue on historical and contemporary incarcerated populations, institutions of confinement and penal cultures as an important area of research, and to promote comparative study, interdisciplinarity and internationalisation. The Translating Penal Cultures research network that the project drew together deliberately sought to work across the disciplines of language, history, cultural studies, law, criminology and sociology. This edited collection is therefore one of the key results of these collaborations.

The volume is nominally structured around three key stages of the criminal justice process: discipline, punishment and desistance, but the chapters do not necessarily map neatly onto this framework. Nor do they conform to a neat linear pattern of development and they have instead been grouped around overlapping and comparative themes and subjects. The transnational perspective that frames this collection and the synergies between and across the individual chapters has also resulted in a more extensive, contextualising opening section on the broad category of discipline which then leads into considerations of punishment policies and practices. The final section, in the shape of a consideration of desistance, provides a reflection back onto many of the issues raised in earlier chapters, further inflecting our understandings of the processes involved in disciplining and punishing societies and individuals. Nevertheless, reading through the different chapters, *discipline* is defined to include the regulation of populations and offenders through law and legal codes, social and racial control, and policing; *punishment* includes flogging, imprisonment, forced labour and banishment; *desistance* refers to the individual offender's movements away from a life of crime, and the structural imperatives that either facilitate or limit this.

Our understandings of these categories are heavily influenced by Michel Foucault's *Discipline and Punish: The Birth of the Prison* – a work that has done more than any other to shape the study of crime and punishment in recent decades. Focusing on the transformation of punishment from the late eighteenth century, Foucault seeks to explain 'the disappearance of torture as a public spectacle,' and the emergence of penitentiary imprisonment as a new form of punishment. Eighteenth-century advocates of the penitentiary depicted the institution as a new form of more rational and humane punishment concerned with the rehabilitation of the convict's soul, but for Foucault the birth of the prison was rooted in new technologies of power, organised around hierarchical observation, normalising judgements, examination and the gaze. However, the prison and indeed the wider carceral system (that included workhouses, asylums) produced new categories including that of delinquency to structure and control crime.[1]

Foucault's scholarship has long been criticised by historians for a lack of empirical rigour. The charge has often been overstated and Foucault's defenders suggest that it wilfully misinterprets the purpose and significance of his work.[2] The chapters included here nonetheless lend weight to the related accusation that Foucault's theoretical framework privileges Western penal traditions and is of limited utility in understanding forms of punishment in non-Western societies, and particularly in colonial and post-colonial settings. As Frank Dikötter and Ian Brown argued in 2007 with reference to the history of non-European penitentiaries, even where Western penal influences were strong, the prison 'was never simply imposed or copied, but was reinvented and transformed by a host of local factors'.[3] The chapters in the *Transnational Penal Cultures* collection present new empirical evidence of these processes of reinvention and transformation, but they broaden the focus in two key ways. First, the collection deliberately incorporates case studies from across the world in order to encourage readers to draw connections across time, space and place. Second, rather than focusing on the prison alone they demonstrate how local contexts and influences shaped penal systems more broadly.

Incorporating case studies from across the continents of Asia, the Americas, Europe, Africa and Australia, the thirteen essays in this collection are based on exciting new research that explores the evolution and adaptation of criminal justice and penal systems largely from the early nineteenth century to the present, although Stephan Steiner's study of internal European deportation and colonisation extends to the late middle ages, and Laura Piacentini briefly

---

[1] Michel Foucault, *Discipline and Punish: The Birth of the Prison*. Trans. Alan Sheridan (New York: Vintage Books, 1979 [1995]).

[2] Randall McGowan, 'Power and Humanity, or Foucault among the Historians', in Roy Porter and Colin Jones (eds), *Reassessing Foucault: Power, Medicine and the Body* (New York: Routledge, 1998), 92.

[3] See, for example, Frank Dikötter and Ian Brown (eds), *Cultures of Confinement: A History of the Prison in Africa, Asia and Latin America* (Ithaca: Cornell University Press, 2007), 1.

touches on the earlier sixteenth-century antecedents of exile in contemporary Russia. The collection draws on the creative and innovative work of younger scholars as well as presenting more established contributors' latest research and reflections on previous work. Ranging across the disciplinary boundaries of history, criminology, law and penology, and drawing on diverse analytical approaches, the chapters in this collection forge new connections between historical and contemporary issues in crime, prisons, policing and penal cultures, and challenge traditional Western democratic historiographies of crime and punishment and categorisations of offenders, police and ex-offenders.

Individual chapters provide new perspectives on race, gender, class, urban space, 'prisonisation' (the process of inmate acceptance or accommodation to the culture and social life of incarceration) and defiance. The gap between imperial and colonial intentions and local outcomes is a key theme of the chapters on Gold Coast prisons, Sudanese police forces, female infanticide in India and penal transportation to Tasmania for example. The expressive penal and political power of the nation state and empire are discussed in chapters on Russian exile, Austrian deportation and colonisation, and Britian's early twentieth-century war on drugs for example. Racial control, surveillance and social control are key themes in the chapters on policing slave cities in the southern United States and Brazil and southern convict leasing, but are also developed in relation to Hong Kong, where racial segregation policies and racial inequities limited the recruitment and promotion of ethnic Chinese and immigrants. 'Prisonisation', desistance, and the relationship of the prison and the imprisoned to the free or outside community are at the centre of the chapters on the UK's licensing system and late modern/contemporary Brazilian prisons.

A range of methodologies have been employed across the collection. The creation of vast penal bureaucracies by nation states, imperial and colonial officialdom, and local administrators to discipline, police, monitor and punish domestic and overseas populations, particularly from the nineteenth century onwards, provide a formidable set of resources for penal and police researchers. Journeying into and unlocking these penal archives has enabled several contributors to present unique and innovative studies of Gold Coast prisons, Austrian deportation colonies, Tasmanian recidivists and English desistors, and indeed detailed life histories of individual offenders. Other chapters have sought to recover the voices of slaves, prisoners and keepers, used slave narratives, convict leasing memoirs, published and first-hand interviews with veteran local Sudanese and Hong Kong police officers, and provided fresh interpretations of media and official reports of immoral and illegal activities, including Indian infanticide cases and Chinese Liverpudlian opium users. Detailed studies of contemporary Russian imprisonment and tropes of exile, and of unique sets of prisons in contemporary Brazil – the Resocialisation Centres (*Centros de Ressocialização* – CRs) in São Paulo state and the APAC (*Associação de Proteção e Assistência ao Condenado* – Association for the Protection and

Assistance of Convicts/the Condemned) prisons in Minas Gerais state – draw heavily on each author's pioneering and innovative fieldwork, including extensive observations, oral interviews and less formalised conversations with a range of different penal, prisoner and official contributors.

Several chapters directly address the ways in which metropolitan cultures of law, policing and imprisonment were translated and adapted to suit various conditions in different parts of empire. Colonial Ghana was a model colony in British Africa but its penal system encompassed reformist as well as disciplinary technologies and discourses, and corporal punishment and convict labour. Gold Coast prisons thus reflected an imperial image of colonial rule as well as its contradictions. In her chapter on the development of colonial prisons in Africa's Gold Coast and differing conceptions of local tribal, colonial and imperial ideas about imprisonment in the nineteenth and twentieth centuries, Stacey Hynd dissects these dialogical tensions between civilisation and violence, and explores the competing imperatives to 'control', 'reform' and 'punish' African convicts. Despite the embrace of modernisation and the emergence of a new 'imperial humanitarianism', violence remained central to colonial disciplinary techniques, particularly amid a hardening of racial attitudes. Hynd thus highlights the effects of the disjuncture between the rhetoric of imperial reform and the reality of continued coercion, control and exploitation on the ground, especially as this became increasingly marked in the twentieth century as colonial governance was threatened by nationalist agitation and amid perceived rising crime rates.

She demonstrates that colonial prisons in British Africa were more than mechanisms of racial and economic coercion, and underscores the changing rather than static colonial perceptions of race, ethnicity and African 'criminality' that shaped moral and political economies of punishment in different decades. Particuarly in the period between the First and Second World Wars, ideas about 'criminal types', fears of detribalisation and changing cultural sensibilities coalesced to produce an important shift away from punitive deterrence toward reformation, hence the greater emphasis on industrial training and resocialisation. Amid the growing nationalist and anti-colonial opposition movements of the 1940s and 1950s, increased imperial influence on local penal culture was also instrumental in the emergence of a new welfarist framework. But it was pragmatism rather than ideology that drove many of these transformations, as well as shifting conceptions of race, deviance and criminality.

Debates over civilisation, progress and appropriate gender roles (as delineated by both imperial racism and local misogyny), and the variances of British imperial, Indian colonial and local tribal views on 'infanticide', and the tensions between civilisation and modernity versus seemingly barbaric local customs are explored in Daniel Grey's chapter. Amid twenty-first century debates over female infanticide and sex-specific abortion in post-colonial and late modern India, Grey reminds us that the wilful killing of unwanted daughters was a central trope in an earlier well-established narrative that emphasised Indian inferiority and justified colonial intervention and correction. The repeated 'discovery' of the murder of daughters in different parts of northern India from the 1790s onwards was documented in travelogues and official sources, while the association between Hinduism and female infanticide (often achieved with an overdose of opium) continued to infuse the nineteenth-century colonial imagination, as well as the views of government officials and journalists. Colonial commentators charged that the unwillingness of upper-caste Hindu families to pay expensive dowries was a leading motivation and that daughter killing was practised regularly by specific tribes in the North-Western provinces.

Grey examines the implementation and effects of the Female Infanticide Act 1870, which was regularly presented as an example of Britain's civilising rule of India but there remained clear official–local discord on the best ways to identify and punish child killing in late nineteenth-century India. Further, colonial officials and the British press understood female infanticide within a broader social and cultural interpretation of tribal women in India centred on the powerlessness and inevitable victimhood of Hindu women. Similarly the effectiveness of the 1870 act was limited by medical, evidential and interpretative issues that were also apparent in newborn murder trials in Britain. However, the argument in 1876 of one civil servant that Indian women convicted of infanticide should not automatically face either a death sentence or transportation for life is suggestive of an imperial humanitarianism that Hynd identified in a later decade. Nevertheless, acknowledging that there were direct parallels between crimes committed in colony and metropole was problematic and would have required explanations that went beyond the race and/or religion of the perpetrator, thus the uniquely Indian crime of female infanticide served different rhetorical and political purposes. This raises essential questions over the ability and intent of imperial administrators based in the metropole and colonial governments to exercise control in the geographic peripheries and to manage effectively different ethnic populations and challenges, which are also at the heart of W.J. Berridge's later chapter on policing in Sudan.

The 1870 legislation increased imperial surveillance of Indian subjects; increasing imperial and state surveillance of local and often non-white populations in the southern United States, Brazil and Sudan, and wartime England is a key theme also in the following chapters on policing. The practical and ideological challenges of policing societies structured by entrenched racial divisions are explored further in these chapters and in relation to Lawrence Ho's comparative study of late colonial and post-return Hong Kong and Macau. James Campbell addresses the commonalities in urban slavery across the Americas as well as diverging mechanisms of policing and punishment in mid-nineteenth-century cities, because they were shaped by specific urban environments as well as broader political and cultural ideas about race, nation, law and slavery. Auerbach demonstrates how cultural relativism, Chinese 'criminality' and political expediency combined to define the treatment of non-white offenders in UK metropolitan centres during the First World War years.

James Campbell's transnational analysis of the cultures of urban policing and punishment in mid-nineteenth-century slave cities in the southern United States and Brazil identifies the essential features of slave law enforcement in key cities, and examines the effects on manpower, law, militarism and municipal government. Campbell grapples with historical and scholarly dissension over the relationship of racial slavery to the nineteenth-century city or urban space. While there was no single model for urban slavery in the Americas, the transience and relative anonymity of urban life enabled city slaves with relatively limited freedoms to engage in diverse independent activities, and to live and participate in vibrant black and interracial communities.

In contrast to the private world of the plantation where the master was authoritarian control – and which provides some parallels with the world of the convict leasing captain discussed in Vivien Miller's chapter – slave cities developed distinctive cultures and practices of policing and punishment and required the routine intervention of the state in matters of slave control. In US slave cities such as Charleston, formalised law enforcement enhanced and often entirely replaced the surveillance and disciplinary power of individual slaveholders as policing and punishment of slaves was a routine part of municipal government. Campbell thus situates the control of urban, white non-slaveholders and free black populations within the wider context of urban slavery but highlights important differences in the national political and policing cultures of Brazil and the United States. In mid-nineteenth-century Brazilian cities, forms of slave policing and punishment merged with oppressive measures used to regulate the free population to create an authoritarian system of control that was enforced against all lower-class city residents. By contrast, in the United States municipal authorities struggled to reconcile local justice systems based explicitly on race and slavery with the crime control needs of urban societies that were increasingly characterised by social disorder and class divisions among the free population. As a result, although slave resistance was particularly threatening to urban Brazilian slaveholders, Campbell underscores the unique ideological challenges to urban slaveholders and the emerging 'pro-slavery' arguments of the late antebellum period in the United States that revered the benevolence and paternalism of the planter class.

In the southern United States and Brazil slaveholder power and slave control was affected by important urban–rural divisions. W.J. Berridge's chapter also illuminates a key centre–periphery divide that undermined British governance in Sudan from the late nineteenth to the mid-twentieth century. Berridge's analysis of the bifurcated police systems of colonial Sudan underlines the ambivalence and shortcomings of British colonial policy towards the police as well as the impossibility of ensuring thorough regulation of Sudanese society. This brings into question whether the British government in London and the Condominium colonial government in Sudan had either the capacity and/or intent to exercise control and to manage effectively different ethnic populations and challenges. The totalizing nature of colonial power as well as its transformative nature, for example, through law and law enforcement, is therefore also in question – as in Grey's chapter on female infanticide in India. The impact of cultural relativism is also clear in both chapters, for example, in the racial ordering of different tribal groups, into martial races (the Rajputs in India, the Shayqiyya in Sudan).

As the police institutions moved away from militaristic (Egyptian Army) control to civil forms, colonial administrators in Sudan actively recruited marginal but literate ethnic groups such as the Shayqiyya to police the urban riverain heartlands. Identified as both a martial and an educated elite, the increasingly professional and educated outlook of such police officers in the principal urban centres put them at odds with officers of the Sudan Political Service (SPS; the specialist governing cadre of the colonial administration) who policed the rural periphery. In the wake of the proto-nationalist White Flag Revolt of 1924, the SPS had become increasingly resistant to educated professional police recruitment (which they equated with pro-Egyptian nationalism or Communism) and were reluctant to embrace modern and rational techniques of policing. However, the pride that provincial officers took in having 'special knowledge' of Sudanese culture as well as the devolution of judicial and police functions to the rulers of various nomadic and then sedentary tribes across Sudan and local resistance to imperial law and legal procedures ensured not only a fragmented system of policing but unsatisfactory investigations of major crimes. The 'administrative' form of police control, bypassing the central legal codes established by the colonial state, continued in the rural peripheries of Sudan while civil policing began to emerge in urban and riverain areas.

Lawrence Ho notes that colonial policing is usually assumed to follow the 'coercive policing' paradigm in which both hard power/physical force and soft power/imperial legislation serves to secure the metropole's interests in its colonies. By contrast, 'policing by consent' where the police constitute a civil institution that works in partnership with citizens is often equated with the metropole. However, Ho's chapter, as well as those of Berridge and Auerbach, suggests that the boundaries between coercive policing and policing by consent are frequently permeable and often overlap. Post-colonial policing was also fraught with the challenges associated with continuity and adaptation, as illustrated in Lawrence Ho's chapter on the transformation of policing systems in Hong Kong and Macau from the later period of British and Portuguese colonial control to the new post-colonial landscape of the twenty-first century in which each territory is now a Special Administrative Region (SAR) of the People's Republic of China.

Ho explores key features of the police forces in each jurisdiction and analyses their coming-of-age from the period of the violent leftist riots of the 1960s through the handovers in 1997 and 1999, and the challenges of the first 'post-return' decade. He charts the evolving relationship of the police to civil society and police involvement in internal security management against both general crime and specific incidents of social unrest. He accounts also for the differing post-1968 developments in the two regions. Events of 1967 pushed the Hong Kong Police Force towards greater professionalism and modernisation, for example through a series of structural reforms to eradicate corruption and improve relationships between police and civil society. Government efforts to build more legitimate, consensual and community-based policing frameworks meant the force was better placed to respond to rising numbers of mass demonstrations, political dissent and protest movements in the post-colonial period, and to deal more effectively with the early twenty-first century challenges of white-collar crime, including commodity smuggling, money laundering, prostitution and drug trafficking, in the SAR. By contrast, Macau's late colonial police remained hampered by lack of resources, language barriers and a Portuguese administration that had neither the capacity nor the intent to exercise control largely because Macau had ceased to have any economic value for Portugal. Somewhat similar to Sudan, Macau was saddled with bifurcated police systems, the Judiciary Police (JP) and Public Security Police (PSP) that were embroiled in jurisdictional disputes; there was significant internal dissension, and little impetus for modernisation. The explosion of violent and syndicated crime associated with Macau's gambling industries eventually exerted acute pressure for change, as did the more recent de-franchising of legal casino operations in the SAR. Yet, Ho provides a more positive assessment of civil policing and citizen trust in late modern Hong Kong and Macau where Chinese populations and European institutions must carve out their futures under the watchful eye of China.

One hundred years earlier, a different Chinese population found itself at odds with a more malignant British police. The role of police in maintaining order and managing internal security during wartime, and the consequent impact on the relationship between police and civil society, is also explored in Sascha Auerbach's chapter. His examination of Britain's early twentieth-century 'war on drugs' – the separate but concurrent anti-opium campaigns and anti-cocaine hysteria – underscores the ways in which criminal behaviours associated with immigrant, foreign-born and differing racial and ethnic communities in the metropole could trigger authoritarian responses in the midst of wartime tensions and anxieties. Growing public anxieties over Chinese 'vice' and the contamination of white Britons, apprehension over declining morals generally and the First World War emergency combined to enable the Home Office to accrue substantially increased powers to monitor and control the domestic UK population, and to investigate, arrest, imprison and deport without trial many Chinese residents.

Chinatowns in the UK (as in the United States) were associated with widespread vice, gambling and immorality, but fears over physical and moral degeneration resulting from opium and narcotics use became more acute amid the wartime military preparedness campaigns. Media reports initially connected cocaine in particular (allegedly introduced to wartime London by

Canadian soldiers) to the corruption of British, thus white, soldiers, but not opium which had been largely associated with Chinese residents in metropolitan centres such as Liverpool and London. However, local police in Liverpool who were anxious to suppress Chinese vice and immorality were able to use wartime legislation to arrest approximately 10 per cent of the small, resident Chinese population for the possession or processing of opium between 1916 and 1918. Several residents were subsequently deported without trial under powers granted to local officials by Regulation 40b (which criminalised the possession or sale of cocaine or opium by anyone besides licensed professionals) of the Defence of the Realm Act 1916 and the earlier Alien Restrictions Act 1914. Others were coerced into 'voluntarily' leaving Liverpool and/or the UK altogether. The campaign of mass arrests and summary deportations – the ability of the state to physically remove select residents without their having effective legal recourse – induced fear and suspicion among Chinese Liverpudlians, as was the apparent intention, but by contrast there were no opium-related deportations in London despite robust anti-vice campaigns in that city.

The physical removal of undesirables – whether common criminals, residents with opium habits, political opponents or homosexuals – to geographic peripheries or overseas penal destinations, often thousands of miles from family and home, were/are central expressions of state and penal power, and are the focus of the next set of chapters. Recent studies have underscored the importance of convict transportation to eighteenth- and nineteenth-century nation states and empires, particularly the UK.[4] However, European deportation practices from the early modern period were intrinsically linked to the idea and practice of internal colonisation. Familiar understandings of transportation are thus complicated by Stephan Steiner's study of the much overlooked internal colonisation of the Austro-Habsburg Empire's political and criminal deportees during the long nineteenth century up to the eve of the First World War. Similarly, the removal of prisoners and their families from European Russia across thousands of miles to the Siberian peripheries is a key feature of Russian imperial, Soviet and post-Soviet history. Russia's elaborate and complex system of banishment and exile – 'in exile imprisonment' – dating back to the nineteenth century is explored in the chapters by Laura Piacentini and Vivien Miller.

Stephan Steiner traces Austria's history of deportation to the late middle ages and the existence of internal European penal colonies of workhouse

[4] See, for example, Clare Anderson, *Convicts in the Indian Ocean: Transportation from South Asia to Mauritius, 1815–53* (Basingstoke: Palgrave Macmillan, 2000); Clare Anderson, *Subaltern Lives: Biographies of Colonialism in the Indian Ocean World, 1790–1920 (Critical Perspectives on Empire)* (Cambridge: Cambridge University Press, 2012); Michael Bogle, *Convicts: Transportation and Australia* (Sydney: Historic Houses Trust of New South Wales, 2009); Gwenda Morgan and Peter Rushton, *Eighteenth-Century Criminal Transportation: The Formation of the Criminal Atlantic* (Basingstoke: Palgrave Macmillan, 2004).

inmates, delinquents and forced labourers often in close proximity to free communities. It was during the eighteenth century that the Austro-Hungarian Hapsburg Empire finally became a *major* European power but did not possess any overseas territories. It was nevertheless able to draw on its historical experiences of internal colonisation – both the voluntary recruitment of new settlers and the forceful displacement of whole groups of delinquents, deviants and dissenters – in its penal disposition of undesirables. From the early nineteenth century, island convict settlements and forced labour in remote fortresses became substitutes for overseas penal settlements, following Hapsburg interest in the Dalmatian coastline as a deportation location and the utilisation of Hungarian fortresses, after 1831 for example, as dumping grounds for problem populations such as the *precettati* (those labelled as insurgents, criminals and deviants) but scandals over their treatment were exposed during the revolutionary movement of 1848. Yet, interest in overseas penal settlements never quite evaporated as there were renewed debates over possible African and South American locations in the wake of the scientific *Novara* Expedition 1857–9, and Austrian interest was again piqued when Germany acquired overseas colonial possessions in Africa in the 1880s. Late nineteenth-century proposals to deport or remove from the centres of empire groups of habitual criminals, repeat offenders, vagrants and, later on, so-called degenerates including political opponents, homosexuals and gypsies, reflected the imprint of social Darwinism and social hygiene ideology. They were also reflected in the bitter debates between two prominent Austrian penologists, Hans Gross (1847–1915) and Hugo Hoegel (1854–1921) that Steiner critiques towards the end of his chapter. Gross supported the introduction of life-long deportation as a punishment for offenders considered to be especially dangerous to the public. Looking eastward, he would have found evidence for his proposals in Russia's system of in exile imprisonment.

The use of exile as a mode of punishment has been widely researched and is often understood as a technical and bureaucratic extension of state power, yet exile *to a prison* has been relatively unexplored. Extending Foucauldian analyses and supplementing traditional criminological emphases with understanding of cultural meanings and metaphor, Laura Piacentini explores the continuing political and cultural resonance of exile in contemporary Russia's collective conscience and national identity. She examines how differing physical forms of incarceration can be experienced as exile and that a renewed sense of understanding of how historical discourse shapes the fates of those punished is crucial to unpacking the dense cultural meanings of exile. Drawing on examples such as the recent Pussy Riot, Khodorkovsky and Greenpeace imprisonment cases, as well as earlier testimonials from women prisoners, Piacentini demonstrates that banishment and penal discipline are not opposites but rather fused through the combination of discipline and display.

As noted in both Piacentini and Miller's chapters, Siberia became a Russian possession and subsequently a penal colony in the same time period that Western European nations and the United States were incorporating imprisonment into their penal and disciplinary portfolios, and throughout the nineteenth and twentieth centuries the banishment and exile of large numbers of Russian citizens continued apace. In the twenty-first century, Moscow continues to export prisoners to other parts of Russia from its ten remand prisons. In Tsarist Russia, penal exile was the by-product of a badly administered and chaotic penal system but in Soviet Russia exile became a primary mode of punishment, and normalised as a legal category of imprisonment by the 1950s. As with the Tasmanian transportees discussed in the chapter by Hamish Maxwell-Stewart and Rebecca Kippen, and the *precattati* in Steiner's chapter, the cleansing of metropolitan centres of undesirable elements and their expulsion to geographic peripheries embodied a profound cultural spectacle of othering. The exile of prisoners in Russia thus had a communicative power that enabled the Tsarist, Soviet and post-Soviet regimes to create and define penal place, penal culture and penal purpose. The sense of abject displacement described by twenty-first century Russian prisoners resonates with the feelings of nineteenth-century transportees to Austrian forts and Australia, but exile like transportation were also liminal spaces of leaving and becoming as transportees and exiles reinvented themselves and created new lives as best they could.

Staying with the transnational influence of Siberia and Russian penal forms in the nineteenth century, Vivien Miller's chapter examines the appropriation of 'Siberia' – where particularly degrading and brutal punishments were inflicted on common criminals and political exiles – by opponents of the convict leasing to cultivate political and popular opposition to late nineteenth-century southern US prison conditions and the mistreatment of prisoners. J.C. Powell's memoir, *American Siberia*, detailed the terrible conditions of life and labour in Florida from the end of post-Civil War Reconstruction through to the New South period as convict leasing became the principal penal arrangement. Former convict captain Powell provided a rare first-hand detailed account of an *emerging* leasing system that contained some explicit comparisons between conditions in late nineteenth-century Florida convict camps and Russo-Siberian forwarding prisons and convict mines that drew heavily on George Kennan's writings on the Russian system of exile to Siberia. This chapter explores the rhetorical linking of the works and the ways in which borrowed ideas, images and forms framed real and imagined penal experiences.

From the 1870s, state prisoners and guards slept in crude log houses in temporary camps and stockades scattered across northern and central Florida and laboured in public, albeit in the backwoods and remote parts of the state. Imprisonment therefore did not mean a permanent place of confinement but forced labour in a remote and temporary place of detention. *American Siberia* contained a compelling portrait of the violent, brutal and bloody world of convict leasing; of the neglect and mistreatment of female convicts, the ubiquity of corporal punishment and flogging, the constant clanking of chains, the unsanitary conditions, poor diet and prevalence of sickness and disease. Guards and captains were generally young white men from local farming families or recent economic migrants to the state while convicts were usually lower-class teenage or young adult African Americans and poor whites. Although racial segregation had yet to be codified, penal and prison hierarchies reflected the expressive power of the state in which white supremacy and black inferiority were central. Convict leasing was supposed to deliver compliant and dependable labour force but the punishment beatings, frequent work stoppages, and other forms of inmate resistance, and the numerous escapes and attempted escapes suggested that ill-discipline and inefficiency were the results. Yet, the promised profitability of convict leasing partly accounted for its durability. The Florida case study highlights further the ideological and geographical distance of sparsely populated frontier states in the United States from metropolitan and nationalising cultures of law, policing and imprisonment.

While convict leasing to private contractors, usually railroad companies, turpentine operators, coal and phosphate mining companies, was a penal system associated with the post-Civil War US South and embedded in the penal and disciplinary apparatus and political economies of many southern states, chain gang labour was found across the globe. Campbell notes Richmond's use of chain gang labour for black and white vagrants in 1856, transportees to Australia provided a source of cheap colonial labour, and even as solitary confinement became more important from the 1840s, there was little abatement of the shackling of convicts and the extraction of labour through the use of ganging. One hundred years later, in the 1940s and 1950s, southern US prison camp models – a descendant of the convict lease system and in which labour subordination remained a key feature – were in effect exported to Burma, Palestine, Tanganyika and the rest of British Africa. Racialised punishments also had clear transnational comparisons. Free blacks were routinely subject to corporal punishment for offences that warranted fines for white offenders in the United States, while in Brazil physical punishment was retained for slaves after 1830. Further, racial categorisation in Gold Coast prisons ensured that African, Asian and European prisoners each received a 'culturally appropriate' diet with different rations. The enduring punitive character of punishment in such places left little room for reform or rehabilitation. Whereas exile to Siberia promised a form of rehabilitation, the rhetoric of reform and rehabilitation was largely absent from the late nineteenth-century South.

Transportation to Australia involved both punishment and subsequent opportunities for reform or for individuals to create lives away from offending. Hamish Maxwell-Stewart and Rebecca Kippen note that between the 1840s and 1860s, 28,000 male convicts passed through probationary gangs in Tasmania before signing pass holder contracts with colonial employers or being issued with tickets of leave. But why were some more successful than others in making the transition from offender to productive citizen? Why do some ex-offenders 'go straight' but others are unable to break the cycle of reoffending? The impacts of mass prisoner transportation to Van Diemen's Land in Tasmania in the early and middle decades of the nineteenth century (it ended in 1853), the factors that assisted desistance and which increased the probability of reoffending, and their relation to the pre-1839 assignment system and the probation system which replaced it, are thus explored in detail in Maxwell-Stewart and Kippen's chapter. They focus on Tasmania, which received 42 per cent of all British convicts transported to Australia and thus was the colony most shaped by the transportation experiment.

Journeying into penal, media and police archives, and drawing on a wide range of sources, Maxwell-Stewart and Kippen collected information on pre-transportation court appearances, sentencing, occupation, marital status, religion, levels of literacy, place of birth, age and height, to conduct detailed analyses of life-cycle offending in a cohort of 1,124 male convicts shipped from Britain. This chapter focuses on a detailed exploration of the life of one transported convict, James Ashcroft, to underline the complexities of the transition from unfree to free labour, and to illustrate the complex reasons behind reoffending and desistance. Born in Manchester, England, in 1809, by the time of his death in Hobart, Tasmania, in 1875, Ashcroft had appeared in a court of some description on at least ninety-six occasions, often on charges of vagrancy or for being idle and disorderly. Yet, while recidivism rates were significant among former probation-era male convicts who remained in Tasmania, Maxwell-Stewart and Kippen found little to physically distinguish those with a record of reconviction from their more law-abiding counterparts. It was thus impossible to identify potential recidivists.

The slowing of penal transportation from the mid-1850s and consequent rise of prison populations in Britain, posed new challenges for the British government. One response was the repatriation of the Australian ticket-of-leave system whereby inmates were released before their sentence had ended, largely so that their labour could be deployed in support of colonial enterprise. From 1850s the majority of offenders in England and Wales were released on licence prior to expiration of sentence, were reintroduced to civil life, and remained free as long as they did not commit any further offences and met other conditions including reporting to police stations at regular intervals; failure to do so would result in their return to prison to serve out rest of their original sentence.

The resulting licence or parole system in Britain – and the questions as to whether it promoted rehabilitation and desistance, how it impacted reoffending and its role as a pressure valve for the whole prison population – are the focus of the chapter by David Cox, Barry Godfrey, Helen Johnston and Joanne Turner. As in the previous chapter, the authors here link individual stories of offending, punishment and desistance to larger macro developments and themes. Navigating their way through the vast English penal bureaucracy, and utilising specific police and punishment records from Birkenhead and Cheshire as well as newspapers, census information and Home Office Criminal

Registers, they focus on the life and criminal stories of three offenders in the period from the 1840s to the 1910s: Richard Edwards (1835–96), Charles Dunning (1886–1967) and Catherine Bowden (1849–1913). By organising material gathered for each offender into life grids – Bowden's grid is included in the chapter – they analyse the relationship of life events such as marriage, having children, gaining employment, and religion, to patterns of offending, incarceration and desistance. In doing so, the authors seek to determine whether the licensing system and significant life events helped or hindered each person's rehabilitation as well as the impact of specific penal practices and policies, such as the Habitual Offender and Preventative Detention Acts, on repeat offenders in order to understand the impact of the relative effects of punishment and surveillance. Cox *et al.* conclude that the Victorian-era licensing system did operate as a pressure valve for the prison population as a whole and it did reduce both numbers of inmates in prisons and penal costs but at the individual level it had no intrinsic value. Nevertheless, for some individual ex-offenders being free on licence did provide a crucial space in which they could desist from criminal offending, thus it had a limited rehabilitative value for select offenders.

Concerns over the role of religion and of the state in the rehabilitation of the offender – including questions of ownership of an inmate's body and soul – and questions about how the community in partnership with the state can reassert some ownership of the criminal justice system, are key themes in the chapters on contemporary Brazilian prisons by Fiona Macaulay and Sacha Darke. Frequently understood as hellholes, where human rights are non-existent and violence is commonplace, the small groups of Brazilian prisons examined here – the so-called Resocialisation Centres (*Centros de Ressocialização* – CRs) in São Paulo state and the Association for the Protection and Assistance of Convicts/the Condemned (*Associação de Proteção e Assistência ao Condenado* – APAC) prisons in Minas Gerais state – offer very different approaches to administration and rehabilitation. Compliant with domestic and international human rights norms, and the sites of little violence and very few escapes, they successfully and cost-effectively reintegrate offenders back into their families and communities. The emergence and existence of these distinctive prisons, at odds with the punitive turn associated with late modernity, relates to both more generally decentralised administrative structures in Brazil and its very limited welfare state, as well as the reconfiguration of state–civil society relations following the late twentieth-century transition to democracy.

Drawing on extensive field research, Macaulay explores the rise and fall from political favour of the state-run CRs, while Darke examines the recent expansion of APACs, particularly in the wake of important enabling legislation passed in 2006. The core disagreement between the founders of each set of institutions concerns the role of religion (and reflects wider social and political tensions between Catholicism and evangelical Protestantism, and indeed Pentecostalism) and the state welfare apparatus in the rehabilitation or desistance of offenders. Macaulay explores the four core elements of the CR model including the creation of an alternative prison culture and support for prisoners' self-esteem that contributed to this ground-breaking model of *good* prison administration. At the same time, because the CRs allow the local community to assert its interest in the fate of 'its' offenders, the NGOs can frequently collide with the state, which remains legally responsible for the custody of an offender. Police remain suspicious and regard the CR model as being 'soft' on offenders.

Taking state abandonment and prisoner collaboration or organisation as their starting points, APACs operate without state presence, thus Darke unravels the complexities of the prison as self-managed community and substitute family, and dissects the central ideological tool of peer-facilitated rehabilitation, as well as the realities of situational control. The focus of this chapter is the self-governing nature of APAC prisons, particularly the role of prisoners, former prisoners and local communities in facilitating rehabilitation and desistance. In building productive and sustained inmate-family-community relationships, by employing local residents, and by housing offenders from the locale, for example, APACs demand that the local community retain ownership of both its lawbreakers and law-abiding citizens, and reinforce inmates' duty, responsibility, and community service in rebuilding their lives. The CR-APAC models are clearly not straight-forward or easy solutions to later modernity's problems of mass incarceration and carceral sprawl. Yet, their existence underlines the need for continued imagination and greater penal invention and innovation, and that "the prison" – like "the police" and the bureaucracies tasked with managing offenders and ex-offenders – is still very much a work in progress.

Collectively, these chapters underscore that the development of modern bureaucratic penal regimes was uneven, fragmented and often rather messy. They complicate and challenge overarching theories about penal reform, whether Foucault's notion of disciplinary power or Norbert Elias's 'civilising process', yet they also illustrate that transnational and comparative approaches to criminal justice history can underpin new interpretations that centre on the interconnectedness and entanglement of ideas, policies and practices about discipline, punishment and desistance across both time and space. They highlight, in particular, that while state violence was recast as corrective and often sanitised from the nineteenth century to the twenty-first century, it remained embedded in the penal bureaucracies of different imperial, colonial and state systems. They demonstrate, too, the tensions that arose as metropolitan and imperial definitions and characterisations of offenders and cultures of imprisonment were translated and adapted to local colonial conditions and the disjunctures between the imagined, the utopian and the intended or officially-conceived penal experience and the realities of prison life and labour. Finally, they also confirm the importance of penal regimes as expressions of state power and intrinsic components of the processes of nation-building and state formation.

Part I
Discipline

1 'Insufficiently cruel' or 'simply inefficient'?

Discipline, punishment and reform in the Gold Coast prison system, c. 1850–1957

Stacey Hynd

The chief object of the Gold Coast Prisons today is reform rather than punishment.[1]

(Governor Guggisberg, 1927)

My experience of fourteen months in prison convinced me moreover, that in a very short time prisoners lose all their individualism and personality ... [and] are so unequipped to meet the outside world that it is little wonder that they hanker for the misery and boredom of their prison cell, a protective shelter for their lost and shattered souls.[2]

(Kwame Nkrumah, 1957)

Although they formed a key component of the coercive networks of colonial states, prisons – and penality more widely – have only recently emerged as a topic of interest in imperial histories.[3] Criminal justice and penal practices across British Africa were characterized by a focus on didactic deterrence and the maintenance of law and order.[4] Historians have generally agreed that colonial prisons differed from the Western penitentiary model in their conscious strategy to constrain bodies rather than discipline minds: these were punitive rather than panoptic institutions.[5] In Florence Bernault's

[1] Frederick G. Guggisberg, *The Gold Coast: A Review of the Events of 1920–1926 and the Prospects of 1927–28* (Accra: Government Printer, 1927), 310.

[2] Kwame Nkrumah, *The Autobiography of Kwame Nkrumah* (London: Thomas Nelson & Sons, 1957), 132.

[3] See Taylor Sherman, 'The Tensions of Colonial Punishment: Perspectives on Recent Developments in the Study of Coercive Networks in Asia, Africa and the Caribbean', *History Compass*, 7.3 (2009), 659–77.

[4] See David Killingray, 'Punishment to Fit the Crime? Penal Policy and Practice in British Colonial Africa', in Florence Bernault (ed.), *Enfermement, Prison et Châtiments en Afrique: du 19e siècle à Nos Jours* (Paris: Karthala, 1999), 181–204.

[5] Florence Bernault, 'De l'Afrique ouverte à l'Afrique fermée: comprendre l'histoire des reclusions continentales', in Bernault, *Enfermement, Prison et Châtiments*, 15–64; Daniel Branch, 'Imprisonment and Colonialism in Kenya, c.1930–52: Escaping the Colonial Archipelago',

field-defining work on African imprisonment, she argues that colonial prisons became experiments in hybridity, moulding Western penal models onto African environments. Prisons were 'tools of social disorder [rather] than civil discipline', geared towards the establishment of colonial control and racial hierarchy, routinizing economic and political coercion.[6] However, whilst existing studies of prisons in Africa have been largely empirical and focused on prisons as mechanisms of racial and economic coercion, this chapter will argue that the figuration of imprisonment in the Gold Coast was also a result of dialogical tensions between 'civilization' and 'violence' within colonial and imperial governance, and that to fully understand the tensions which shaped punishment historians need to consider the interconnections between penal, political and moral economies of empire in Africa at local, colonial and imperial levels. A political economy analysis of colonial punishment alone does not fully explain the development of colonial prisons: the cultural and discursive norms which shaped penal policy must also be considered. Certainly, although the reports of individual colonial governments concentrate on committals and costs, the gaze of the imperial archive is also focused on the image conveyed by practices of imprisonment in Africa. Did the modernizing Governor Guggisberg's rhetoric of 'reform' translate into action, or was the reality of imprisonment closer to Nkrumah's account of 'lost and shattered souls'?

During the early stages of conquest and pacification across nineteenth- and twentieth-century Africa, imperialism was marked by the idea of a 'civilizing mission' that tied Africa's integration into a global capitalist economy with the liberation of the continent from its 'primitive' status.[7] This period saw the importation of imprisonment from England as a punitive but also modernizing measure, and the mobilization of prison labour to develop colonial economic and political infrastructure. In the inter-war years, however, the apparent failure of the 'civilizing mission' led to the adoption of a policy of indirect rule through which Africa was to develop under British guidance, and African cultures were to be protected from the degenerative effects of too rapid social change and exposure to Western, urbanized cultures.[8] The inter-war years were therefore marked by an unresolved tension between colonial efforts to modernize, capitalize and industrialize Africa, and the fear that such efforts would 'detribalize' African communities, destroying social stability

---

International Journal of African Historical Studies, 38.2 (2005), 239–66; Stacey Hynd, 'Law, Violence and Penal Reform: State Responses to Crime and Disorder in Colonial Malawi, c.1900–59', *Journal of Southern African Studies*, 37.3 (2011), 431–47.

[6] Florence Bernault, 'Shadow of Rule: Colonial Power and Modern Punishment in Africa', in Frank Dikötter and Ian Brown (eds), *Cultures of Confinement: A History of the Prison in Africa, Asia and Latin America* (Ithaca: Cornell University Press, 2007), 55–94.

[7] Megan Vaughan, 'Africa and the Birth of the Modern World', *Transactions of the Royal Historical Society,* 16 (2006), 143–62.

[8] Frederick Lugard, *The Dual Mandate in British Tropical Africa* (Edinburgh: W. Blackwood & Sons, 1923).

and culture, as well as endangering the colonial project. These tensions were replicated within prisons in the competing imperatives to 'control', 'reform' and 'punish' African convicts. By the late 1930s, and particularly after 1945, the emergence of anti-colonialism, African nationalism and the welfare state in Britain pushed the British Empire into a new welfarist, interventionist, developmental model of colonialism in order to justify its continued rule.[9] At this point, new technologies of rule and an increasingly universalist colonial penal model emerged, which stressed the need to reform offenders rather than punish them, and called for the widespread introduction of industrial training and education in prisons to create modern, economically productive and disciplined colonial subjects. This however proved more difficult to enact than London had anticipated. There was frequently a disconnect between the rhetoric of imperial reform and the reality of continued coercion and exploitation on the ground, particularly as colonial control came under threat from nationalist agitation and rising crime rates.

In the Gold Coast more specifically, a longer history of colonialism exposed the colony to a wide range of imperial influences, from the punitive early nineteenth-century uses of penal labour and the 'cat o' nine tails', to late nineteenth-century reforms and the economic mobilization of convict labour during the high point of imperialism in the early twentieth century, before the modernization and Africanization of prisons as the Gold Coast became the first black African colony to transition towards independence in 1957. Discourses and practices surrounding the translation of British models of imprisonment into the Gold Coast were indelibly marked by the perceived need to both 'control' and 'civilize' the local population, leading the aims of imprisonment to be more political than penal, with a focus on punishment/severity, productivity/efficiency and reform/welfare. To investigate these ideas, imprisonment will here be analysed as a lens on the tensions permeating colonial states and societies from an imperial to a local level: between the universalist policies of the Colonial Office in London and the particularist practices of colonial governments; between reformist and retributive tendencies within penal systems, and between African and colonial conceptions of crime and punishment. This chapter will draw on archival records from London and Accra to investigate how metropolitan cultures of imprisonment were translated in the colony and these developments will be contextualized against the socio-legal background of shifting conceptions of race, deviance and crime in the colony.

There is limited historical evidence available on patterns of punishment in the pre-colonial period. The lands that became the Gold Coast have a long history of transnational contact from regional migration, trading and multiple imperialisms, leading to cosmopolitan legal cultures.[10] Many local African systems of justice were primarily based on restitutive principles, with a focus on

---

[9] See Frederick Cooper, *Decolonization and African Society: The Labour Question in French and British Africa* (Cambridge: Cambridge University Press, 1996).
[10] Roger Gocking, *The History of Ghana* (Westport: Greenwood Press, 2005).

compensation and reconciliation between parties rather than the punishment of an individual offender by the state. Control over people, not space, was key and consequently judicial strategies did not prioritize spatial confinement.[11] Social isolation through enslavement, spiritual sanctions and physical punishment, including pinioning, mutilation and execution, instead dominated methods of punishing serious offences.[12] As the Gold Coast became a central node in the transatlantic slave trade, however, there emerged a regional history of physical confinement and detention for economic, if not judicial, purposes as slaves were held in fort dungeons before being transported.[13]

The development of criminal justice and imprisonment in the British Gold Coast was intermittent. In the early 1780s, with US independence cutting off previous routes for transportation, Britain sent a small number of convicts from England to the Gold Coast and Senegambia as soldiers and agricultural labourers to establish a British presence, highlighting the political function of colonial penality from the outset. The failure of these settlements, however, with gross immorality and crime in convict-staffed forts, led to public scandal and the collapse of the venture.[14] With the expansion of British imperialism in the nineteenth century, legal and penal systems in British West Africa were directly imported from the metropole and then adapted to local conditions through pragmatism rather than ideological commitment to the 'majesty' of British law or penal modernity. In the aftermath of the abolition of the slave trade, from 1828 to 1842 British rule centred on coastal trade forts governed by a Committee of Merchants who aimed to promote the growth of 'legitimate trade' in the region.[15] The slave dungeons of coastal forts at Accra, Elmina and Cape Coast were transformed into gaol cells filled with inmates, who were often held in chains. These prisons however were largely custodial affairs, and many inmates were incarcerated for debt rather than criminal offences: flogging and fines were preferred as methods of punishment and discipline.[16] With the re-establishment of formal imperial control in 1843, the implementation of English common law was formalized in the Bond of 1844 between Britain and the 'Protected Tribes', which established that 'murders, robberies and other crimes and offences [should] be tried and inquired of before the Queen's

---

[11] Bernault, 'Shadow of Rule', 56.
[12] See J.E. Casely-Hayford, *Gold Coast Native Constitutions* (London: Frank Cass & Co., [1903] 1970); R.S. Rattray, *Ashanti Law and Constitution* (Oxford: Clarendon Press, 1929).
[13] Paul E. Lovejoy, *Transformations in Slavery: A History of Slavery in Africa*, 2nd edn (Cambridge: Cambridge University Press, 2000).
[14] Emma Christopher, *A Merciless Place: The Lost Story of Britain's Convict Disaster in Africa* (Oxford: Oxford University Press, 2011).
[15] David Kimble, *A Political History of Ghana: The Rise of Gold Coast Nationalism, 1850–1928* (Oxford: Clarendon, 1963), 204.
[16] Great Britain, *Report of Her Majesty's Commissioner of Inquiry on the State of the British Settlements of the Gold Coast, at Sierra Leone and the Gambia, 1841*, Parl Papers Session 1842, vol. 12, p. 15. See R. Rathbone, 'Locking Up or Locking Out?' (unpublished conference paper, in author's possession).

judicial officers and the chiefs of the district'. British officials had jurisdiction in and around the forts and gradually took over the punishment of offenders from local chiefs, whom it was feared were using convicted criminals as human sacrifices to bolster their ritual authority.[17] Prisons thus became a marker of the 'civilization' and 'modernity' supposedly brought to the Gold Coast by British rule against the purported 'barbaric' violence of local custom.

As colonial rule became more firmly established in the coastal region, so did its mechanisms of social control, from the Supreme Court to Gold Coast police and the prisons.[18] By the 1860s Colonial Office circulars requested that colonial prisons be placed on the same basis as English gaols: the separate system, a minimum diet and penal labour.[19] These structures however quickly proved unworkable. Officials presumed solitude to be particularly hard for 'communal' Africans to bear and thus the separate system seemed appropriate to the punishment of African criminals. But as the main available detention sites were communal cells in fort dungeons, it proved impossible 'adequately to make the prisoners feel the want of social intercourse which every prisoner should experience', with inmates working and sleeping together in gangs of four to twenty men.[20] The individualizing nature of the Western penitentiary was almost entirely absent. The 1896 Blue Book noted that Accra, Elmina and the Dutch forts cells had proven 'not suitable for modern prison discipline', but the 'swish' [rammed earth] prisons which emerged upcountry were also built around communal cells and conditions were even less sanitary or secure.[21] The minimum diet was also difficult to translate into an African context: with malnourishment common in many communities, any diet severe enough to be worse than a normal diet outside of the prison was likely to be potentially hazardous to health, and a colonial government which declared itself a 'civilizing' force could not legitimately allow prisoners under its direct care to suffer such illness, leading to protracted debates over the rations accorded to African prisoners.[22] More broadly, prison diets in Africa were not simply punitive but served to racially categorize convicts, with African, Asian and European prisoners receiving 'culturally appropriate' diets. Most significantly, however, the third pillar of the separate system, penal labour, ran counter to the economic imperatives of colonialism. In a

[17] Bond of 1844 cited in J.J. Crooks, *Records Relating to the Gold Coast Settlements from 1750–1874* (1923; reprint, London: Routledge, 1973), 296.
[18] Gold Coast, *A Note on the History of the British Courts in the Gold Coast Colony* (Accra: Government Printer, [1904] 1936); W.H. Gillespie, *The Gold Coast Police, 1844–1938* (Accra: Government Printer, 1955).
[19] See Government of the Gold Coast, *Prisons Ordinance, 1876*.
[20] Government of the Gold Coast, *Annual Report of the Prisons Deparment 1897* (Accra: HMSO, 1898) [hereafter Prisons Annual Report], Government of the Gold Coast, *Annual Report[s] for the Year Ending 1900–06* (Accra: HMSO, 1901–7) [hereafter *Blue Book[s]*).
[21] *Blue Book 1896.*
[22] See shifting rations awarded between diets recorded in 1872 and 1876 *Blue Books*; the National Archives, Kew [TNA] CO 859/378 Prison Diet 1953.

post-slave trading economy which required the creation of a new capitalistic labour market, local authorities preferred to put Africans into productive labour rather than seeing them toil uselessly on the treadmill, crank or shot drill, highlighting tensions between 'punishment' and 'productivity'.[23] Imprisonment was to be didactic, teaching the value of hard work to 'lazy' Africans. The archival record reveals that by the 1850s prisoner chain-gangs were already being deployed to build and maintain roads.[24] In 1902 Acting Superintendent of Prisons Major Kitson combined punitive and productive aims by ordering that Africans should work any hours in any job 'so long as the work he is doing is objectionable and hard to him', with convicts working in everything from 'scavenging' to sanitation, agriculture and conservancy.[25] Meanwhile, the treadmill and crank drill built at Ussher Fort broke down and were left to rot.

During the scramble for Africa at the turn of the twentieth century, British control of the region expanded with the purchase of the Dutch Gold Coast in 1872 and the annexation of Ashanti and the Northern Territories in 1902–3. Imperial expansion was accompanied by a hardening of racial attitudes, particularly during the era of scientific racism. Colonial law and punishment at this point fulfilled military and political needs to establish control rather than to deter crime. Initial political resistance was met with military force, exile or execution, but once control had been established the focus of penality shifted to the routinization of colonial hegemony and the production of African subjects.[26] Colonial perceptions of race, ethnicity and African 'criminality' shaped the moral and political economies of imprisonment. As legal and bureaucratic authority increased, a growing number of Africans found themselves captured by expanding spaces and categories of colonial criminality. By 1895 approximately half of the 2,006 persons in gaol were in penal imprisonment, with only one in six being debtors.[27] Criminalization expanded as the colonial state developed, with rates of penal imprisonment averaging around 1:500 between 1925 and 1955, whilst committal rates were closer to 1:300.[28] The majority of these were short, arbitrary detentions, with between 70 to 90 per cent of inmates annually sentenced to less than six months of imprisonment. Many of these sentences were for petty theft or infringement of colonial bye-laws, or served in default of payment of fines or taxes. Consequently, many Africans were imprisoned for offences they did not recognize as 'crimes',

---

[23] Stacey Hynd, "'… A Weapon of Immense Value": Convict Labour in British Colonial Africa, c.1850–1950s', in Alex Lichtenstein and C. de Vito (eds), *Global Histories of Convict Labour* (Leiden: Brill, 2015), 419–59.

[24] *Blue Book 1850.*

[25] *Prisons Annual Report 1902.*

[26] See TNA CO 96/362/80 Ashanti Political Prisoners 1902–3; A. Adu Boahen, *Yaa Asantewa and the Asante-British War of 1900–1* (Oxford: James Currey, 2003).

[27] *Blue Book 1895.*

[28] This is in line with other colonies in British Africa, but much higher than England and Wales, where rates were between 1:1,100 to 1:2,700 in the same period.

morally or within customary law. For colonial states, deviance became a racial trait, encompassing the entire spectrum of the African population.[29] Gold Coast prisons certainly followed the general colonial model of prioritizing racial segregation within prison walls, with European and Asian prisoners held separately from Africans.[30] But with the Gold Coast lacking a large settler population, racial ordering was perhaps a less significant penal imperative than in colonies like Kenya or Rhodesia. Ethnic stereotypes instead strongly shaped sentencing: whilst colonial courts were more likely to find Ga, Fante and Asante offenders capable of premeditated offences, tribes such as the Dagomba from the Northern Territories were regarded as particularly prone to violence. Lagosians, and Nigerians more generally, were regarded by both colonial and Gold Coast Africans to have marked criminal tendencies and were notably overrepresented in prisons.[31] Local discourses of power also shaped structures of imprisonment. African agency in translating imprisonment can be seen in the development by African chiefs of 'bush prisons' attached to their Native Courts. Chiefs came to view these prisons as a vital adjunct to their power and forced Gold Coast authorities to formalize their existence in the 1910 Native Jurisdiction Bill and Native Prisons Ordinance.[32] These 'bush prisons' worried prison officials as they were largely unregulated by central authority, and were prone to corruption and poor conditions, but as they provided vital labour for local economies they were retained throughout the colonial period.[33]

Imperial, as well as local colonial, politics shaped the nature of imprisonment and penal reform in the Gold Coast with metropolitan precedent informing not only the initial infrastructure and ethos of prisons, but the impetus for reform. In 1895, the Gladstone Committee on Prisons in England declared that deterrence and reform were to be the joint objectives of prison, and advocated the abolition of the penal reform and the separate system.[34] Although its reforms were not intended for imperial consumption, they were gradually, if fitfully, adopted across British Africa during the 1900s to 1930s. With its established systems of punishments and self-professed status as a model colony, the Gold Coast quickly adopted the rhetoric of modern penal reform in its annual

---

[29] Bernault, 'Shadow of Rule', 65.
[30] Europeans sentenced to long terms of imprisonment were usually transported back to England to serve out their sentence.
[31] *Prisons Department Report 1938–9*. It may also have been due to Nigerians being less able to pay fines, either through poverty or lack of social networks within the Gold Coast.
[32] See Casely-Hayford, *Gold Coast Native Institutions*, 274.
[33] In a system similar to that used in Britian, prisoners would work for the Native Authorities who ran the prisons, usually either on prison maintenance or growing food supplies, working on the Native Authority's properties, or providing communal labour for the village. (NB – the archive contains little detail about the specifics of this labour.) Gold Coast, Sessional Paper VIII 1919–20, *Report on the Prison Department and Proposals for its Reorganisation*.
[34] Great Britain, *Report from the Departmental Committee on Prisons*, C. 7702, Parliamentary Papers, 1895.

reports, memoranda and new prison regulations in 1922.[35] Implementing such reform in practice however proved a protracted struggle. As in many other fields, there was a distinct discrepancy between official rhetoric and the reality of colonial reform in prison. Reform was limited by institutional inertia and financial constraints, with Prisons Departments treated as the 'Cinderella service' of colonial administrations.[36] Prison administration in the 1900s to 1920s was marked by a lack of any clear philosophy of treatment at a local level, and as such many prisons 'degenerate[d] into mere caretaking institutions' which were badly run and underfunded.[37] The 1920 report which initiated the reform and modernization of the prison system in the Gold Coast notably documented 'strange tales … told of the Gold Coast Prisons':

> is it not true that their gates are commonly opened to visitors by the prison clerk? And what of the escort warder who was sent out in charge of a firewood gang, and having been observed stealing cassava from a farm, returned to gaol, his hands tied with rope, under escort of his own prisoners? Again, was it at Axim or Winnebah that convict prisoner 'Ace of Spades' on being told that his time had come for discharge, remonstrated in this wise [sic] 'what for you go sack me'.[38]

As such tales indicate, although colonial law formally 'criminalized' large numbers of Africans by convicting them of minor offences, local officials often regarded such people as 'primitive', 'deviant' or simply disobedient rather than innately criminal, because many felt Africans lacked the intellectual and cultural sophistication to harbour criminal intent. Governor Nathan had argued to Secretary of State Joseph Chamberlain in 1901 that '[t]he British Prison System as adopted in Africa had failed as a deterrent for crime, not because it was insufficiently cruel but because the large group of people with but faintly developed criminal instincts were not deterred by the disgrace of prison as they were in England'. Both prisons and colonial categories of 'crime' did not translate easily into African idioms of control and deviance. Administrative reports routinely noted that aside from petty theft and 'homicides during sudden gusts of passion' there was little serious crime.[39] The main categories of criminal offence resulting in imprisonment

---

[35] Government of the Gold Coast, *Prison Regulations of 1922*.

[36] J.C. Hamilton, *Crime and Punishment in West Africa* (Accra: Staples Press, 1953), 13; TNA CO 912/3, Treatment of Offenders Sub-Committee Draft Minutes 21 December 1937, Colonial Penal Advisory Committee Papers Distributed 1937–40.

[37] ADM 14/15 Sessional Paper VIII Leg Co 1919–20, cited in R.B. Seidman, 'The Ghana Prison System: An Historical Perspective', in A. Milner (ed.), *African Penal Systems* (London: Routledge & K. Paul, 1969), 442.

[38] Gold Coast, Sessional Paper VIII 1919–20, *Report on the Prison Department and Proposals for its Reorganisation*.

[39] Cited in Seidman, 'The Ghana Prison System', 431–69; GNA ADM 5/1/62 Northern Territories of the Gold Coast Annual Report 1922–3.

were larceny, housebreaking, wounding and assault. Many prisoners were migrant labourers from the Northern Territories who had travelled south but been unable to find work and tended 'to offend more from circumstances than innate criminality'.[40] Within judicial and penal administrations there was a certain sympathy for short-term inmates, many of whom were incarcerated after failing to pay fines or taxes, and it was generally recognized that imprisonment did such men more harm than good by exposing them to 'moral contagion'. Such sympathy facilitated the adoption of reformist discourse, even if the resources for actual change were severely limited. It was only in the 1920s and 1930s that 'criminal types' emerged in colonial discourses, as part of wider fears concerning detribalization and unemployment in urban environments. Only these 'habitual offenders' or recidivists were regarded as having a criminal mindset, and therefore deserving of firm discipline.[41] With recidivism rates running at over 20 per cent by the 1930s, repeat offending was blamed by colonial officials on a growing criminal culture in urban areas, difficulties for ex-convicts in finding employment on discharge, and the lack of stigma attached to imprisonment among local communities. As a prison report noted in the mid-1930s, 'among a very large proportion of inhabitants a term in prison is no disgrace, on discharge a convict is welcomed everywhere by his friends and relations who regard his imprisonment as a bit of bad luck, consequently he feels no moral obligation to keep out of prison in future'.[42]

The need to transform both the wider prison population and burgeoning 'criminal elements' into colonial subjects drove reformist policies in the inter-war years. The arrival of a new technocratic, reformist governor, F. G. Guggisberg, in 1927 kickstarted local reform in the colony. Governor Guggisberg stated in a 1927 report that '[t]he chief object of the Gold Coast Prisons today is reform rather than punishment … [primarily] through trade training'.[43] The following year's Blue Book report to London asserted that prisons were 'gradually emerging from a system of negative prevention to one of training and reformation'.[44] The major focus on imprisonment was thus ostensibly shifted from punitive deterrence to disciplining and re-socialization through the teaching of a trade to create economically productive citizen-subjects. Although Seidman argues that this shift occurred 'not from any clearly articulated concept of penology but to explain what was being done in fact', it can equally be read as part of a larger re-orientation of colonial penology as officials drew on emerging networks of professional knowledge and metropolitan overview of criminal justice increased in the wake of various

---

[40] Government of the Gold Coast, *Prison Regulations of 1922*.

[41] Alexander Paterson, *Report on a Visit to the Prisons of Kenya, Uganda, Tanganyika, Zanzibar, Aden and Somaliland* (Morija: Government Printer, 1944), 27.

[42] *Prisons Department Report 1934–5*.

[43] Frederick G. Guggisberg, *The Gold Coast: A Review of the Events of 1920–1926 and the Prospects of 1927–28* (Accra: Government Printer, 1927), 310.

[44] Gold Coast, *Blue Book, 1928–9*.

scandals.[45] In addition, the effects of the Great Depression and changing ideas of African labour drove reconceptualizations of the form and function of prison labour.[46]

Bernault argues that colonial prisons were not supposed to reclaim and transform individual Africans, but rather to promote the reproduction of the dominant power through racial hierarchy and economic development.[47] The economic determinants of penality however shifted over time, being most significant during the early colonial period. Courts normatively handed sentences of imprisonment 'with hard labour' but the content of this labour was not specified. Prisoners formed a reserve pool of cheap labour for the Gold Coast government, which was particularly useful during the expansion of colonial rule from the 1890s to the 1920s as slave and forced labour decreased: in effect, penal labour became a hidden form of forced labour.[48] In the early nineteenth century, unskilled labour dominated, with 'degrading' sanitation and conservancy work that could not easily be filled with free labour comprising the majority of man-hours, before there was a shift to agricultural production and semi-skilled service labour.[49] Prisoners worked at both the coalface and the ornamental façade of colonialism: the 1902 report noted that prisoners at James Fort Accra were employed at the polo and cricket grounds, the racecourse, Christiansborg gardens and in tending the Governor's yard.[50]

Convict labour proved a crucial financial fillip to early colonial governments striving to meet imperial demands for self-sufficiency and efficiency, with the Prisons Commissioner proudly noting that the gross value of labour in 1902 was £8,117 against a total cost for the department of £10,215.[51] Penal labour was formally abolished as unworkable and inappropriate in 1907 and officially replaced with the idea of prison labour as a financial asset to the colonial state.[52] As part of this shift to productive labour, industrial training was introduced to create a pool of semi-skilled workers, with convicts being trained as masons, carpenters, tailors, brickmakers and other trades. In the Gold Coast, annual reports noted with pride the growth in prison industry outputs from £413 in 1904 to £2,693 in 1908.[53] Commodities production

[45] TNA CO 544/90/13, Visit of H.G. Bushe to West Africa: Report, 1932.
[46] See G. St. Orde Browne, *The African Labourer* (Oxford: Oxford University Press, 1933).
[47] Bernault, 'De l'Afrique ouverte', 40.
[48] Kwabena O. Akurang-Parry, 'Colonial Forced Labor Policies for Road-Building in Southern Ghana and International Anti-Forced Labor Pressures, 1900–1940', *African Economic History*, 8 (2000), 1–25.
[49] *Prisons Department Report 1935–6*.
[50] *Prisons Department Report 1902*. Prisoners also routinely provided labour for District Officers. See Laura Boyle, *Diary of A District Officer's Wife* (Oxford: Alden Press, 1968), 18.
[51] *Prisons Report 1902*.
[52] Killingray, 'Punishment to Fit the Crime?', 191; S. Coldham, 'Crime and Punishment in British Colonial Africa', in *Punishment: Transactions of the Jean Bodin Society for Comparative Institutional History, LVIII* (Brussels: De Boeck University, 1991), 57–66; Gold Coast, *Prisons Report 1908*.
[53] *Prisons Report 1908*.

aimed to boost flows of material goods and encourage African 'wants' to draw communities further into the capitalist global economy. Annual prison reports kept careful and detailed records of the number of items produced and the costs saved to government departments from both prison labour and industries: this could be a significant percentage of the outlay, with gross revenue of 1929–30 of £32,658 against £50,013 total expenditure.[54] The reformist impact of trade education was however negated by limited training facilities, skills which were inappropriate for local markets – such as book-binding and bootmaking – and by the simple fact that the majority of prisoners were serving sentences which were too short to allow effective training.[55] Agriculture had always been a major occupation for African convict labour. But with inter-war concerns about whether industrial training was appropriate and effective for ordinary Africans, and growing fears about detribalization and criminalization in urban areas, prison agriculture took on new moral and political dimensions. Many senior prison officials held that rather than being given industrial training, African convicts should be taught modern agricultural methods to make them 'better peasants', reclaiming them from crime through encouraging them to return to their 'natural', rural lifestyles. It is unclear, however, how many officials truly believed this, and how many were simply seeking a justification for the lack of reform within their prisons, or looking to use agricultural labour to keep costs down as the Depression took hold of colonial economies and budgets.[56]

The colonial archive of the inter-war years reveals a shift in the colonial and imperial gaze, from a primarily political and economic approach, to an increasingly humanitarian consideration of the nature of imprisonment. Moral economies of reform were strongly shaped by the tension between 'civilization' and the perceived necessity of violence in colonial disciplinary techniques. Prison discipline regulations were copied directly from the English model, but adapted to local conditions for practical and ideological reasons. There was a persistent dichotomy in colonial penality between the desire for 'harsh' discipline to punish and maintain order, and the desire for a more 'humane', modern disciplinary regime that operated in accordance with metropolitan standards of penality. According to departmental reports, in 1901 there were 3,231 punishments for 482 prisoners (a ratio of 6:1), including 71 floggings, 1,416 shot drills, 145 crank drills and 339 encasements in leg irons. The twentieth century however saw the emergence of a new 'imperial humanitarianism' which drove changing attitudes towards the infliction of pain on the colonized body.[57] In prison discipline this translated into a shift

---

[54] *Prisons Report 1929–30.*
[55] Only prisoners serving over six months' imprisonment were eligible for trade training. However, in 1954–5 it was estimated that 70 per cent of those eligible were released before training was completed.
[56] *Prisons Report 1931–2.*
[57] Rob Skinner and Alan Lester, 'Humanitarianism and Empire: New Research Agendas', *Journal of Imperial and Commonwealth History,* 40.5 (2012), 729–47.

from physical discipline to 'modern' disciplinary techniques.[58] In line with metropolitan humanitarian sentiment, crank drills and leg irons were quickly phased out, despite Prison Superintendent Kitson's protests that discipline was being weakened by 'the lightness of the present punishments inflicted on half-civilized prisoners'.[59] Shot drills dropped from 1,416 in 1902 to 183 in 1903, and ended entirely by 1934. Instead, a marks system and the removal of privileges – including prisoners' earnings, visitations, and permission to play warri [boardgame] in cells or listen to wireless broadcasts – emerged in the inter-war years as key disciplinary tools.[60]

Corporal punishment had long been regarded as particularly appropriate for Africans, both as an 'indigenous practice' and as a language of discipline that Africans could understand, with many colonial officials believing that Africans understood pain but lacked the intelligence to respond to psychological means of behavioural change. In colonial penology, physical punishment served to construct and demarcate racial difference, with only non-white colonial subjects flogged.[61] In the Gold Coast whipping and flogging with the 'cat o' nine tails' were incorporated from maritime penal traditions and were frequently used in the nineteenth century as both a judicial penalty and within prison discipline, before corporal punishment declined in the twentieth century.[62] This shift in penal violence can be viewed as part of a wider colonial shift towards restricting – or at least routinizing and sanitizing – the use of corporal punishment, as changing cultural sensibilities and humanitarian pressure made officials increasingly uncomfortable with the infliction of non-essential, direct physical violence by the state on subject African bodies.[63] However, this was no unilinear 'civilizing process' and there remained a persistent vein of coercive violence in imprisonment, defying Foucault's model of a transition away from 'sovereign', physical punishment in modern penal regimes.[64] Prisons remained central sites of colonial violence, as evinced by the centralization of executions at Accra, Sekondi and Tamale, and the enforcement of court-awarded sentences of corporal punishment within prison precincts. Violence was sanitized, bureaucratized and discursively recast, not eradicated. Canings and whippings continued to be widely used for juvenile delinquents and in Native Courts, although they were officially standardized and medicalized, with regulation instruments, a normative limit of twelve lashes and a doctor to check the offender's health was good

---

[58] Michel Foucault, *Surveiller et Punir: Naissance de la Prison* (Paris: Gallimard, 1975).
[59] GNA CSO 15/9/92, Mechanical Means of Restraint in Prison, 1935; *Prisons Report 1903*.
[60] *Prisons Report 1937–8*.
[61] Steven Pierce, 'Punishment and the Political Body: Flogging and Colonialism in Northern Nigeria', *Interventions*, 3.2 (2001), 206–21; Bernault, 'A Shadow of Rule'.
[62] See Judicial Department Reports, Prison Department Reports, *Blue Books*.
[63] TNA CO 323/1399/3, Penal Reform in the Colonies: Corporal Punishment, 1936–7.
[64] Norbert Elias, *The Civilizing Process: Sociogenetic and Psychogenetic Investigations* (Oxford: Blackwell, [1939] 2000); Foucault, *Surveiller et Punir*.

enough to safely withstand the sentence.[65] Even in the post-war welfaristic period, the 'cat' remained a significant symbolic marker of colonial power, with over thirty floggings handed down for mutiny, incitement and gross personal violence against warders within prisons in the 1950s, in addition to its use as a court sentence.

Prison discipline remained contested throughout the colonial period, although annual rates of punishment dropped to 1:15 from 1:10 inmates from the 1920s to the 1950s. One reason for continued disputes over disciplinary issues was the questionable relationship between prisoners and their guards. The poor quality of warder staff had been noted by government officials since the nineteenth century, as European warders tended to drink themselves to death upon arriving on the Gold Coast, whilst African warders were prone to ill-discipline and corruption.[66] An investigation into a 'fracas' at Kumasi prison in September 1946 among 200 recidivists revealed that key among their complaints was misconduct of the warders and allegations that warders were stealing food.[67] Prisoners were often thought to be 'more intelligent and of a superior class' than their warders, leading to the inversion of power structures.[68] Micro-relations of power dictated the daily realities of imprisonment. Some convicts were able to effectively establish informal relations with guards which disrupted the hierarchies of power. Warders could be awed by the supernatural powers claimed by some inmates. Max Fohtung, a Chief Warder in the 1940s, told of how one prisoner, Mubanga, used demonstrations of his 'magic' – escaping from handcuffs, making padlocks open by themselves, making police guards fall asleep and stealing their guns – to demand extra rations and blankets, £5 in cash, cigarettes and gin or whisky from his guards.[69] Prison walls could be porous, in both physical and cultural senses.[70] Escapes were certainly common, particularly from 'swish' prisons and labour gangs, but inmates who remained in prison were also not always isolated from society. Ideas of power and subjecthood from outside could affect prisoners' experiences, from fears of magic to ideas of rights, dignities and citizenship, particularly in the late-colonial era as prisoners increasingly began to collectively protest about their treatment, mirroring protests in the streets outside.[71]

---

[65] GNA CSO 15/1/108, Corporal Punishment Returns 1937–42.
[66] Annual Report of 1902; GNA, ADM 1/50, Despatch No. 239, Governor to Secretary of State, 25 August 1901.
[67] GNA CSO 15/9/377, Fracas between prisoners, DC Kumasi to Chief Commissioner Ashanti, 23 September 1946. See also *Prisons Department Report 1934–5* for a similar occurrence in September 1934.
[68] *Annual Report of 1902*. Discipline among prison staff remained poor throughout the period, for example, in 1954–5 there were 1,253 disciplinary offences committed by 1,324 staff, and 49 staff were dismissed.
[69] Rhodes House Library, Oxford MSS.Afr.s. 2137/1 Chilver, 'Autobiography of Max Fohtung'.
[70] Branch, 'Imprisonment and Colonialism', 242.
[71] See GNA CSO 15/9/377, Fracas between prisoners, DC Kumasi to Chief Commissioner Ashanti, 23 September 1946.

The Second World War forced the rejustification of Britain's empire in the face of global calls for self-determination and domestic needs to harness the economic potential of colonies, propelling a move towards a new 'welfaristic', developmental model of colonialism.[72] In legal and penal arenas this translated into increased imperial influence on penal policy, particularly with the establishment of the Colonial Office's Advisory Committee on the Treatment of Offenders, which espoused a universal reformist model for colonial penality and drew extensively on metropolitan penal models and expertise, counting Margery Fry and Alexander Patterson as key consultants.[73] Like many countries, the Gold Coast experienced a sharp post-war crime boom.[74] Previous fears of 'detribalization' intensified amidst economic development, rapid urbanization, post-war unemployment, and burgeoning political unrest. For Prison and Welfare officials, the causes of criminality were firmly located in the dangers of burgeoning urban environments and rapid cultural change. According to J.C. Hamilton, Assistant Director of Probation Services:

> Criminals are not born … [but] are made so, as a result of their environment and upbringing … In West Africa today we have a threat of an increase in crime in the future due to many causes, not least being the sudden rush to large towns, with its consequent overcrowding and poverty and the impersonal life of the community.[75]

It was a combination of post-war disruption and burgeoning nationalist, anti-colonial agitation that brought the Gold Coast prison system to crisis point. Before the war, the average daily prison population had been around 1,900 persons, but by 1951 it was 3,300 and increasing. Overall committals rose from 9,548 in government prisons in 1938–9 to 20,087 in 1954–5. There were also 3,000–4,000 committals annually to the thirty-six Native Authority Prisons. By 1957 the daily average was 4,412 prisoners, with overcrowding running at 148 per cent. Reformist impulses simply could not cope with this rapid expansion and, as Hamilton admitted in his 1953 pamphlet, '[o]vercrowding, drabness and enforced idleness are the hallmarks of too many of our prisons'.[76] In an attempt to maintain

---

[72] S. Miers and R. Roberts, 'Introduction', S. Miers and R. Roberts (eds), *The End of Slavery in Africa* (Madison: University of Wisconsin Press, 1988), 16.

[73] See Colonial Office, *Report of the Committee on the Treatment of Offenders* (London: HMSO, 1954); TNA CO 912 series. Late-imperial models of imprisonment were also shaped by wider global discourses of modern penology including the United Nations' International Penal and Penitentiary Commission.

[74] See Richard Rathbone, 'The Government of the Gold Coast after the Second World War', *African Affairs*, 67.268 (1968), 209–18; Gold Coast, *Statement of the Gold Coast Government on the Report upon the Gold Coast Police by Colonel A. E. Young, Commissioner of the Police for the City of London* (Accra: Government Printer, 1952).

[75] Hamilton, *Crime and Punishment*, 3–10.

[76] Ibid., 15.

order after 1947, recidivists and 'bad hats' were transferred to Ussher Fort, Accra, where 'strict discipline, which had been relaxed in proportion to modern standards of reform' was again imposed.[77]

With economic development and post-war unemployment, the role of prisons in colonial economies declined. This, combined with the imperial development turn, brought penal reform to the fore once more. The Prisons Service was almost entirely 'Africanized' in the run up to independence, with C.B. Moses taking over as Director of Prisons in 1953.[78] The Prisons Department continued to draw heavily, if unsuccessfully, on metropolitan policies however. Attempts were made to inculcate a reformist concern among African public opinion and better reintegrate prisoners into society with the introduction of Prison Visitors, probation and 'after-care' systems, but these measures were very limited in effect.[79] Modernizing post-war reform efforts included creative and intellectual activities with the introduction of adult education classes, guest lectures, quizzes, libraries (although it was noted that the donated *Tunnelers of Holzminden* was probably not suitable reading), films and radio broadcasts. Such efforts, however, remained concentrated at central prisons, and later reports were forced to concede that, behind the rhetoric, education programmes had 'failed lamentably'.[80]

The aim of prison reform was less to produce better, educated citizens than to assuage metropolitan criticism of the 'primitive' nature of colonial imprisonment. With limited resources, reformist efforts refocused on a manageable, malleable, sub-category of offenders: juvenile delinquents. The post-war era saw the rapid development of juvenile courts and reformatories, based on metropolitan borstals, to combat the perceived rise in delinquency. Delinquency was taken as symptomatic of wider social crisis, and thus 'reforming' deviant youth served to secure the 'future' of the colonial project.[81] Similarly, with rising numbers of women imprisoned on revenue, health and price control or profiteering offences, there was a renewed focus on health, hygiene and domestic training in the reform of female inmates, which aimed to turn economically productive women into 'good mothers' and wives. To combat the sharp increase in prison inmates, and tap the potential reservoir of labour they constituted without interfering with 'free labour' markets, colonial states increasingly turned to building low-security camps – a 'prison without walls' – for first offenders in rural locations.[82] The prison camp system had been appropriated from the southern United States, and introduced into Burma and Palestine for infrastructure projects, before transferring

---

[77] Government of the Gold Coast, *Annual Report on the Treatment of Offenders during the Year 1953–4* (Accra: HMSO, 1954) [hereafter *Treatment of Offenders Report*].
[78] *Treatment of Offenders Reports, 1950–57*; Seidman, 'Prisons in Ghana', 461.
[79] *Prisons Report 1938–9*.
[80] *Prisons Report 1944–5*.
[81] See Department of Social Welfare and Community Development, 'Problem Children of the Gold Coast' (unpublished, undated paper, c.1954).
[82] *Prisons Report 1944–5*.

across to Tanganyika and then spreading to the rest of British Africa.[83] Combining modern approaches and supposedly 'traditional' employment, the prison camps at Ankaful and Maaombi became symbols of reform and were regarded as an 'invaluable aid towards further development', with prisoners trained in modern agricultural methods like contour farming, crop rotation and soil conservation.[84] These reforms, however, barely scratched the surface of imprisonment, and a climate of internment, violence and dehumanisation continued to shape the majority of prisoners' experiences.[85]

In the run up to independence, prisons became not simply sites of colonial power but also a focus of anti-colonial protest. During the Accra riots on Sunday 29 February 1948, liquor bottles were thrown over the walls of Ussher Fort and the prisoners who were on exercise 'rapidly became unmanageable'. The mob forced open the outer gates and a large number of prisoners escaped.[86] Prisons became even more significant as a site of anti-colonial protest when, after the Accra riots, leading nationalists including future Prime Minister Kwame Nkrumah were incarcerated, with crowds gathering outside James Fort prison to sing 'Kwame Nkrumah lies mouldering in a cell'. Nkrumah's writing provides a rare insight into African experiences of imprisonment, if from a privileged perspective. He wrote that 'it was something of a shock to me to discover that, as a political prisoner, I was treated as a criminal ... It was difficult to imagine that there could be worse treatment if the minimum of health and sanity of the inmate were to be preserved'. Nkrumah recounts frequent complaints about poor food and hygiene, the demoralizing effects of boredom and privation, and the constant struggle to find writing materials.[87] However, if colonial officials intended imprisonment to destroy nationalist sentiment, this plan backfired. Political prisoners routinely formulated political statements and strategies, which were written on toilet paper and smuggled out of the jail, and Nkrumah even won the 1951 general election from within prison, his election to the Legislative Council immediately forcing his release.[88]

[83]   TNA CO 323/1344/3, Prison Labour Camps in Colonies, 1935; TNA CO 912/2, Offenders Sub-Committee Circulars 1947–59.

[84]   *Treatment of Offenders Report 1947–8.*

[85]   See Gold Coast, *Report of the Committee on Prisons* (Accra: Government Printers, 1951), No III of 1951.

[86]   S. E. Hutchings, *Life in the Colonial Prison Service: The Memoirs of S. E. Hutchings* (Ilfracombe: Arthur H. Stockwell, 1987), 20–34.

[87]   Nkrumah, *The Autobiography of Kwame Nkrumah*, 126–36.

[88]   After independence in 1957, punishment had to be re-translated to fit new post-colonial contexts. Like most other African nations, Ghana retained the general penal and legal infrastructures inherited from colonialism. There was, however, an increase in penal severity to protect Ghana's social and economic development, with the introduction of harsh minimum sentences, and the use of political imprisonment against Nkrumah's opponents. See R.B. Seidman and J.D. Abaka Eyison, 'Ghana', in Milner, *African Penal Systems*, 61–87; GNA ADM 5/3/164, White Paper on the Report of the Committee of Inquiry into Ghana Prisons WP 14/68; D. Odotei Thompson, *I Was Nkrumah Prisoner* (Accra, undated).

In conclusion, prisons in the Gold Coast served not simply to contain, or punish, or reform the African body, but also reflected the image of colonial rule and its contradictions: between civilization and violence, exploitation and reform, punishment and humanitarianism. This chapter has highlighted the tensions between individual reform, the need for 'discipline' and the creation of productive labour, particularly when the prison system became increasingly overcrowded with short-term inmates. As the colonial period progressed, prisons became less about confinement and more about control. Whilst nineteenth-century prisons were largely custodial institutions, marked by poor conditions and discipline which could oscillate between harsh and inept, by the twentieth century, as British colonial rule expanded, the political and economic functions of imprisonment came to the fore. Whether prisoners were being used to carry buckets of 'nightsoil', build roads or manicure the Governor's lawn, prison labour proved an invaluable source of income for the colonial state, but the imperial as well as colonial contexts were also critical to the development of imprisonment in the Gold Coast. Pressure from London to reform prison systems across British Africa increased throughout the inter-war period, with prison administrators caught between the conflicting needs to reform the system on more modern and 'civilized' lines in accordance with Colonial Office instructions, and to make imprisonment harsh enough to meet local demands for social and crime control. For much of the colonial period, the impetus for reform in the Gold Coast went hand-in-hand with calls for stronger penal discipline, indicating the continued belief in 'civilizing violence' among some colonial authorities. Rhetorics of reform were adopted from metropolitan and global penal policies but failed to disrupt the inefficiencies and violence inherent in colonial prisons in the Gold Coast, even in the years preceding independence: there was a translation of penal policy rather than practice in many instances. Whilst the rhetoric of reform was rarely matched by its reality, a focus on colonial discourses highlights for the historian the shifting position of imprisonment in colonial penality and concerns about how continued violence and exploitation reflected negatively on the supposed 'modernizing' and 'civilizing' nature of colonialism. In their failure to eradicate crime and reform individuals, prisons demonstrated the limits both of colonial power and reformist impulses. More detailed research in the Ghanaian archives, particularly on upcountry and Native Authority imprisonment, would allow for a more nuanced analysis of the limits of reform and the daily experiences of African prisoners. Ultimately, prisons here have been shown to serve as a microcosm of the colonial state in its contradictions, its criminalization of African subjects and its lasting coercion.

2 'Who's really wicked and immoral, women or men?'

Uneasy classifications, Hindu gender roles and infanticide in late nineteenth-century India

Daniel J. R. Grey

In 1882, a woman from Buldhana in the Central Provinces published a biting denunciation in Marathi of contemporary attitudes towards women in India, entitled *A Comparison Between Women and Men*.[1] As Rosalind O'Hanlon has noted in her critical translation of this work, it would probably be an overstatement to describe Tarabai Shinde as a 'feminist', given that her text is in many ways a conservative one.[2] Nonetheless, Shinde's pamphlet provided a witty and incisive critique of both colonial racism and Hindu sexism, and complained that a significant proportion of male social reformers – regardless of caste, class, faith or ethnicity – were ultimately hypocrites uninterested in Indian women's welfare. As she bluntly exclaimed:

> These phoney reform societies of yours have been around for thirty, thirty-five years. What's the use of them? You're all there patting yourselves on the back, but if we look closely, they're about as much use as a spare tit on a goat.[3]

Shinde's writing was inspired by her fury at the popular (and frequently sanctimonious) response to the high-profile conviction of a widow named

Research conducted at the National Archives of India for this chapter was made possible by the generous support of the John Fell Oxford University Press Fund, to whom I am indebted. I am very grateful to Padma Anagol, Esme Cleall, Vivien Miller and James Campbell for their helpful suggestions on how best to improve it.

[1] Rosalind O'Hanlon, *A Comparison Between Women and Men: Tarabai Shinde and the Critique of Gender Relations in Colonial India* (New Delhi: Oxford University Press, 1994). Although from a lower caste background, Shinde's father was relatively prosperous. I am grateful to Padma Anagol for providing me with additional information on Shinde during our conversations about infanticide in colonial India.

[2] O'Hanlon, *A Comparison*. On indigenous feminist and anti-feminist women's writing and activism in late nineteenth-century India, see variously Padma Anagol, *The Emergence of Feminism in India, 1850–1920* (Aldershot: Ashgate, 2005); and Padma Anagol, 'Gender, Religion and Anti-Feminism in Hindu Right Wing Writings: Notes from a Nineteenth Century Indian Woman-Patriot's Text "Essays in the Service of a Nation"', *Women's Studies International Forum*, 37 (2013): 107–13.

[3] O'Hanlon, *A Comparison*, 85.

Vijaylakshmi for the murder of her newborn child in April 1881.[4] The trial sparked heated debate about the most appropriate judicial treatment of infanticide and the broader social and cultural position of women in India, drawing substantial commentary not only across South Asia but in the United Kingdom as well.[5] Crucially, Vijaylakshmi's case was not one of those perennially reported instances where the sex of the infant was a factor.[6] Rather, the killing had resulted from the fact that as a Hindu widow (already stigmatised as a bringer of misfortune) she was expected by her community to remain chaste and subject to strict rules of behaviour until her own death. If these codes of conduct were breached, a widow would suffer even greater economic and emotional hardship than was already true of women in her uncomfortable social position.[7] Nor was Vijaylakshmi's crime an isolated incident. Clare Anderson has noted that during the early nineteenth century, 'the overwhelming majority of female convicts transported to Southeast Asia were convicted of infanticide', and this seems to have been part of a trend that continued across the colonial period.[8] One writer in 1895 suggested that 'fully fourth-fifths' of all female convicts in India had been found guilty of the murder of their infants and had then had the resulting sentence of death commuted to transportation or imprisonment.[9] As Anshu Malhotra has demonstrated, despite the radical views of popular *bhakti* sects in nineteenth-century India, even those groups which deliberately set out to challenge established religious

---

[4] British Library Asia, Pacific and Africa Collections: India Office Records [henceforth APAC IOR] P/1796. See entries 6 July 1881 and 18 July 1881; *Times of India*, 21 May 1881, 2; *Times of India*, 27 May 1881, 3; *Times of India*, 31 May 1881, 2; *Times of India*, 13 June 1881, 3.

[5] Padma Anagol, 'The Emergence of the Female Criminal in India: Infanticide and Survival Under the Raj', *History Workshop Journal*, 53 (2002), 73–93.

[6] On sex-specific infanticide in this period see L.S. Vishwanath, *Female Infanticide and Social Structure: A Socio-Historical Study in Western and Northern India* (New Delhi: Hindustan Publishing Corporation, 2000); Anagol, 'The Emergence of the Female Criminal'; Veena Talwar Oldenburg, *Dowry Murder: The Imperial Origins of a Cultural Crime* (New Delhi: Oxford University Press, 2002), 41–72; Anshu Malhotra, 'Shameful Continuities: The Practice of Female Infanticide in Colonial Punjab', in Doris Jakobsh (ed.), *Sikhism and Women* (New Delhi: Oxford University Press, 2010), 83–114; Daniel J.R. Grey, 'Gender, Religion, and Infanticide in Colonial India, 1870–1906', *Victorian Review* 37.2 (2011), 107–20.

[7] On widowhood and attempted social reforms, see variously Ishvarchandra Vidyasagar, *Hindu Widow Marriage*, trans. Brian A. Hatcher (New York: Columbia University Press, [1855] 2012); Lucy Carroll, 'Law, Custom, and Statutory Social Reform: The Hindu Widows' Remarriage Act of 1856', *Indian Economic & Social History Review*, 20 (1983), 363–88; O'Hanlon, *A Comparison*, 20–38; Tanika Sarkar, *Rebels, Wives, Saints: Designing Selves and Nations in Colonial Times* (Ranikhet: Permanent Black, 2009); Mytheli Sreenivas, *Wives, Widows, and Concubines: The Conjugal Family Ideal in Colonial India* (Bloomington: Indiana University Press, 2008); Nita Verma Prasad, 'The Litigious Widow: Inheritance Disputes in Colonial North India, 1875–1911', in Anindita Ghosh (ed.), *Behind the Veil: Resistance, Women and the Everyday in Colonial South Asia* (Basingstoke: Palgrave Macmillan, 2008), 161–90.

[8] Clare Anderson, *Convicts in the Indian Ocean: Transportation from South Asia to Mauritius, 1815–53* (Basingstoke: Macmillan, 2000), 145n45.

[9] Mary Frances Billington, *Woman in India* (London: Chapman and Hall, 1895), 243.

and social norms could often retain inherently conservative attitudes towards gender and sexuality.[10]

Similarly, although the most stereotypical view of an infanticide defendant in late nineteenth-century Britain and Ireland remained the figure of a young and unmarried woman who had been seduced and deserted by her paramour, cases of widows killing their illegitimate newborns in order to try and retain their respectability and socio-economic status were certainly not unknown.[11] In the same year as Vijaylakshmi was put on trial, Esther Bishop, a 35-year-old soldier's widow who had been supporting herself by working as a cook, was charged with the murder of her illegitimate newborn daughter at her employer's home at Colchester, England.[12] The body of the child had been found in a laundry copper that was partially filled with water, and the post-mortem examination strongly suggested that the baby had been born alive and died from drowning, both of which were crucial elements in attempting to meet the stringent tests for proof of life according to the law that were a requirement for infanticide convictions.[13] During her trial at the Essex Winter Assizes in January 1882, the jury eventually decided that there was insufficient medico-legal evidence that the baby had been born alive to convict Bishop of either murder or manslaughter, but she was found guilty of concealment of birth.[14] As Margaret Arnot has noted, conviction on this lesser offence was common in suspected infanticide cases during the nineteenth century, since English juries were notoriously averse to handing down the mandatory death sentence that a murder conviction would entail.[15] Yet the relatively severe sentence of fifteen months' hard labour given to Bishop suggests that the judge, at least, took a less lenient view of her particular circumstances.[16]

---

[10] Anshu Malhotra, '*Bhakti* and the Gendered Self: A Courtesan and a Consort in Mid Nineteenth Century Punjab', *Modern Asian Studies* 46.6 (2012), 1506–39.

[11] Elaine Farrell, '*A Most Diabolical Deed': Infanticide and Irish Society, 1850–1900* (Manchester: Manchester University Press, 2013); Daniel J.R. Grey, 'Discourses of Infanticide in England, 1880–1922' (unpublished PhD thesis, Roehampton University, 2008).

[12] The National Archives (henceforth TNA) ASSI 95/322. See Essex Assizes January 1882, Nos. 8 & 9, TNA ASSI 36/25. *R. v. Bishop.*

[13] *The Essex Standard, West Suffolk Gazette, and Eastern Counties' Advertiser*, 12 November 1881, 8.

[14] *The Essex Standard, West Suffolk Gazette, and Eastern Counties' Advertiser*, 28 January 1882, 2.

[15] Margaret L. Arnot, 'Understanding Women Committing Newborn Child Murder in Victorian England', in Shani D'Cruze (ed.), *Everyday Violence in Britain, 1850–1950: Gender & Class* (London: Longman, 2000), 55–69.

[16] TNA ASSI 31/39. See 23 January 1882, 226. Theoretically 'concealment of birth' could be punished with up to two years' imprisonment – with or without hard labour – but this was unusual. Of the fifty men and women who were convicted of concealment of birth in England and Wales during 1882, the majority (twenty-seven defendants, or 54 per cent) were sentenced to one month's imprisonment or less. Bishop was one of just four people (8 per cent of the total) to be sentenced to more than a year's imprisonment for this offence. Regrettably, as the compilers of the judicial statistics themselves noted, it is impossible to determine from these figures how many such convictions were actually the results of the jury concluding that

In comparison, Vijaylakshmi's murder trial and the broader debate that it generated sat uneasily on the discursive boundary between acts of violence that could be represented by colonial officials as 'uniquely Indian' (such as *sati* or 'widow-burning', 'thuggee' or female infanticide), and those crimes which more obviously resembled offences committed in Britain.[17] Such instances were particularly troubling for colonial commentators both at home and abroad. British writers had regularly devoted substantial attention since the eighteenth century to violence which could be labelled easily as 'Hindu' in nature, but remained acutely uncomfortable when direct parallels could be drawn between crimes committed in colony and metropole and these also defied explanations that were based on the race and/or religion of the perpetrator.[18] As Esme Cleall has observed, a sizeable proportion of missionary activism and authorship during the nineteenth century rested on constructions of African and South Asian people as fundamentally incapable of providing either 'normal' emotional relationships or physical safety from sickness, violence and even death without the benefit of Christian – and above all *British* – interventions.[19]

This chapter explores the different ways in which colonial commentators negotiated the uneasy and permeable boundaries between infanticide cases in late nineteenth-century India where the sex of a newborn was understood to have been a motivating factor in commission of the crime, as well as in those where it was deemed irrelevant. Significantly, the association between Hinduism and the murder of daughters remained fixed in the colonial imagination. This was despite the open acknowledgement by officials that: 'Infant sacrifice is not required by the Shastras, nor tolerated by Hinduism. The murder of a female infant is indeed declared to be a sin above all sins.'[20] There were also potentially significant differences, both rhetorical and practical, between the relatively abstract labelling of an entire region or tribe in order 'to determine the localities, or the clans and families, to which the [1870 Female Infanticide] Act shall be applied',[21] and attempts by the authorities to prosecute and punish individual cases of child homicide. The latter were

---

someone on trial for murder should instead be found guilty of concealment of birth, and how many of these represented indictments on the lesser offence only. See 'Judicial Statistics of England and Wales for 1882', *Parliamentary Papers*, 1883, C.3763, Vol. LXXVII, 103.

[17] Daniel J.R. Grey, 'Creating the "Problem Hindu": *Sati*, Thuggee & Female Infanticide in India, 1800–1860', *Gender & History* 25.3 (2013), 496–508.

[18] Grey, 'Gender, Religion, and Infanticide'.

[19] Esme Cleall, *Missionary Discourses of Difference: Negotiating Otherness in the British Empire, c. 1840–1900* (Basingstoke: Palgrave Macmillan, 2012).

[20] Henry Reade Cooke, *Repression of Female Infanticide in the Bombay Presidency* (Bombay: Government Central Press, 1875), 1. The *Śāstras* are ancient Hindu texts setting out rules of behaviour and written in Sanskrit. For an analytical overview of these and related scriptures see especially Wendy Doniger, *The Hindus: An Alternative History* (New York: Penguin, 2009).

[21] APAC IOR P/92. See Circular No. 24A, from the Secretary of Government for the North-Western Provinces to all District Officers, 1 June 1870.

beset by many of the same issues, both evidential and discursive, that routinely impacted upon newborn murder trials in the United Kingdom, but these parallels were rarely (if ever) explicitly acknowledged by government officials or newspaper editors. To do so, in fact, could have seriously undermined the oft-repeated justification for 'beneficent' imperial rule: namely that 'English Councils, an English army and English courts secure and maintain order, safety, justice for all classes and all interests'.[22] In both India and Britain, cases of infanticide prompted uncomfortable questions and vociferous debates over appropriate gender roles, sexual morality, 'civilisation' and its progress, how such defendants should best be identified and punished, and the nature of 'deviance', or, as Tarabai Shinde demanded to know in the subtitle to her pamphlet, 'who's really wicked and immoral, women or men?'[23] Yet it was also clear that there were not any simple answers to these issues, or that ideas about and perceived solutions to the problem could be translated easily from Britain to its empire or vice versa. As one civil servant from the Central Provinces reflected wearily in 1868, 'I have always looked on this subject as one of very extreme difficulty'.[24]

Part of this 'very extreme difficulty' was that, as Padma Anagol has illustrated, the British authorities and other interested commentators had for some time lumped together what were actually several different, if nonetheless closely related, issues under the broad heading of 'Indian infanticide'.[25] This included those instances of child homicide where the sex of the infant was irrelevant but the stigma against single motherhood and its material consequences was a central factor; those where upper-caste Hindus were alleged to be killing their daughters out of 'caste pride'; and those South Asian tribes who, regardless of whether or not they were actually Hindus, were nonetheless widely believed to practice human sacrifice as part of local customary and/or religious rites.[26] In a sense, this grouping together was logical, particularly as all these crimes dealt with the murder of young children. But colonial critics were rarely themselves clear about what the practical distinctions between them meant in terms of either motivation on the part of the offenders, or what would constitute the most appropriate (and indeed, 'just') solution to any of these crimes. Tellingly, the first of these 'types' of infanticide seems to have been covered by colonial commentators in far less detail than the latter two, where it was possible to make stories of malevolent Hindu precepts or more generic 'Indian inferiority' a key part of such narratives. Cases where

---

[22] London Missionary Society, *Report of the London Missionary Society for 1876* (London: Yates and Alexander, 1876), 33.

[23] O'Hanlon, *A Comparison*, 72.

[24] National Archives of India (henceforth NAI) Home Judicial 19 May 1870, Nos. 21–35. See memo by G. Campbell, Chief Commissioner of Central Provinces, 18 January 1868.

[25] Anagol, 'The Emergence of the Female Criminal'.

[26] John Campbell, *Narrative by Major-General John Campbell, C.B., Of His Operations in the Hill Tracts of Orissa, for the Suppression of Human Sacrifices and Female Infanticide* (London: Hurst and Blackett, 1861).

an illegitimate child was killed, either boy or girl, because its very existence proved a lack of chastity on the part of an unmarried or widowed woman who would then suffer significant reputational and potentially economic damage occurred just as often in Britain as in India, as the 1882 trial of Esther Bishop demonstrates. Tales of child sacrifice or the deliberate singling out of *daughters* for murder by married couples simultaneously anxious for the birth of a son, however, allowed British critics to maintain a comfortable rhetorical distance from an 'alien' set of crimes practised by colonial subjects.

The Female Infanticide Act of 1870 passed by the Government of India was a measure that had, to a greater or lesser extent, been constantly agitated for by colonial critics since the late eighteenth century.[27] British writers from a variety of perspectives – missionary, military, administrative and feminist – had repeatedly 'discovered' the phenomenon of the murder of daughters in different parts of northern India from the 1790s onwards and identified it as a pressing issue in need of eradication by legal means as well as moral re-education.[28] As Rashmi Dube Bhatnagar and her co-authors have suggested, 'the recurrent trope of discovery is less about the material realities of this anti-woman practice, and far more about the generic convention of the eighteenth-century travelogue to which the official document faithfully adheres'.[29] These literary conventions enabled British commentators to fit their impressions, regardless of whether these were based in painstaking observation or gossip and hearsay, into a well-established narrative format which emphasised Indian inferiority and the need for paternalistic colonial interventions. Such reports of female infanticide rapidly became a key element of the 'problem Hindu' story which identified the Hindu faith as posing unique dangers to, in the most literal of senses, its female adherents, and claimed that Hindu men could for the most part be divided between the majority who were enervated in body and mind by their faith to become effete and weak-willed, and a minority who became bloodthirsty savages.[30] Implicitly, this also denied the existence of cases where it was women, rather than men, who were responsible for making the decision as to whether or not a baby girl would be permitted to survive. Yet, as Veena Oldenburg has noted, in many instances it was likely that Indian women ultimately made many of the 'pragmatic, ruthless, and …

[27] Lalita Panigrahi, *British Social Policy and Female Infanticide in India* (New Delhi: Munishiram Manoharlal, 1972).

[28] Although India was arguably the most notable and frequently used example of such rhetoric during the long nineteenth century, this process was paralleled elsewhere in the British Empire, since infanticide acted as a useful shorthand for demonstrating the 'savagery' of colonial subjects. See Marguerita Stephens, 'A Word of Evidence: Shared Tales about Infanticide and Others-Not-Us in Colonial Victoria', in Jane Carey and Claire McLisky (eds), *Creating White Australia* (Sydney: Sydney University Press, 2009), 175–94.

[29] Rashmi Dube Bhatnagar, Renu Dube and Reena Dube, *Female Infanticide in India: A Feminist Cultural History* (Albany: State University of New York Press, 2005), 39.

[30] Grey, 'Creating the "Problem Hindu"'; Mrinalini Sinha, *Colonial Masculinity: The 'Manly' Englishman and the 'Effeminate' Bengali in the Late Nineteenth Century* (Manchester: Manchester University Press, 1995).

necessary' choices about whether or not the family could afford to provide for a third daughter in place of a potential son.[31] Presenting female infanticide as a crime that resulted entirely and absolutely from the decision of a malevolent *paterfamilias*, even if the actual deed itself was carried out by a midwife or older female relative, further reinforced colonial assumptions about the powerlessness and inevitable victimhood of Hindu women in the nineteenth century.

Given these long-standing arguments it is perhaps surprising on one level that the 1870 infanticide legislation took so long to be passed, but this can perhaps best be explained by the perceived regional specificity of the crime. It is important to note that in many instances, despite the collective trauma and anxieties induced by the Great Rebellion in 1857, the colonial regime frequently remained willing in practice to flout the 'non-interference with religion' that was repeatedly avowed as the cornerstone of their policy in India.[32] The area most notoriously associated with female infanticide from the late eighteenth century onwards was the North-Western Provinces, corresponding to areas of the Subcontinent such as Rajasthan or the Punjab.[33] While the killing of daughters was acknowledged to also occur in southern India, incidents in that region were generally perceived to be aberrations. For example, the anthropologist and Indian Army officer William Marshall directly linked the practice of female infanticide and other customs such as polyandry in one South Indian mountain tribe with their especially 'primitive' nature, which he considered not only exceptional but likely to disappear entirely as India gradually became more 'civilised'.[34] Colonial commentators overwhelmingly associated the crime with upper-caste Hindu families in the North-West, where it was commonly held that even the *potential* for any girl to marry into a lower-ranking family and pay an expensive dowry was so destructive to both individual pride and the respect of the wider community that parents were willing to murder their daughters at birth.[35] Solving the ongoing 'dowry problem' was seen as central to reducing female

---

[31] Oldenburg, *Dowry Murder*, 172.

[32] On the Rebellion and its broader socio-political implications see especially Clare Anderson, *The Indian Uprising of 1857–8: Prisons, Prisoners and Rebellion* (London: Anthem, 2007); Kim A. Wagner, *The Great Fear of 1857: Rumours, Conspiracies and the Making of the Indian Uprising* (Oxford: Peter Lang, 2010) and Kim A. Wagner, 'Treading Upon Fires: The "Mutiny-Motif" and Colonial Anxieties in British India', *Past and Present*, 218 (2013), 159–97.

[33] See, for example, 'Female Infanticide Among the Rajputs', *Church Missionary Gleaner*, 1 March 1852, 33; and key discussion in Oldenburg, *Dowry Murder*, 41–72; Malhotra, 'Shameful Continuities'. On the broader context of the Punjab see also the collected essays in Anshu Malhotra and Farina Mir (eds), *Punjab Reconsidered: History, Culture, and Practice* (New Delhi: Oxford University Press, 2012).

[34] William E. Marshall, *A Phrenologist Amongst the Todas, Or The Study of a Primitive Tribe in South India: History, Character, Customs, Religion, Infanticide, Polyandry, Language* (London: Longmans, Green & Co., 1873), 190–202.

[35] Norman Chevers, *A Manual of Medical Jurisprudence for India* (Calcutta: Thacker, Spink & Co., 1870), 756–8.

infanticide throughout the nineteenth century, and colonial officials were routinely expected to secure the agreement of high-caste men that their families would 'put a stop to the bad practice and remove the shame and indignity brought on [themselves] by needless expenses'.[36] Rather than accusing all upper-caste Hindus, however, the authorities focused in still further and claimed that the killing of daughters was a regular practice among specific tribal affiliations such as the Jats and Rajputs and in regions in which these caste customs were adhered to with special fervour. It was this combination of traits, rather than Hinduism in general, or being either high-caste or a Rajput in particular, which was alleged to create a sort of 'perfect storm' where female infanticide was the inevitable and gruesome result.[37] Some writers such as J.P. Willoughby went still further and observed significant differences in the practice and its perceived acceptability *between* high-caste Rajput tribes that were located in different areas. According to Willoughby, families among the 'Somburree' Rajputs allegedly committed female infanticide but were nonetheless considered to be tainted after the killing of a daughter, and shunned by their peers until they underwent a ritual in which they were publicly granted absolution by a Hindu priest. By contrast, the equally influential Dhankarra Rajputs were praised as 'really the only tribe of Rajpoots, among whom no family destroys its infant daughters in Oude'.[38]

Stamping out sex-specific child murder in India was not a simple matter, despite the fact that it was a practice that played beautifully into the hands of those authors keen to demonstrate the need for Britain's 'civilising rule'. *Sati* served a very similar rhetorical purpose for the colonial administration and had also been widely associated with the North-Western Provinces, as well as its famous associations with, and eventual abolition in, Bengal.[39] Yet, as Andrea Major has demonstrated, because of strategic concerns the East India Company had hesitated to enforce its prohibition on widow-burning in the North-Western Provinces during the mid-nineteenth century in a way that was conspicuously absent from their dealings with Bengal and the adjoining north-eastern parts of India.[40] Rajputs had the dubious honour to fall under the classification of 'martial races' in the British lexicon on racial traits: those Indian men, who while undoubtedly considered to be inferior to Europeans as a result

[36] APAC IOR P/234/26. North-Western Provinces Criminal Judicial Proceedings, 25 August 1856. Copy of translated agreement between Shooratum Singh and others, 30 November 1855. See also key context in Oldenburg, *Dowry Murder*.

[37] Grey, 'Gender, Religion, and Infanticide'.

[38] British Library Asia, Pacific and Africa Collections: Mss. Eur. E293/227, c 1856. Minutes by J.P. Willoughby regarding the laws, infanticide customs etc. of India (unpaginated).

[39] Lata Mani, *Contentious Traditions: The Debate on Sati in Colonial India* (Berkeley: University of California Press, 1998).

[40] Andrea Major, *Sovereignty and Social Reform in India: British Colonialism and the Campaign against Sati, 1830–60* (New York: Routledge, 2011).

of their ethnicity and religion, were also fierce and dangerous warriors.[41] As such, especially after 1857, colonial officials were anxious to avoid actions that could be seen as provocation or which would stir up protests against British interference. It is worth noting that when it was revealed that certain civil servants based in the North-Western Provinces had published a tract claiming – in terms considered offensive even by contemporaries – that, essentially, Indians should be grateful for British rule and it would be best to enforce an openly despotic regime for the greater good of the Empire, this was perceived as a monumental breach of accepted practice and discipline. The Governor General immediately dispatched a furious memo in July 1860 asserting that 'were it not for the evidence of the papers the Governor General in Council would have refused to believe that British Officers could be so ignorant or so unmindful of the duty of their country to the people of India'.[42]

For the 1870 Act to be passed and implemented, the colonial authorities had to feel secure enough in their hold over north-west India and its surrounding regions to risk stirring up overt opposition to British rule. Essentially, under the terms of the Female Infanticide Act, in areas where the census revealed a worrying dearth of daughters (especially in those cases where families claimed when questioned that they could not even remember a case of daughters being born within the tribe for generations, as many reputedly did), the village would be subject to strict surveillance and ongoing sanctions until the sex ratios of children began to approach more normal levels. These strictures were intended to be instrumental in changing attitudes to the value of female children, as well as starkly reducing the number of child homicides. The point, as the *Birmingham Daily Post* noted approvingly in 1871, was that under such careful observation and enforcement it would be far more difficult for the guilty to evade justice. Indeed, the newspaper remarked that judging by recent infanticide and baby-farming scandals in Britain and Ireland,[43] it was a shame such a law could not be introduced 'to the British metropolis, where, if Coroners may be credited, this most accursed of the great sins of great cities still flourishes in rank and scarcely heeded luxuriance'.[44]

The Act of 1870, however, worked at a regional and tribal level rather than an individual one. It did nothing whatsoever to alter – much less improve – the chances of prevention, detection and punishment for those who killed infants not only because they were girls, but because their existence would potentially bring ruin to one or both of the parents. Regardless of the circumstances

[41] On the ideology of 'martial races' see Heather Streets, *Martial Races: The Military, Race and Masculinity in British Imperial Culture, 1857–1914* (Manchester: Manchester University Press, 2004); Gavin Rand, '"Martial Races" and "Imperial Subjects": Violence and Governance in Colonial India, 1857–1914', *European Review of History* 13.1 (2006), 1–20.
[42] NAI Home Public 7 July 1860 No. 17.
[43] See Margaret L. Arnot, 'Infant Death, Child Care and the State: The Baby-Farming Scandal and the First Infant Life Protection Legislation of 1872', *Continuity & Change* 9.2 (1994), 271–311; Farrell, *'A Most Diabolical Deed'*; Grey 'Discourses'.
[44] *Birmingham Daily Post*, 22 September 1871, 4.

of the case, defendants accused of killing a baby were still tried for murder or manslaughter under the Indian Penal Code in the usual manner, without any reference to the provisions of the Female Infanticide Act. Likewise, although instances of married women killing their legitimate children were more unusual than alleged infanticides by widows or unmarried women, such cases were certainly not unknown in colonial India.[45] This was a factor that potentially further complicated debates over the causes and solutions of the crime, since the motivation of 'avoiding shame' and its very real economic and social consequences was naturally irrelevant for either British or Indian married defendants. While this did not inevitably equate to harsher treatment of married women before the courts in either nation, since some important elements of the discourses which allowed infanticidal women to be perceived as worthy of popular and official sympathy could be translated to women who killed their legitimate children, it did generally increase the likelihood of conviction.[46] For the authorities to then consider a reduction in the severity of the sentence passed naturally meant that alternative explanations for what seemed an unnatural and especially heinous crime had to be sought.[47] Just as in Britain, there were also individual instances in which magistrates became concerned that mentally ill Indian women accused of actual or attempted child homicide were being unfairly dealt with by the judicial system despite the fact 'that while the accused was under trial she appeared ... to be of unsound mind'.[48] In such cases the presiding magistrate registered an appeal with the Local Government that the defendants be transferred to an asylum for psychiatric treatment, rather than simply being incarcerated or transported. For example, in one case in January 1892, the authorities agreed that 'Bannoo, woman', who had been charged before Mr Richardson with the unlawful abandonment and exposure of her infant, should be sent as a patient to Colába Lunatic Asylum.[49]

Further, the 1870 legislation had limited impact in a case where an individual parent *did* make the decision to kill their female child because she was not the hoped-for son. In 1889, the Deputy Commissioner of Rae Bareli, V.A. Smith, bitterly recounted to his superiors his failure to secure the conviction of 35-year-old farmer Chauharja Singh for the murder of his eight-week-old daughter.[50] The surgeon who performed the post-mortem confirmed that her

---

[45] Padma Anagol, 'From the Symbolic to the Open: Women's Resistance in Colonial Maharashtra', in Anindita Ghosh (ed.), *Behind the Veil: Resistance, Women and the Everyday in Colonial South Asia* (Basingstoke: Palgrave Macmillan, 2008), 48.

[46] See variously Anagol, 'The Emergence of the Female Criminal'; Anagol, 'From the Symbolic to the Open'; Farrell, *'A Most Diabolical Deed'*; Grey 'Discourses'.

[47] One convenient way of doing this was for the authorities to assert that 'obviously' a husband had forced his wife to kill the child, even to the point of directly contradicting witness testimony or confessions. See Grey, 'Creating the "Problem Hindu"', 506.

[48] APAC IOR P/4264. Bombay Judicial Department Proceedings. Letter from Mr C.W. Richardson, Third Presidency Magistrate, 11 January 1892.

[49] Ibid.

[50] APAC IOR P/4514. Memo from V.A. Smith, Deputy Commissioner, Rae Bareli, to Commissioner of Rae Bareli Division, 23 August 1889.

death was due to an overdose of opium – notorious in India as a favoured method of dispatching unwanted infants[51] – and that there was simply no way the poison could have been accidentally administered. When questioned, Singh insisted that his daughter had died from a fever and that he could not account for the presence of the drug. Determining whether or not an infant had died from natural causes, or from accidental or deliberate means, had been internationally acknowledged as a major problem in nineteenth-century medical jurisprudence.[52] In the case above, although Smith charged Singh with murder, he was ultimately forced to drop the case for lack of evidence before it came to trial. Thus, while there had been a deliberate attempt in the crafting and explanations of the 1860 Penal Code to try and avoid the regular disputes over case law and rules of evidence which generated so many problems for British and Irish infanticide trials during this period, in practice, the crime continued to be interpreted with relative liberality by the judicial system and convictions were relatively rare in India, just as they remained low in the United Kingdom.[53] Adding insult to injury from Smith's perspective, the murder of Singh's daughter had occurred in a village he described as already being determined as 'specially [*sic*] guilty on the infanticide register' according to the official statistics. The area was already operating under the harshest possible strictures of the 1870 Act.[54] All in all, Smith concluded angrily, Singh's case proved that the Act was utterly useless for the purposes of either saving the lives of female infants or punishing their murderers.[55]

Ongoing problems with the application of the 1870 legislation meant that amendments to the laws dealing with infanticide were debated at regular intervals in late nineteenth-century India, both in the press and in letters and memos shuttled between government officials. Occasionally, such discussions focused on the treatment of those cases which held direct parallels with British ones.[56] Sir Madhava Rao, the chief revenue officer of Baroda, argued in 1876 that there should be some reform of the law so that women convicted of the killing of their infants would not automatically face either the death penalty or transportation for life.[57] While colonial government officials felt that there was no need for the law to be amended, they did quietly agree in 1879 that an

---

[51] Cooke, *Repression*, 5; I.B. Lyon, *A Text-Book of Medical Jurisprudence for India* (Calcutta: Thacker, Spink & Co., 1889), 368.

[52] See Katherine D. Watson, *Forensic Medicine in Western Society: A History* (New York: Routledge, 2011), 105–11. For specific reference to this issue in India see Lyon, *A Text-Book*, 351–69; J.D.B. Gribble and Patrick Hehir, *Outlines of Medical Jurisprudence for India*, 3rd edn (Madras: Higginbotham & Co., 1892), 269–81.

[53] Grey, 'Gender, Religion, and Infanticide'.

[54] APAC IOR P/4514. Memo from V.A. Smith, Deputy Commissioner, Rae Bareli, to Commissioner of Rae Bareli Division, 23 August 1889.

[55] Ibid.

[56] Anagol, 'The Emergence of the Female Criminal'.

[57] Sir Madava Rao, 'Considerations on the Crime of Infanticide and its Punishment in India', *Journal of the National Indian Association*, 65, May (1876), 131–7.

existing informal arrangement, whereby all sentences passed on women found guilty of child homicide were reviewed by the relevant provincial High Court and by the local government, should be made an essential part of the criminal justice system across India.[58] To ensure that this arrangement was adhered to, a circular was released in 1882 that required that any case in which a woman was convicted of killing her child be forwarded to the Government of India as part of the annual police reports.[59] Details were to include what course of action had been taken after the woman's sentence was locally reviewed. Delivered in tabular format and providing no information whatsoever about the individual circumstances of the crime, these reports offer no clues to the reader about what led regional court or government officials to determine what would be the most appropriate commuted sentence for the women so recorded. In the case of those ten women found guilty of murdering their infants in the North-West Provinces and Oudh during 1884, it is perhaps telling that the 'Remarks' section of the tables has almost universally been left blank by the official who created it (see Table 2.1). It is therefore impossible to tell whether the woman in question was (or had been) married; whether the sex of the murdered infant was – rightly or wrongly – believed by the authorities to have had any part in the motivation for the crime, or what details of an individual case led them to either alter or confirm the original sentence.[60]

Possibly, this tendency to omit any further details was in part a reflection of unconscious disquiet about the similarities which could be traced between many of these women and the circumstances of British infanticides, but it may also have been due to practical considerations regarding constraints of time and space when filing reports. A terse reminder was issued in September 1900 that the records of *all* infanticide convictions and their particular circumstances were supposed to be passed to the Government for officials' perusal, and not only those where the victims were illegitimate newborns, suggesting that some local civil servants had assumed there was in practice a significant difference between how married and unmarried infanticidal women should be perceived and treated by the criminal justice system.[61] It was, however, remarked that in cases where the defendant had killed their legitimate offspring

---

[58] APAC IOR P/6066. Reprinted extract from Proceedings of the Government of India in the Home (Revenue and Agricultural) Department (Judicial), 26 September 1879.

[59] APAC IOR P/6066. Reprinted Home Department Circular, originally issued 19 October 1882. Following the events of 1857 and the implementation of the Indian Penal Code in 1860, the existing colonial court system was dramatically overhauled and the High Courts – most of which dealt with appeal cases – were established in 1862. See M.P. Singh, *Outlines of Indian Legal and Constitutional History*, 8th edn (New Delhi: Universal Law Publishing Co., 2006), 92–100.

[60] Given the severity of the commuted sentences in question, it is important to note that 'sympathy' for individual defendants was very much relative. See Anagol, 'The Emergence of the Female Criminal'.

[61] APAC IOR P/6066. Letter from J.P. Hewett, Secretary to the Government of India, to the Secretary to Government of NW Provinces and Oudh, 16 September 1900.

Table 2.1 Statement of cases in which women were found guilty of murdering their infant children and which were reported to Government during 1884

Sessions division	Name of prisoner	Sentence passed	Sentence as modified by Local Government	Remarks
North-Western Provinces				
Gorakhpur	Mussamat Rachpali	Transportation for life	Fourteen years' transportation	
Gházipur	Ditto Sanichari	Ditto	Twelve years' transportation	
Gorakhpur	Ditto ditto	Ditto	Seven years' transportation	
Ditto	Ditto Munna *alias* Munia	Ditto	Five years' rigorous imprisonment	
Cawnpore	Mussamat Bhagwania	Ditto	Sentence allowed to stand	No orders have yet been passed
Oudh				
Lucknow	Ditto Rukia	Transportation for life	Seven years' transportation	
Rae Bareli	Ditto Bachia	Ditto	Sentence allowed to stand	
Sessions Division not known	Ditto Kailasa	Ditto	Twelve years' transportation	
Fyzabad	Ditto Gobinda	Ditto	Five years' rigorous imprisonment	
Sítápur	Ditto Jheria	Ditto	Ditto	

Source: Table reproduced directly from APAC IOR P/6066. North-Western and Oudh Judicial Proceedings, January 1901.

it would be useful to note down whether or not the presiding sessions judge had recommended a reduction in the sentence. This tacitly endorsed the view that such cases were indeed not as invariably deserving of official sympathy as those of unmarried or long-widowed women, and reflected the complex ways in which such defendants were officially and popularly represented.[62]

Invariably, whenever the subject of infanticide was raised by concerned British or Indian commentators during the late nineteenth century, the colonial government preferred to focus on the workings and supposed successes of the 1870 Act, which was regularly held up in Britain as part of a wider imperial model of 'civilising rule'.[63] Debates in fact continued throughout this period as to whether further amendments to specific sections of this legislation

[62] Ibid.
[63] See for example *Times of India*, 12 November 1900, 4.

would lead to better management of the 'problem' of female infanticide, or if a lesser degree of evidence of unequal birth rates should be required before the strictures of the Female Infanticide Act were implemented.[64] Further, the ongoing focus on female infanticide as a practice supposedly unique across South Asia to Hindus (and, in the Punjab, certain Sikh groups, a religious distinction the colonial regime was not itself always clear about) was also occasionally – if unsuccessfully – questioned both within and outside the government of India.[65] As one anonymous critic acidly pointed out in the January 1897 edition of the *Calcutta Review*, all religions in India roundly condemned the killing of infants and warned the perpetrators of horrific consequences in the afterlife for their crime even if they escaped justice on earth.[66] The 1870 Act was in fact quietly abolished in 1906, after more than thirty years in force, supposedly on the grounds it had succeeded in its stated aim of eliminating female infanticide.[67] Indeed, the *Times of India* proudly claimed the following year: 'As an approved and established custom the crime has disappeared.'[68] In practice, however, the systematic neglect (up to and including death) of female infants has remained a live issue across North India right into the twenty-first century.[69] Given the British concerns about imperial strength and what constituted 'just rule' that had been brought explosively to the forefront by events in Southern Africa over the preceding decade, the belief that the 1870 Act had succeeded in its aims and could be safely repealed was a very welcome success story for the British Empire.[70]

Today India remains one of a relatively small number of jurisdictions worldwide, such as the United States, not to have passed laws formally separating this crime from other types of homicide. In contrast, a very different sort of Infanticide Act – one which formally took into account the possibility

---

[64] Demonstrating the complexity of this issue, the Government of the Punjab devoted 120 pages to reproducing four years' worth of detailed discussion between civil servants of how best to eradicate female infanticide from the province. See APAC IOR P/5834. Arrangements for the Suppression of Female Infanticide by Medical Agency, February 1900.

[65] On Sikh religion and culture see Tony Ballantyne, *Between Colonialism and Diaspora: Sikh Cultural Formations in an Imperial World* (Durham, NC: Duke University Press, 2006) and the essays in Jakobsh, *Sikhism and Women*.

[66] M.L., 'Female Infanticide in the Punjab', *The Calcutta Review*, 1 January 1897, 144–76.

[67] Oldenburg, *Dowry Murder*.

[68] *Times of India*, 15 April 1907, 5.

[69] Grey, 'Gender, Religion, and Infanticide', 116; Sunita Kishor, '"May God Give Sons to All": Gender and Child Mortality in India', *American Sociological Review* 58.2 (1993), 247–65.

[70] Esme Cleall, '"In Defiance of the Highest Principles of Justice, Principles of Righteousness": The Indenturing of the Bechuana Rebels and the Ideals of Empire, 1897–1900', *Journal of Imperial and Commonwealth History* 40.4 (2012), 601–18; Liz Stanley, *Mourning Becomes … Post/Memory and the Concentration Camps of the South African War* (Manchester: Manchester University Press, 2006). On the politics of childhood in South Africa during the period covered by this chapter, see Sarah Emily Duff, 'What will this Child be? Children, Childhood, and the Dutch Reformed Church in the Cape Colony, 1860–1894' (unpublished PhD thesis, University of London, 2010).

of violent women suffering from postnatal mental illness, removing the death penalty from such cases – was implemented in England, Wales and Northern Ireland in 1922, and still remains in force as of 2014.[71] Despite the rhetoric surrounding repeal in 1906, female infanticide and the associated practice of sex-specific abortion have continued to be a pressing concern in the post-colonial republic, in the face of repeated attempts over the course of the twentieth century to eradicate these crimes.[72] Easy for British commentators to explain away as a mark of intrinsic South Asian racial and religious inferiority, and convenient as a marker of why India did not deserve self-rule, sex-specific infanticide remained an issue which did not challenge the gendered or racialised late Victorian status quo, or demand practical (and likely expensive and contentious) reforms rather than empty platitudes in response to Tarabai Shinde's question: 'Who's really wicked and immoral, women or men?'[73] Indian women continue to report that illegal ultrasound screening to determine foetal sex in defiance of the 1994 law that prohibits this practice, and intense familial pressure to terminate pregnancies if they are not carrying sons, both remain common practices.[74] To have successfully dealt with these issues in the late nineteenth century would have first meant unpicking assumptions built up over several decades about the interplay between faith, gender and custom in India, or indeed the ways in which colonial rule had crystallised these ideas by placing heavy emphasis on 'tradition' as a (not unproblematic) signifier of status.

[71] Daniel J.R. Grey, 'Women's Policy Networks and the Infanticide Act 1922', *Twentieth Century British History* 21.4 (2010), 441–63. Although initially this only dealt with victims who were 'newly born', in 1938 the age limit for children covered by the act was extended to twelve months.

[72] Elisabeth Croll, *Endangered Daughters: Discrimination and Development in Asia* (London: Routledge, 2000), 52–63; M. Shahid Perwez, 'Death before Birth: Negotiating Reproduction, Female Infanticide and Sex Selective Abortion in Tamil Nadu, South India' (unpublished PhD thesis, University of Edinburgh, 2009).

[73] O'Hanlon, *A Comparison*, 72.

[74] '"My Husband Tried to Force Me to Abort My Twin Girls": Doctor's Charge Inflames India's Fight for Gender Equality', *Independent*, 11 August 2013, www.independent.co.uk/news/world/asia/my-husband-tried-to-force-me-to-abort-my-twin-girls-doctors-charge-inflames-indias-fight-for-gender-equality-8755942.html (accessed 13 August 2013).

3   At "war against our institutions"

Policing and punishment in the slave cities of the United States and Brazil

James Campbell

Slavery in the Americas developed distinctive features in cities. Across the varied built environments and political, cultural and economic landscapes of cities in the United States, the Caribbean and Central and South America there was no single model for urban slavery, but forms of enslaved labour, demography, culture and resistance always differed markedly from rural settings. In particular, cities provided spaces in which at least some slaves could lead lives marked by a degree of autonomy that was beyond the ordinary expectations of their rural counterparts. Urban labour demands saw slaves loading and carrying goods, running errands and toiling in manufacturing trades and factories. Some slaves worked as skilled artisans and many were hired out, sometimes earning wages and even making their own living arrangements. For example, as a young man enslaved in antebellum Louisville, Isaac Throgmorton, a barber, lived with free people and passed most of his days almost as a free man himself. "I served my apprenticeship of seven years," Throgmorton recalled in an 1863 interview, "and then kept shop for myself one or two years, & then I was one year steamboating up the river."[1] Throgmorton recognised that he had been particularly fortunate, for even in cities slavery could be a brutal and oppressive institution, but the transience and anonymity of urban life nonetheless enabled even slaves with relatively limited freedoms, such as domestic servants, to engage in diverse independent activities. Urban slaves participated in vibrant black and interracial communities, bought and sold goods in city markets, and joined large church congregations. They also joined in more explicitly subversive activities. They read of slave rebellions and political debates about liberty and abolition; accessed underground liquor establishments, gambling and dance halls; attempted to steal away on board ships, stage coaches and trains; passed themselves off as free people; and planned and staged violent uprisings.[2]

---

[1] Isaac Throgmorton, interviewed in Canada, 1863. John Blassingame, *Slave Testimony: Two Centuries of Letters, Speeches, Interviews, and Autobiographies* (Baton Rouge: Louisiana State University Press, 1977), 432.

[2] There are numerous studies of urban slavery in the Americas. See, for example, Douglas R. Egerton, "Slaves to the Marketplace: Economic Liberty and Black Rebelliousness in the Atlantic World," *Journal of the Early Republic* 26.4 (2006); Christine Hünefeldt, *Paying the*

One consequence of these circumstances was that slave cities developed distinctive cultures and practices of policing and punishment. Whereas law enforcement on farms and plantations was the preserve of slaveholders, supplemented by overseers and slave patrols whose actions were almost entirely unconstrained by law, the nature of slavery in cities required the routine intervention of the state in matters of slave control. Hence, the former slave and abolitionist Frederick Douglass could describe an early-nineteenth century plantation in Maryland as "a little nation of its own" untouched by the "laws and institutions of the state," but when Frederick Law Olmsted visited Charleston in the 1850s he found a city where "citadels, sentries, passports, grapeshotted cannon, and daily public whippings" were evidence of "more arbitrary and cruel power than any police in Europe."[3] The mechanisms of policing and punishment that developed in mid-nineteenth-century slave cities are the focus of this chapter, which seeks to develop two lines of enquiry that have been marginalised in previous studies. First, it outlines key features of slave law enforcement in cities and situates the policing of urban nonslaveholders – particularly poor whites – as a central part of the story of slave control. Second, it adds a transnational perspective through a comparative analysis of urban slavery, policing and punishment in the United States and Brazil. Drawing on original research and a review of existing literature, the chapter proposes that while the policing of slaves shared notable commonalities throughout the urban Americas, the policing of white nonslaveholders in cities proceeded along very different lines and in ways that generated particular ideological and political challenges for the pro-slavery arguments that developed in the pre-Civil War southern United States.

Urbanisation and slavery in the Americas

Throughout the Americas, slavery was primarily a rural institution and though it adapted readily and profitably to urban environments, there were social and political tensions inherent in the growth of slave cities. In a pioneering study in the 1960s, Richard Wade argued that from the 1820s until the outbreak of the Civil War, slavery was "disintegrating" in the urban US South, as slaveholders' capacity to control their human chattel was fundamentally compromised by

Price of Freedom: Family and Labor among Lima's Slaves, 1800–1854 (Berkeley: University of California Press, 1994); Mary C. Karasch, *Slave Life in Rio de Janeiro, 1808–1850* (Princeton: Princeton University Press, 1987); Seth Rockman, *Scraping By: Wage Labor, Slavery, and Survival in Early Baltimore* (Baltimore: Johns Hopkins University Press, 2009); Richard C. Wade, *Slavery in the Cities: The South, 1820–1860* (Oxford: Oxford University Press, 1967); Daniel E. Walker, *No More, No More: Slavery and Cultural Resistance in Havana and New Orleans* (Minneapolis: University of Minnesota Press, 2004); Pedro L.V. Welch, *Slave Society in the City: Bridgetown, Barbados, 1680–1834* (Kingston: I. Randle, 2004).
[3] Herbert Aptheker, *American Negro Slave Revolts*, 5th edition (New York: International Publishers, 1987), 69. On slave patrols, see Sally E. Hadden, *Slave Patrols: Law and Violence in Virginia and the Carolinas* (Cambridge, MA: Harvard University Press, 2001).

the inherent autonomy of city spaces and labour demands. In support of his argument, Wade noted that urban expansion in the mid-nineteenth-century South proceeded in conjunction with declining urban slave populations. The largest southern cities by 1860 were Baltimore, New Orleans and St. Louis, each with a population of more than 150,000 people, but these were principally white cities with large communities of European immigrants and relatively limited numbers of slaves. In both Baltimore and St. Louis, slaves comprised barely 1 per cent of the total population in 1860, and only 8 per cent in New Orleans, compared to 23 per cent in 1840. The slave population of smaller cities was also in decline by the eve of the American Civil War, either in absolute terms or relative to the number of whites. Charleston, South Carolina, for example, had a population of around 45,000 by 1860, of which about 33 per cent were slaves, but this was down from 50 per cent just ten years earlier.[4]

In a 1985 study of Baltimore, Maryland, Barbara Fields pushed Wade's argument further. She claimed that although individual slaves could be made to work profitably in city conditions, there was a "profound basis for antagonism" between urban development and slavery as a system. Other historians have similarly argued that slaveholders struggled to reconcile the competing labour demands of the commercial marketplace on the one hand, with the maintenance of white supremacy and effective slave control on the other. Employing slaves in cities might serve the economic interests of individual slaveholders, but all too often it did so in ways inconsistent with slaveholders' collective interests as a ruling class. As Midori Takagi explains with reference to Richmond, "to tighten the lax slave system would threaten the success of the economy, while failing to do so might encourage resistance and rebellion." In William Link's assessment, slavery was strong in urban Virginia, but "its political defences were weakened" by the forces of market capitalism.[5] For Douglas Egerton, who notes that the "vast majority" of slaves who led rebellions were wage-earning hired hands who lived away from their masters, the critical weakness of urban slavery across the Americas was that it exposed slaves to "a different class system ... in which class position was based upon initiative and economic advancement rather than on the more sluggish, agrarian plantation-based society in the countryside."[6]

The "inherent instability" thesis was first challenged in 1976 by Claudia Golden who argued that slavery was limited in cities not because of opportunities for resistance, but due to the greater profits that derived from

---

[4] Wade, *Slavery in the Cities*, 326.
[5] Barbara Fields, *Slavery and Freedom on the Middle Ground: Maryland during the Nineteenth Century* (New Haven: Yale University Press, 1985); John Ashworth, *Slavery, Capitalism, and Politics in the Antebellum Republic / Volume 1: Commerce and Compromise, 1820–1850* (Cambridge: Cambridge University Press, 1995); Midori Takagi, *Rearing Wolves to Our Own Destruction: Slavery in Richmond, Virginia, 1782–1865* (Charlottesville: University of Virginia Press, 1999), 6; William A. Link, *Roots of Secession: Slavery and Politics in Antebellum Virginia* (Chapel Hill: University of North Carolina Press, 2003), 76.
[6] Egerton, "Slaves to the Marketplace," 618.

employing slaves on rural plantations producing staple crops such as cotton, rice and sugar. Subsequent works by Stephen Whitman, David Goldfield, Frank Towers and William Dusinberre support the idea that urbanisation did not "undermine the solidity of the slave system" in any meaningful sense. Towers argues, for example, that cities in fact performed functions essential to the very survival of slavery, including facilitating the domestic slave trade and connecting the plantations of the southern interior to global economic markets. He also describes cities as "research and development laboratories," where new forms of slavery evolved that were compatible with industrialisation and market capitalism, complete with flexible labour patterns, factories and even a life insurance industry that protected slaveholders against losing their valuable human property in industrial accidents.[7]

From a Latin American perspective, the idea of a fundamental incompatibility between cities and slavery appears profoundly misplaced. In a 2009 study of Baltimore, Maryland, and Sabará, Brazil, Mariana Dantas noted that all of the problems that Wade attributed to urban slavery in the United States were present in Brazil (and were more acute in many cases), but there they did not inhibit the development of vast slave cities by the mid-nineteenth century.[8] Brazilian cities, for example, experienced acts of collective violent slave resistance on a scale unknown in the United States. Salvador – Brazil's second city – was struck by a series of major slave rebellions during the nineteenth century including an uprising of several hundred Muslim slaves in 1835 that left 70 people dead, while in Rio de Janeiro, urban slave discipline was further compromised by maroon communities established by slave runaways that surrounded the city. Known as *Quilombos*, these communities were, in Thomas Holloway's assessment, "close enough to the urban center that *quilombolas* could sneak into the city at night to forage for supplies, and their twinkling campfires and throbbing drums left the downtown residents jittery."[9]

---

[7] T. Stephen Whitman, *The Price of Freedom: Slavery and Manumission in Baltimore and Early National Maryland* (Lexington: University Press of Kentucky, 1997); David Goldfield, *Cotton Fields and Skyscrapers: Southern City and Region, 1607–1980* (Baton Rouge: Louisiana State University Press, 1982); William Dusinberre, *Strategies for Survival: Recollections of Bondage in Antebellum Virginia* (Charlottesville: University of Virginia Press, 2009), 50; Frank Towers, "The Southern Path to Modern Cities: Urbanization in the Slave States," in L. Diane Barnes, Brian Schoen and Frank Towers (eds), *The Old South's Modern Worlds: Slavery, Region, and Nation in the Age of Progress* (Oxford: Oxford University Press, 2011), 157.

[8] Mariana L.R. Dantas, *Black Townsmen: Urban Slavery and Freedom in the Eighteenth Century Americas* (New York: Palgrave Macmillan, 2008), 96. Keila Grinberg also emphasises similarities between slave cities in Brazil and the United States in "Freedom Suits and Civil Law in Brazil and the United States," *Slavery and Abolition* 22.3 (2001), 67.

[9] Thomas H. Holloway, *Policing Rio de Janeiro: Repression and Resistance in a 19th-Century City* (Stanford: Stanford University Press, 1993), 35. By contrast, the most extensive rebellions plotted by urban slaves in the United States were uncovered and crushed before they even began, including Gabriel's rebellion in Richmond in 1800 and the Denmark Vesey plot in Charleston in 1822.

Even so, in 1850 Rio's population stood at 200,000 people, including 78,000 slaves and in Salvador, there were around 35,000 slaves among 90,000 city residents.[10] Slavery in Brazilian cities did decline after mid-century, but, as in the United States, this can be explained by growing abolitionist influences (slavery was abolished in Brazil in 1888) and the economic lure of western territories. Whereas slaves in the United States were sold to meet the booming demand for labour in the emerging cotton plantation regions of Alabama and Mississippi, so in Brazil they were transferred to work in the coffee-growing regions of western São Paulo.[11]

Policing urban slaves

In the slave cities of the United States, formalised law enforcement enhanced and often entirely replaced the surveillance and disciplinary power of individual slaveholders. The demands of slave control led southern cities including Charleston, New Orleans and Richmond to establish the nation's first police forces in the late eighteenth and early nineteenth centuries, far earlier than northern cities with much larger populations.[12] Urban police in the South enforced state criminal laws against slaves, but spent much of their time regulating slave conduct in accordance with wide-ranging municipal ordinances that reflected the particular demands of slave control in city environments. A New Orleans ordinance passed in 1817 was representative. On pain of arrest and whipping, slaves were prohibited from residing or sleeping in any building that was not the property of their owner or hirer without a ticket granting explicit permission. They could not assemble in public spaces except for purposes of "divine worship" during specified hours and for approved sports and dances on Sundays, which were to take place only during daylight hours in locations specified by the mayor. Slaves could not appear in public carrying a cane, club or other stick unless they were blind or infirm, and nor could they make any "clamorous noise," sing indecent songs or show disrespect to any white person. Additionally, hired slaves employed by the day were required to wear an official badge indicating their status.[13] The Black Code of the District of Columbia contained even more detailed

[10] Joao J. Reis, "The Revolution of the Ganhadores: Urban Labour, Ethnicity and the African Strike of 1857 in Bahia, Brazil," *Journal of Latin American Studies* 29.2 (1997), 357–8.

[11] Laird W. Bergad, "American Slave Markets During the 1850s: Slave Price Rises in the United States, Cuba, and Brazil in Comparative Perspective," in David Eltis, Frank D. Lewis and Kenneth L. Sokoloff (eds), *Slavery in the Development of the Americas* (Cambridge: Cambridge University Press, 2004), 224–5. Recent research has begun to challenge traditional distinctions between urban and rural slaves. See, for example, Ian Read, *The Hierarchies of Slavery in Santos, Brazil, 1822–1888* (Stanford: Stanford University Press, 2012), 4–5 and Timothy Lockley, "Slaveholders and Slaves in Savannah's 1860 Census," *Urban History*, Available on CJO 2014 doi:10.1017/S096392681400012.

[12] Dennis C. Rousey, *Policing the Southern City: New Orleans, 1805–1889* (Baton Rouge: Louisiana State University Press, 1996), 13–28.

[13] *A General Digest of the Ordinances and Resolutions of the Corporation of New-Orleans* (1831), 133–7.

provisions for the nation's capital. In addition to criminal laws enacted by the state of Maryland, under city ordinances slaves faced the lash for racing or maltreating horses on city streets; bathing in the city's rivers or canals; damaging public water pumps, walls, fences or street lamps; gathering in disorderly assemblages at any time or for religious worship after 10 o'clock at night; going "at large" after 10 o'clock at night without carrying a pass from a justice of the peace or other respectable person; causing a false alarm of fire; setting off fire-crackers, or violating any of the ordinances that regulated the city's markets.[14]

In practice, most slaves were arrested for violating city curfews and other restrictions on their freedom of movement designed to police runaways, or, somewhat less often, for drunkenness and disorderly conduct. Reflecting the role of the police as a surrogate for the slaveholders' rule, it was relatively rare that officers arrested slaves for more serious criminal offences. Commonly, arrested slaves were held overnight in the city jail in anticipation of an appearance before the mayor or justice of the peace the following morning for a swift and summary hearing of the case. In the event that the accused was judged to be guilty, corporal sentences were normally carried out the same day so that slaves could quickly be returned to work.[15]

The policing and punishment of slaves was, then, a routine part of municipal governance in the US South during the nineteenth century. Due to the imperatives of slave control, southern police forces were roughly double the size of their northern counterparts relative to population by the 1850s, and though they still had insufficient manpower to keep watch over slaves and free African Americans in all of the clandestine spaces that cities offered for illicit gatherings, the system worked well enough to provide a basic stability to urban slavery. There were, nonetheless, inherent practical and ideological problems with an institutionalised system of slave control that rested on law rather than the mastery of slaveholders. First, for all that slaveholders demanded strict regulation of urban slaves in the abstract, they regularly opposed excessive police interference in their slaves' affairs, which threatened their personal authority over the enslaved and potentially compromised their slaves' productivity when it interrupted their working lives. An editorial in the New Orleans *Daily Picayune* in 1859 complained that slaves were "frequently arrested when there are not the slightest grounds for supposing them to be fugitives from service, and positive losses and annoyances to their owners are the result."[16] Slaveholders also had reason to oppose the imposition of corporal punishments on slaves by the state, as the scars of the lash and the branding

[14] Worthington G. Snethen, *Black Code of the District of Columbia* (1848), 34–47.
[15] Howell M. Henry, *The Police Control of the Slave in South Carolina* (Emory, VA, 1914), 49; Betty C. Wood, "Prisons, Workhouses, and the Control of Slave Labour in Low Country Georgia, 1763 to 1815," *Slavery and Abolition* 8.3 (1987), 261–2.
[16] Cited in Stacy K. McGoldrick, "The Policing of Slavery in New Orleans, 1852–1860," *Journal of Historical Sociology* 14.4 (2001), 411–12.

iron remained on the bodies of enslaved convicts as permanent symbols of their criminality and resistance to white authority and could affect the price they commanded on the auction block. As Andrew Boone, a former slave in North Carolina explained, "[a] nigger scarred up or whaled an' welted up wus considered a bad nigger an' did not bring much. If his body wus not scarred, he brought a good price."[17] Some slaves in state custody never returned to their owners at all. One enslaved man sent to the New Orleans calaboose to be whipped slit his own throat rather than endure a flogging, while the slave Jesse, secured in a Virginia jail by his owner "for safe keeping and correction," died a few days after returning home due, in his owner's opinion, to being "unnecessarily exposed to cold and wet" conditions and inadequately cared for by the jail keeper. In each of these cases, state Supreme Court justices rejected slaveholders' claims for damages.[18]

By the mid-nineteenth century, the policing of slaves in the southern United States was also inconsistent with developments in pro-slavery thought. In response to the growing strength of the anti-slavery movement and calls for slavery's immediate abolition from the 1830s, southern politicians and writers constructed a range of new "pro-slavery" arguments that depicted the institution as a "positive good." Their defence of slavery rested on diverse claims, including that it was superior to the free labour system of the northern states, underpinned the freedom of all southern whites, and was justified by Christian theology. The most important component of pro-slavery ideology, however, was the contention that slavery was a moral institution in which slaveholders practised a benevolent and paternalistic form of mastery that nurtured and civilised slaves who in turn were docile and content in their submissive condition.[19] The reality was everywhere very different, but in cities the autonomy of hired slaves and the central roles of municipal authorities and law in slave control meant that even the pretence of paternalism was unsustainable. As Georgia planter John Stoddard complained in the 1850s, many slaveholders in Savannah could not even "tell where their servants are, or what they are doing," while an article in the Mobile *Advertiser* suggested that negligent masters were the principle reason for slave insubordination and crime in the city.[20]

---

[17] Walter Johnson, "Inconsistency, Contradiction, and Complete Confusion: The Everyday Life of the Law of Slavery," *Law and Social Inquiry* 22.2 (1997), 423–4; *Slave Narratives, vol. XI, North Carolina Narratives, Part I*, 134–5.

[18] *Lewis v. New Orleans* (1857), in Helen Catterall, *Judicial Cases Concerning American Slavery and the Negro*, III (New York: Octagon Books, 1968 [1936]), 653.

[19] For a critique of pro-slavery thought, see Ashworth, *Slavery, Capitalism, and Politics*, 192–285.

[20] Richard H. Haunton, "Law and Order in Savannah, 1850–1860," *Georgia Historical Quarterly* 56 (1972), 3. On the relationship between paternalism, policing and urban slavery, see James M. Campbell, *Slavery on Trial: Race, Class, and Criminal Justice in Antebellum Richmond, Virginia* (Gainesville: University Press of Florida, 2007), 34–5.

Nonslaveholding whites and urban slavery in the United States

The complexities of law enforcement in southern cities were not limited to the treatment of African Americans. On the contrary, for all that slave control was the primary justification for the expansion of southern police forces, in practice regulation of the enslaved was often entangled with the policing and punishment of free nonslaveholders. Free African Americans – who were a substantial minority of the black population of southern cities – were subject to many similar municipal regulations as slaves, as well as comparable punishments including public whippings for myriad minor offences. This was entirely consistent with southern racial and pro-slavery ideology, but regulating the myriad interactions that took place between poor whites and slaves in urban environments presented a very different challenge. By the 1850s, substantial poor and ethnically diverse white populations were a feature of cities across the South, and their meagre living conditions, coupled with the growing concentration of slaveownership among a wealthy urban elite, were at odds with the claims of pro-slavery politicians such as James Henry Hammond that slavery was the basis of an unparalleled social equality among southern whites. In part, these developments were offset by slave hiring, but even such a short-term form of mastery that did not require substantial capital was beyond the reach of many city residents. As a result, whites often encountered slaves almost as social equals in lower-class neighbourhoods, drinking houses and even workplaces, and this could generate both interracial conflict and opportunities for criminal activities that crossed the colour line and compromised slave discipline. The Savannah *Republican* claimed in 1860, for example, that 90 per cent of thefts in the city were the result of white men trading stolen goods with slaves, and argued that the illegal, interracial trade in liquor was responsible for compromising the morals and destroying the value of the slave population.[21]

Policing interracial criminality was therefore a pressing concern for municipal authorities, but the arrest and incarceration of white people could raise troubling questions about the meaning of whiteness, freedom and republican government. Writing on the comparative history of slave law in the Americas, Robert Cottrol has argued that in Anglo-American regions, the "procedures and institutions" of law enforcement "came to take on cultural and moral significances beyond the simple protection of the citizenry. They became affirmations of the rightness of the common law culture and the essential correctness of the Anglo-American social order."[22] Cottrol notes that in the slave South the commitment to common law could ensure a degree of due process in the trial and punishment of slaves, but more routinely a system of criminal laws that was starkly divided by race guaranteed the rights of white

---

[21] *Savannah Republican*, 28 July 1860.
[22] Robert J. Cottrol, "Outlawing Outcasts: Comparative Perspectives on the Differing Functions of the Criminal Law of Slavery in the Americas," *Cardozo Law Review* 18 (1996), 722–3.

southerners and thereby gave meaning to the ideology of white supremacy on which slavery was based. This was evident, for example, in the fact that as the nineteenth century progressed, free African Americans were increasingly treated by the courts in the same manner as slaves, on account of their race, rather than as whites in recognition of their freedom. In the aftermath of Nat Turner's rebellion in 1831, in which several dozen slaves killed nearly 60 white men, women and children in Southampton County, Virginia, for example, free African Americans in the state – which was the most heavily urbanised in the South – lost the right to trial by jury, except in capital cases, while neighbouring Maryland allowed free blacks to be sold into slavery for a second felony conviction and imposed fixed-terms of enslavement for free blacks convicted of misdemeanours including petty theft. Across the South, free blacks were also routinely subject to corporal punishment for offences that brought only fines when committed by whites, and they were prevented in almost all cases from testifying against whites in courts of law.[23]

Although the racial bifurcation of the criminal law was clearly enshrined in southern statute books, however, in practice the competing demands of controlling slaves and protecting the legal rights of nonslaveholding whites were not always easily reconciled. As fears of slave resistance grew amidst heightened tensions over slavery's future in the mid-nineteenth century, slaveholders pushed for an expansion of criminal justice provisions to control the white poor in their dealings with slaves. In South Carolina, for example, whites could be sentenced to 39 lashes for gambling with slaves or free African Americans and petitions were submitted calling for the disfranchisement and public whipping of whites who illegally traded with slaves, a penalty that was eventually introduced in 1857 for those convicted of a second offence. Other states increased fines and prison terms for trading with slaves and relaxed the standard of proof required for a guilty verdict in an attempt to counter low conviction rates that stemmed from laws that prohibited black witnesses from testifying against white defendants in southern law courts.[24]

Such moves to police the white poor went furthest in southern cities, but it was there that they were also most politically explosive due to the increasingly stark divisions along lines of class and ethnicity that characterised urban white populations. In Richmond, municipal authorities established a chain gang in 1856, on which black and white vagrants and petty criminals laboured side-by-side. According to city officials, the chain gang was necessary to discourage the European immigrants and northern workers who were moving to the city in their thousands and contributing to growing rates of poverty and disorder. The sight of white men shackled and forced to labour on the city streets,

---

[23] See Edward Ayers, *Vengeance and Justice: Crime and Punishment in the 19th-Century American South* (New York: Oxford University Press, 1984), 62; Christopher Phillips, *Freedom's Port: the African American Community of Baltimore, 1790–1860* (Urbana: University of Illinois Press, 1997), 204.

[24] Jeff Forret, *Race Relations at the Margins: Slaves and Poor Whites in the Antebellum Southern Countryside* (Baton Rouge: Louisiana State University Press, 2006), 111–12.

however, also stood as a monument to the crass claims of pro-slavery advocates that slavery elevated all whites and made the South immune from the types of social dislocation that plagued the free labour cities of the North. William Vest, a white veteran of the Mexican War, was sentenced to the Richmond chain gang following a string of convictions for property crimes. He successfully appealed for clemency from the governor of Virginia on the grounds that the chain gang was the "height of degradation" and "a barbarous torture." In upholding the appeal, the governor expressed his disagreement with city authorities over what constituted appropriate punishment for white men.[25]

There were similar tensions over the punishment of white men and women in other southern cities. In Charleston, the commissioners of the poor-house recommended in 1838 that white paupers should be forced to grind corn on a treadmill, but the proposal was rejected on the grounds that "the long established connection of such an establishment with the Work House has rendered it one of the modes of punishment for slaves and other colored persons." As Cynthia Kennedy has shown, judges in Charleston also routinely failed to note the name, race or gender of white women who appeared before them on criminal charges in order to avoid undermining established racial assumptions that only black women committed crimes in the city.[26] In New Orleans, meanwhile, a paramilitary police force established in 1805 to control the slave population was reformed in the 1830s, as demographic changes in the city meant that whites rather than slaves became the primary targets of police surveillance and arrests. In this context, the practices of police carrying firearms and wearing military-style uniforms came to appear not as necessary protections against slave insurrection, but rather as threats to white liberty and republican values and thus from 1836 officers patrolled in civilian clothes instead of uniforms and their guns were replaced with nightsticks.[27] This new form of policing was consistent with the ideas of pro-slavery writers, such as Thornton Stringfellow, who condemned the need for "standing armies of policemen" in northern cities, such as New York, as evidence of the superiority of slavery over free labour, and George Fitzhugh, perhaps the most extreme of the pro-slavery intellectuals, who argued that in the cities of England only "a bloody code, a standing army and efficient police" was sufficient to regulate the working poor.[28] From a similar standpoint, the Mayor of Richmond, Joseph Mayo, wrote with pride in 1861 that his city of nearly 50,000 inhabitants had "but eight day policemen, not one armed," but he neglected to mention that a night watch and a state Public Guard of more than 100 men were also stationed in the city and served principally to police

[25] Campbell, *Slavery on Trial*, 71–2.
[26] Cynthia M. Kennedy, *Braided Relations, Entwined Lives: The Women of Charleston's Urban Slave Society* (Bloomington: Indiana University Press, 2005), 182–8.
[27] Rousey, *Policing the Southern City*, 13–28.
[28] Thornton Stringfellow, *Scriptural and Spiritual Views in Favor of Slavery* (Richmond: J.W. Randolph, 1856), 143; George Fitzhugh, *Sociology for the South, Or the Failure of Free Society* (Richmond: A. Morris, 1854), 35.

the enslaved.[29] Hinton Rowan Helper, a critic of slavery, viewed crime control in Virginia rather differently, noting that the combined cost of compensating slaveholders for the execution of slaves and maintaining the state public guard to police slaves in Richmond amounted to $46,000 in 1856 alone, which he considered an unjustifiable tax on the poor.

Slave cities, policing and punishment in Brazil

Evidence from Brazil suggests that the forms and functions of slave policing in cities followed similar patterns to the United States, with police serving as "urban overseers" and courts imposing regular whippings for violations of municipal ordinances and criminal laws.[30] In Rio de Janeiro slaves accounted for about 80 per cent of approximately 5,000 arrests made between 1808 and 1821. Most had committed relatively trivial offences that in many cases were a function of their slave status. Almost two-thirds were charged with being runaways or with public order offences, notably disorderly conduct, carrying a weapon and participating in the African martial art of capoeira.[31] Similarly in Recife, the largest city in the northern province of Pernambuco, 62 per cent of slaves held in the House of Detention between 1860 and 1885 were charged with public order offences, while in late 1870s Santos generic charges of "disorder" and "disobedience" accounted for more than 28 per cent of arrests of male slaves and 48 per cent of female slaves, and a further 30 per cent of total slave arrests involved curfew violations and attempted flight.[32]

Brazil also saw moves to privatise urban slave punishments in the nineteenth century. In 1829, the whipping of slaves arrested on the orders of their owners was removed from public gaze in the city squares to the Calabouço and Aljube jails. Similarly at the state level, the Criminal Code of 1830 abolished torture and all forms of physical punishment, apart from the whipping of slaves.[33] Some believed that further reforms were necessary. In 1856, Rio's police chief felt compelled to comment that the Aljube prison was "in flagrant contradiction with the humanitarian sentiments that distinguish the Brazilian population." Particularly disconcerting was that the institution stood in the nation's capital city, a location that was, in the police chief's words, "the center

---

[29] "The Reception of the Prince in Richmond," *Daily Dispatch* [Richmond, VA.], 10 January 1861. On the public guard, see Takagi, *Rearing Wolves*, 136.

[30] Alexandra K. Brown, "'A Black Mark on our Legislation': Slavery, Punishment, and the Politics of Death in Nineteenth-Century Brazil," *Luso-Brazilian Review* 37.2 (2000), 96.

[31] Leila M. Algranti, "Slave Crimes: The Use of Police Power to Control the Slave Population of Rio de Janeiro," *Luso-Brazilian Review* 25.1 (1988), 33, 39–40; Holloway, *Policing Rio de Janeiro*, 296–7.

[32] Martha K. Huggins, *From Slavery to Vagrancy in Brazil: Crime and Social Control in the Third World* (New Brunswick: Rutgers University Press, 1985), 90; Ian Read, *The Hierarchies of Slavery in Santos, Brazil, 1822–1888* (Stanford: Stanford University Press, 2012), 116.

[33] Thomas H. Holloway, 'The Brazilian "Judicial Police" in Florianópolis, Santa Catarina, 1841–1871', *Journal of Social History* 20.4 (1987), 735–6.

of our civilization."[34] Daniel Walker's research suggests that the people of Havana, Cuba, shared similar concerns. A whipping house was built outside the city walls to protect the public from views of "streaming blood and lacerated flesh." According to the British consul to Cuba in the 1840s, however, the city was still exposed to the "piercing screams and piteous shrieks for mercy" that emanated from within the whipping house walls.[35] The practice of slaveholders paying police officers to jail and inflict corporal punishment on slaves was a further aspect of urban slave control that transcended national boundaries. For a small charge, officers at the Calabouço prison in Rio de Janeiro inflicted hundreds of lashes on slaves with no questions asked, and there is evidence of similar practices in the southern town of Florianópolis.[36]

By contrast, the form, meaning and implications for slavery of policing and imprisoning free people differed sharply in Brazil from the southern United States. Whereas southern whites in the United States viewed standing armies and municipal police as a threat to republican liberty, in Brazil, government forces were routinely deployed to protect the state against attacks from insurgencies launched by both enslaved and free persons. The extensive police provisions of Brazilian cities did not stand as the anomalous institutions they were in the southern United States, therefore, but rather were consistent with national political and policing cultures. In part, this was a consequence of the greater fluidity and flexibility of racial categories in Brazil, where the binary associations of black/slave and white/free were less entrenched than in the United States. The majority of free people subjected to arrest and prosecution in Brazilian cities during the slave era were non-white and ideas of white supremacy – which were in any case less integral to the slave system in Brazil – consequently were not threatened by the enforcement of criminal law against poor and nonslaveholding free labourers. What is more, slave ownership was more broadly diffused among urban populations in Brazil than in the United States and was an important mechanism of social mobility even for people of colour in a city like Rio de Janeiro, and particularly in the first half of the nineteenth century before the abolition of the Atlantic slave trade to Brazil pushed up slave prices after 1851. Historian Zephyr Frank has argued that slaves were the most evenly distributed form of property among what he calls the "middling groups" of Rio de Janeiro, and slaveholding was accessible even to individuals who had once been slaves themselves on a scale unknown in the United States. In one notable example, Antonio Dutra, formerly an enslaved barber, purchased his own freedom, and by the time of his death in 1849 owned 13 slaves and had achieved a solidly middle-class status.[37]

---

[34] Holloway, *Policing Rio de Janeiro*, 204.
[35] Walker, *No More, No More*, 28.
[36] For an example of a mistress who privately flogged her slaves despite complaints from her neighbours, see A. Toussaint-Samson (ed.) *A Parisian in Brazil* (Boston: James H. Earle, 1891), 43–4.
[37] Zephyr L. Frank, *Dutra's World: Wealth and Family in Nineteenth-Century Rio de Janeiro* (Alberquerque: University of New Mexico Press, 2004), 56.

Even if the forms and functions of slave policing and punishment were similar in both Brazilian and US cities, therefore, the broader political and ideological demands placed upon systems of law enforcement were distinct. As such, police forces in Brazilian cities dwarfed those in the southern United States. Rio de Janeiro, for example, developed the most extensive police provisions of any city in the Americas in the nineteenth century, with the possible exception of Havana, and state power was routinely deployed not only to protect against slave resistance but also to defend the emergent nation state from popular uprisings involving free people. The power of the Brazilian state was especially evident in the first two decades after independence in the 1820s. Historian Hendrik Kraay has characterised this era as a time when "the elite project for the new state was vigorously contested by excluded groups" and government troops were regularly used to crush opposition movements. In 1838, for example, troops massacred at least 1,000 people in Salvador following the Sabinada revolt. This was an uprising involving people of diverse backgrounds and interests, including radical liberals and military officers, as well as free and enslaved people of African descent. These latter groups comprised most of the dead and Kraay notes that although the substantial numbers of middle- and upper-class persons of European descent who were involved in the revolt were treated more leniently by the government than slaves, as authorities sought to reassert control over Salvador they nonetheless restricted the constitutional rights of hundreds of free people who were arbitrarily arrested and faced summary deportation to other provinces.[38] Within this repressive political context, there was little that seemed new or problematic about using prisons and police forces to regulate the lives of the free urban poor.

In post-independence Brazil, therefore, state and municipal authorities treated the nation's urban lower classes, whether enslaved or free, as what historian Thomas Holloway has called "a largely undifferentiated group." The gradual amelioration of slave punishments in the mid-nineteenth century was part of this process,[39] as was the conservative reaction (*Regreso*) of the 1840s, which saw individual police chiefs empowered to examine suspects and impose sentences on free people without a trial and with minimal due process in all but the most serious cases. In practice, this meant that free Brazilians could be imprisoned or exiled for up to six months without ever coming before a judge or jury.[40] Some did not even make it to prison. From the 1820s, individuals

---

[38] On the Sabinada, see H. Kraay, "'As Terrifying as Unexpected': The Bahian Sabinada, 1837–1838," *The Hispanic American Historical Review* 72.4 (1992), 502.

[39] Criminal law in Brazil distinguished between slaves and free people, albeit less starkly and consistently than in the United States. In 1824, for example, corporal punishments were abolished for free people but retained for slaves, while under the 1831 criminal code slaves could be executed for crimes unique to their status, including insurrection and, from 1835, the murder of a master, overseer or member of the master's family. Brown, "A Black Mark on our Legislation," 101–3.

[40] Holloway, *Policing Rio de Janeiro*, 168, 324n5.

categorised as vagrants, idlers or disorderly elements, could be conscripted into the army, irrespective of their race or civil status, without any court procedures. Thomas Flory has argued that this practice represented a new concern in Brazilian law enforcement with "behavioural and social categories" rather than "civil status and the overt discrimination of racial criteria," while Sandra Graham found that, by the 1870s, "slavery's terms permeated, and corroded all social relations, and extended to free persons."[41]

Even as the slave population declined, policing in Brazilian cities took on an increasingly militaristic air. By the 1870s, Salvador was policed by nearly 2,000 men belonging to the provincial police and a separate city guard, and it was also patrolled by the army, while the urban guard in Rio de Janeiro was abolished in 1885 and the city's military police – described by an Italian visitor to the city as the most "brutal," "despotic" and "arbitrary" to be found anywhere in the world – expanded from 560 to 1,008 men.[42] Rio's police system had responded to changing urban demography by applying the autocratic tradition of slave policing to all lower-class residents in the city whether they were enslaved or free. This was apparent in the response of the Rio authorities to the Vintem Riot of 1880. When a crowd of 4,000 protestors marched in opposition to new taxes imposed on tram passengers in the city, they were attacked by police officers and army infantry and cavalry armed with guns and swords, and by nightfall three protestors had been killed. In the years following the abolition of slavery in 1888 the repressive policing of Brazil's urban poor persisted.[43] Historian Peter Beattie has shown that impressment into military service remained a common, alternative form of incarceration in response to crime in Brazil into the late nineteenth century, while research by Martha Huggins and Boris Fausto on the cities of, respectively, Recife and São Paulo, shows an increasing reliance on criminal vagrancy statutes to secure a pliant labour force. After emancipation in the United States, similar legislation was used primarily to coerce labour from former slaves, but in Brazil it equally targeted the thousands of European immigrants – mostly Italians and Portuguese – who entered the country from the late nineteenth century.[44]

[41] Thomas Flory, "Race and Social Control in Independent Brazil," *Journal of Latin American Studies* 9.2 (1977), 204. Graham notes that, "in order to gain the necessary city license, free people who hired themselves out as casual labor supplied a sponsor or guarantor just as slaves did." See Sandra L. Graham, *House and Street: The Domestic World of Servants and Masters in Nineteenth-Century Rio de Janeiro* (Cambridge: Cambridge University Press, 1988), 110.

[42] Brown, "A Black Mark on our Legislation," 99; Holloway, *Policing Rio de Janeiro*, 241, 282–3.

[43] Holloway, *Policing Rio de Janeiro*, 241, 282–3; Sandra L. Graham, "The Vintem Riot and Political Culture: Rio de Janeiro, 1880," *The Hispanic American Historical Review* 60.3 (1980), 436–7.

[44] Peter M. Beattie, "Conscription versus Penal Servitude: Army Reform's Influence on the Brazilian State's Management of Social Control, 1870–1930," *Journal of Social History* 32.4 (1999), 847–9; Huggins, *From Slavery to Vagrancy*; Boris Fausto, *Urban Crime in Brazil: The Case of São Paulo, 1880–1924* (Latin American Program, Wilson Center, 1981). Keri L. Merritt

Conclusion

While historians have recently highlighted the commonalities in urban slavery across the Americas, the cultural meanings and ideological implications of policing and punishment could diverge sharply in mid-nineteenth century cities, because they were shaped not only by urban environments, but also by broader political and cultural ideas about race, nation, law and slavery. This was especially apparent in the policing of free people, which in the cities of the southern United States was essential to the regulation of slaves, but also constrained by pro-slavery ideology and the political imperative of upholding white solidarity in the face of a growing abolitionist threat. By contrast, developments in urban policing and punishment in Brazil were informed by different political priorities that centred on state-building and the emergence and consolidation of the Brazilian nation. As a result, while forms of urban slave resistance, control and punishment were similar across the Americas, municipal authorities in Brazil were able to institute far more extensive provisions for policing slaves than were their counterparts in the United States. While the historiography on urban slavery has in recent years become very rich in its analysis of slave life and particularly the impact of manumission, this transnational history of law enforcement suggests a need for further understanding in the comparative literature of free nonslaveholders of all ethnic and racial identities and their political, social and economic connections with the enslaved, slaveholders and the state.

has shown that vagrancy laws in Georgia were "overwhelmingly" enforced against whites during slavery and against blacks after emancipation. See Merritt, "'A Vile, Immoral, and Profligate Course of Life': Poor Whites and the Enforcement of Vagrancy Laws in Antebellum Georgia," in Susanna Delfino, Michele Gillespie and Louis Kyriakoudes (eds), *New Currents in the History of Southern Economy and Society: Southern Society and Its Transformations, 1790–1860* (Columbia: University of Missouri Press, 2011), 40.

4 'Thank goodness Habeas Corpus did not run in Nahud'

Bifurcated systems of policing in Condominium Sudan, 1898–c.1956

W.J. Berridge

This chapter explores how capable the colonial state in Sudan was of policing its subject populations. The extent to which the twentieth-century colonial governments were capable of exercising control over those they ruled is a much debated question in the wider scholarship on Africa. Berman argues that there are two contending models of the colonial state in Africa. One depicts the state as a 'paternalistic mediator' with few resources and limited coercive capacity, whereas the second represents a state with an expansive bureaucratic apparatus intervening in ever-widening areas of the political economy.[1]

Such an emphasis on the totalizing nature of colonial power reflects the broader theoretical concerns of interpreters of colonialism such as David Scott, whose article 'Colonial Governmentality', developing the Foucauldian notion of 'governmentality', emphasizes the transformative nature of colonial power. For Scott, the development of the colonial state in Asia, Africa and the Middle East in the nineteenth and twentieth centuries represented an extension of the modern state and modern power. For the purpose of this chapter it is particularly important to explore some of Scott's statements about the nature of colonial legal power. For him, 'colonial governmentality' represented a shift away from eighteenth and early nineteenth century modes of colonialism, whereby the colonial state was characterized by 'extractive domination', towards an attempt to regulate wider colonial society through the introduction of European law codes in order to regulate individual behaviour. Scott emphasizes 'the introduction of a new game of politics' which depended on 'the constitution of a legally instituted space where legally defined subjects could exercise rights, however limited those might have been'.[2]

This chapter will challenge Scott's analysis by contending that the colonial state in twentieth-century Sudan was fundamentally conflicted over whether or not to introduce a new and transformative system of policing. The British colonial administration in Sudan possessed its own specialist governing

---

[1] Bruce Berman, *Control and Crisis in Colonial Kenya: the Dialectic of Domination* (London: Currey, 1990), 424–5.

[2] David Scott, 'Colonial Governmentality', *Social Text* 43.2 (1995), 191–220 at 208.

cadre, the Sudan Political Service (SPS). The SPS was unique in that most of its members spent their entire careers in Sudan, in contrast with more itinerant administrators who served elsewhere in the empire working under the Colonial Office. As a result, Political Service officers often developed a quite intense attachment both to their position in Sudan and to each other.[3] They feared that the emergence of a professional cadre of policemen applying the civil policing models developed in Britain, together with the modern legal codes favoured by the Sudan judiciary, would not only bolster the nationalist movement but cause a clash with their own, more conservative understanding of the methods of policing that Sudan required.

The administration thus made strenuous efforts to isolate these educated and professional men, both British and Sudanese, from the provincial police forces. The provincial governors and 'inspectors' of the Political Service had possessed direct control over provincial police units ever since the government transferred authority over the police from the Egyptian Army to the Political Service in 1905. These administrators often emphasized their own peculiar 'understanding' of 'the Sudanese' as a justification for maintaining a position of authority over the colonial constabulary, and consequently marginalized specialist British police professionals whose desires to modernize the Sudanese police system were deemed inappropriate. It will be seen that administrators expounded ideals about 'the Sudanese' which fitted in with their own crude notions of cultural relativism, and the supposed peculiarity of the Sudanese environment and its resistance to modern and rational techniques of policing. In contrast, police and judicial professionals increasingly tried to forge a modern, disciplined, literate and legally-knowledgeable institution out of Sudan's police. Understanding these conflicts, in which the administration usually retained the upper hand, enables us to explain precisely why colonial governance of Sudanese society was so restricted. The British had limited resources to govern Sudanese society, but also limited intent. This chapter will argue that the colonizers focused primarily on policing the 'gateways' of the colonial economy and not on developing a 'governmentalist' approach based on regulating Sudanese society as a whole.[4]

Focusing on colonial policy towards the police will also allow us to study the extent to which the Condominium (established by the British in 1898 as a theoretical exercise of joint rule in unequal partnership with their own informal possession, Egypt) had a role in perpetuating the divide between the centres and peripheries of Sudanese society. In recent years academic specialists on Sudan have emphasized the explanatory power of the 'centre–periphery' concept in understanding conflict in nineteenth- and twentieth-century Sudan, using it to challenge interpretations that emphasize culture, religion and

---

[3] Martin Daly, *Imperial Sudan: The Anglo-Egyptian Condominium, 1934–1956* (Cambridge: Cambridge University Press, 1991), 399.

[4] Frederick Cooper, *Africa since 1940: The Past of the Present* (Cambridge: Cambridge University Press, 2002), 5.

politics. The 'centre–periphery' explanation posits that conflict in Sudan in the last two centuries has been the product of a regional imbalance of power between the urbanized, mercantile, affluent 'centre' of Sudan along the Nile and marginalized, exploited peripheries such as Darfur, southern Kordofan and (the now seceded) southern region of the country.[5] This chapter will argue that the Condominium actively exacerbated this divide, as its disjointed policy towards the Sudanese constabulary effectively ensured that the colonial state subjected Sudanese outside the main urban centres located along the Nile, such as Khartoum, Shendi, Wad Medani and Atbara, to an 'administrative' form of police control, bypassing the central legal codes established by the colonial state and creating what Alice Hills has termed an 'institutional bifurcation'.[6] Administrative policing did not pursue the Foucauldian logic of individuating criminals by subjecting them to targeted investigations and 'avoiding distribution in groups' so as to prevent group solidarity; rather, it treated the inhabitants of the rural peripheries as Mamdani's de-individuated 'subjects', whereas in the urban and riverain north the idea of civil policing slowly began to grow.[7]

Policing, 'martial race' ideology and nationalism in Sudan

Police forces in early colonial Africa usually took on a military character, and Sudan was no exception.[8] The police force emerged gradually out of the Egyptian Army, which the British had used to reconquer Sudan in 1898, ensuring that from its very inception it served the political aims of the colonial state. In the first two and a half decades of Condominium rule in Sudan, its principal tasks were to assist the army in crushing Mahdist uprisings and spying on educated Sudanese who were perceived to be pro-Egyptian nationalist or pro-Communist agitators. The internal organization of the police also retained a military character. Officers were divided into the infantry (*biyada*), whose job was guarding markets and ensuring security in the individual *merkaz* (government headquarters), and the cavalry (*al-quwwa al-rakiba*), further divided into horse riders (*khayyala*) and camel riders (*hajjana*), which functioned in the countryside.[9] Furthermore, the police had

[5] Amir Idris, *Conflict and Politics of Identity in Sudan* (New York: Palgrave Macmillan, 2005), 10–14. Douglas Johnson, *The Root Causes of Sudan's Civil Wars* (Oxford: James Currey, 2003), xvii.

[6] Alice Hills, *Policing Africa: Internal Security and the Limits of Liberalization* (Boulder: Lynne Rienner, 2000), 27.

[7] Mahmood Mamdani, *Citizen and Subject: Contemporary Africa and the Limits of Late Colonialism* (London: James Currey, 1996), 109.

[8] 'Consent, Co-ercion and Colonial Control', in David M. Anderson and David Killingray (eds), *Policing the Empire: Government, Authority and Control, 1830–1940* (Manchester: Manchester University Press, 1991), 6.

[9] Omer Salih Abu Bakr, *Tarikh al-Shurta fi-Sudan* (Riyadh: Dar an-Nushr bi'l-markaz al-arabi li'l-dirasat al-'amniyya wa'l-tadrib, 1990), 36.

military ranks, such as *askari, nafar, shawish, bash-shawish*, based on the Ottoman titles that were used by the Egyptian Army.

The colonial state's weak presence and reliance on the set of power structures inherited from the Egyptian Army was also evidenced by its inability to adjust ethnic imbalances in Sudanese state structures to suit its own purpose. In other British African territories, such as Nigeria, Ghana and Kenya, the British bound the police more closely to the state by recruiting marginal ethnic groups into the central police forces.[10] In spite of the British government's politicization of the police force, this was not the case in Sudan, where the central police was dominated by the Shayqiyya, an 'Arab'-identified ethnic group from the riverain region to the north of Khartoum. This group posed a particular threat to the colonial state because of its close identification with other branches of the riverain elite.

Together with other 'Arab'-identified groups from the riverain region to the north of Sudan that possessed literacy in Arabic, such as the Ja'aliin and the Danagla, the Shayqiyya came to dominate the main branches of government in colonial and post-colonial Sudan. The Shayqiyya largely dominated the officer corps of the police (and the army) throughout the country, as well as the rank-and-file in the riverain areas of the north. Alleyne Nicholson recalled that when he recruited police in Shendi and Merowe, he would only accept recruits if they could read and write Arabic, thus giving the Shayqiyya 'a great sense of responsibility'.[11] L.M. Buchanan remembered that the migration of the inhabitants of the northern Nile to the rest of Sudan seeking their fortune was common during the colonial era. This was especially true of 'the Shaigia, who enjoyed a strong martial tradition ... and were proud to form the backbone of the S.D.F [Sudan Defense Force] and the Police in the Northern Sudan'.[12]

There was a key difference in the British strategy of employing the Shayqiyya as a 'martial race' and the use of such tactics in other parts of the empire. Elsewhere, the British cultivated 'masculine' and 'rugged' types from the rural peripheries of a colonial territory to police the literate and educated population of the towns, and who formed the bulk of the nationalist movement.[13]

---

[10] Philip Ahire, *Imperial Policing: the Emergence and Role of the Police in Colonial Nigeria 1860–1960* (Milton Keynes: Open University Press, 1991), 56; David Killingray, 'Guarding the Extending Frontier: Policing the Gold Coast, 1865–1913' in Anderson and Killingray, *Policing the Empire*, 107.

[11] Deborah Lavin (ed.), *The Condominium Remembered: Proceedings of the Durham Historical Records Conference, 1982. Vol. 1, The Making of the Sudanese State* (Durham: Centre for Middle Eastern and Islamic Studies, 1991), 90.

[12] L.M. Buchanan Memoirs, 10 May 1982, 797/8/29, Sudan Archives, Durham, Durham, UK. Hereafter cited as SAD.

[13] Heather Streets-Salter, *Martial Races: The Military, Race and Masculinity in British Imperial Culture, 1857–1914* (Manchester: Manchester University Press, 2004), 162–8; P. Robb, 'The Ordering of Rural India', in Anderson and Killingray, *Policing the Empire*, 128.

In Sudan, however, the Shayqiyya overlapped with both these groups. For instance, the first Sudanese chief justice, Muhammad Abu Rannat (1956–64), the first military president, Ibrahim Abboud (1958–64), and a pioneering nationalist politician, Ahmad Kheir, were all Shayqiyya.[14] The Sudanese police at the riverain centre had relatively high levels of literacy. A police training school was opened in 1926,[15] and 62 per cent of the Khartoum police force could read and write by 1937.[16] It was this versatility in the role of the Shayqiyya, both as a 'martial race' and educated elite, that would complicate British policies towards the development of the police in Sudan.

After the proto-nationalist White Flag Revolt of 1924, the Political Service became increasingly focused on preventing the spread of the educated or 'effendi' class of nationalist and often pro-Egyptian Sudanese, including professional policemen, throughout Sudan's provinces. The British feared that expanding the central system of government would empower this 'effendi' class, as well as create a sizeable category of 'detribalized' Sudanese from the peripheries who – having been removed from their more local ethnic ties – would become more inclined towards nationalism. Indeed, Abu Bakr claims that a number of young educated police professionals had been sympathetic to the Revolt.[17] This fear of the educated 'effendi' elite clearly had an effect on the structure of the police force in Sudan. While the increasing numbers of educated policemen in the urban riverain areas led to the growth of a police force at the centre that was becoming increasingly centralized and professionalized, in the provinces British administrators attempted to keep the police as an adjunct to the administration or to delegate policing to local notables.

Police–administration tensions and the limited growth of the central force

The administrators' contempt for educated policemen led to a series of tensions with the modernizing British professionals who were keen to develop the force. These frictions first came into evidence after the dismissal of J.H. Plumbridge in 1920 following a falling-out with the then civil secretary. This disagreement focused on the two principal issues that caused frictions between the administration and police professionals: police education and the right of the professionals to exercise independent control over provincial forces. Initially, the disagreement was caused by the civil secretary's refusal to accept Plumbridge's proposal that police officers and Non-Commissioned Officers (NCOs) be sent to Egypt and England for further training.[18] The

---

[14] Peter M. Holt and Martin W. Daly, *A History of the Sudan: From the Coming of Islam to the Present Day* (New York: Longman, 2000), 151.

[15] Governor-General Annual Report for 1927, 17 [hereafter GGAR], accessed 11 November 2009, www.dur.ac.uk/library/asc/sudan/gov-genl_reports/.

[16] GGAR 1937, 222.

[17] Abu Bakr, *Tarikh al-Shurta*, 40.

[18] Abu Haraz Mu'tader, *Kitab Muqtasir fi Tarikh al-Shurta* (Khartoum: s.n., 2008), 44.

civil secretary argued that there simply were not enough funds for such a mission, although it is more likely that the administration was worried about the potential politicization that could result from officers visiting Egypt in particular, which was in the throes of anti-British nationalist agitation. The administration turned down a similar request from Jose Penney when he was commandant of the Police School in 1927.[19] Mu'tader claims that the civil secretary had also repeatedly written to Plumbridge requesting that he not interfere with the provincial forces, and it was rumoured that Plumbridge was aspiring to become commissioner of police, a position which did not exist at this time.[20] This was something the civil secretary resisted, since creating a commissioner of police would hamper the administration's unchecked control over the police forces of Sudan.[21]

K.C.P. Struvé, governor of Upper Nile, wrote in 1926 that police officers and administrators rarely got on well.[22] This was often due to different attitudes towards the 'Sudanese character'. Struvé complained of his local police officer, Coryton, that he 'does not understand Sudanese, and always favours any man who has a tinge of yellow in him ... Coryton cannot see any virtue in the Sudani's qualities, and denies them even courage'.[23] District Commanders (DCs) thus asserted their own 'special knowledge' of Sudanese culture. They often took great pride in their police forces and disliked the possibility that they might fall into the hands of those who were less familiar with the local languages and people.[24] They also often reacted negatively to the education of policemen and demanded more 'martial' qualities.[25]

The limited governmental ambitions of the colonial administration and its combined fear of, and contempt for, educated Sudanese also explain why the numbers of officers passing through the Police School remained extremely limited. Just as expansion of educational facilities for training clerks and civil servants was reined in as a result of the White Flag Revolt, the Police School remained largely stillborn after it opened in 1926, as the number of officers graduating each year in the late 1930s remained in single figures.[26] Apprehension about police education culminated in 1937 with the closure of the Police School out of fears that the newly-educated generation of policemen were becoming too attracted to the nationalist movement, although the school was re-opened later in the same year, albeit as a school for the training of administrators as well as policemen.[27]

[19] Ibid., 51.
[20] Ibid., 44.
[21] Ibid., 44.
[22] K.C.P. Struvé, Handing-Over Notes for Upper Nile, 11 August 1926, SAD 212/9/3.
[23] Ibid.
[24] H.A. Nicholson Memoirs, n. d., SAD 777/10/45.
[25] Owen Memoirs, c.1960–1, SAD 769/11/43.
[26] Abu Bakr, *Tarikh al-Shurta*, 52.
[27] Ibid., 50–1.

The provincial and district administrators of the Political Service theoretically retained executive control over the police in the exercise of their crime-fighting duties. Nevertheless, the professional British police commandants who were appointed by the governor-general in the wake of the White Flag Revolt were later made responsible to the commissioner of police – a newly created post for the head of the Police Department that encompassed responsibility for matters of internal administration. The Police Headquarters first started sending out circulars to provincial police forces in 1930 and after this its bureaucracy gradually expanded as a regular regime for reporting criminal cases was established.[28] In the urban areas, which presented more opportunities for a 'professional' style of policing, Owen recalled that 'the Police became a distinct organisation merely co-operating with the Administration'.[29] However, the areas in which this obtained were relatively few. In 1934 the governor-general observed of the police: 'Except at Khartoum, Port Sudan, and, to some extent, in Darfur and the Blue Nile Provinces, this force is being administered as a part time function by Political Officers.'[30] In 1937 the governor-general appointed senior members of the Political Service as 'Inspectors of Police' in every province except Equatoria, which was still left without any inspector, and Khartoum and Port Sudan, which possessed a 'Commandant of Police' with the 'requisite professional qualifications'. The railway police also possessed such a commandant.[31] In other words, the only places where specialized professionals were in charge of the police were the capital and the colonial state's major port, where the Department of Public Security had assumed direct control over law and order in 1923.[32] This demonstrated the state's focus on 'gatekeeper' security.

Administrative control over the police in the provinces

In the provinces, members of the Political Service attempted to stall the growth of this centralized police force by using government policemen for their own administrative purposes. Owen recalled that in the rural areas the police remained to a large extent 'the district commissioner's men'.[33] Sudanese 'police officers' in the countryside were never quite sure what their title implied. In the 1920s they were frequently recruited from the training school for administrative 'sub-Mamurs', rather than the Police School, and their functions overlapped with those of administrators.[34] British administrators

[28] Abu Haraz, *Kitab*, 54.
[29] Owen Memoirs, SAD 769/11/44.
[30] Note on Police by Governor-General, Stewart Symes, dated 14 July 1934, NRO Civ Sec (1) 99/1/3.
[31] GGAR 1937, 12.
[32] K.J. Perkins, *Port Sudan: The Evolution of a Colonial City* (Boulder: Westview Press, 1993), 156.
[33] Owen Memoirs, SAD 769/11/44.
[34] Note on 'Mamurs + Sub Mamurs The Future of the Mamur', A. Redfern to J. Madden, 15 September 1929, NRO Civ Sec (1) 50/3/12.

argued that the police officer who possessed exclusively criminal functions was too much of a 'one line man' except in major towns.[35] The demand for 'police officers' with more administrative specialisms began to shape the evolution of the Police School itself, which was re-organized as a joint administrative and police training centre in 1935. Until it was re-organized as a 'Police College' once more in 1948, it would absorb students from Gordon College, the school established by the colonial government for the purpose of training local Sudanese to serve in the administration, and would thus produce far less technically specialized officers.[36]

Meanwhile, both the rank and file (*anfar*) and NCOs would be recruited locally and trained in local depots, although they could be sent to the Police School for specialized courses.[37] Local administrators often assigned them multiple roles, including serving as drivers, prison warders, tax collectors, labour organizers and locust exterminators – and guards for ginning factories in the Gezira Scheme, prisoners on guarantee schemes, and even to protect the DC's children from crocodiles.[38] Often, too, they acted as a sort of 'retinue' for the DC, escorting him while out on trek and chivvying the baggage animals.[39] This was typical of colonial administrative cadres, who often exploited their position to live out militaristic and aristocratic ideals and exercise a form of authority that had fallen into abeyance in Europe.[40] Rowton Simpson, a former DC, recalls that in al-Ubayyid he and other administrators were accompanied by mounted policemen on a 'town ride' bearing the British and Egyptian national flags, sometimes briefly arresting a town inhabitant for 'failing to stand up or for not dismounting from his donkey or otherwise not displaying proper respect'.[41] Thus administrators preferred a personal force which prioritized loyalty above literacy and would sacrifice professional police specialization to participate in the general administration.

There was little place in this system for Police School graduates with technical training in criminal investigation. Although Plumbridge's training school – and after 1926 the Police School as well – increasingly started to turn out trained Sudanese who would from 1923 take up roles as 'Police Officers'[42]

[35] Note on 'Future of sub-Mamur' by Angus Gillan, El Obeid, 31 December 1928, NRO Civ Sec (1) 50/3/12.
[36] 'Abdallah Hasan Salim, *Tarikh al-Shurta* (Khartoum: s.n., 2008), 23.
[37] L. James, 'The Sudan Police Force in the Final Years of the Condominium', in D. Lavin (ed.), *The Condominium Remembered: Proceedings of the Durham Historical Records Conference, 1982. Vol. 1, The Making of the Sudanese State* (Durham: University of Durham, 1991), 54–9.
[38] D. Evans, Western District Annual Report for 1939, 14 January 1940, SAD 710/7/26. G. Bell, *Shadows in the Sand* (London: Hurst, c.1983), p. 66. Winder Memoirs, n.d., c.1930s, SAD 104/15/17. Longe, Handing-Over Notes, Northern Gezira, Nov.-Dec. 1934, SAD 641/5/33. Peggy Vidler Memoirs, 1987, SAD 890/9/8. Evelyn Simpson Memoirs, 1987, SAD 890/8/25.
[39] T. Owen Memoirs, SAD 769/11/40.
[40] Bruce Berman and John Lonsdale, *Unhappy Valley: Conflict in Kenya and Africa*, vol. 1 (Athens: Ohio University Press, 1992), 237.
[41] Rowton Simpson Memoirs, c.1976, p. 40, SAD 720/4.
[42] Salim, *Tarikh al-Shurta*, 15.

under either British commandants of police or British DCs, the administration preferred that such officers should be restricted to the riverain areas. In 1934, the governor-general observed that recent Police School graduates dispatched to serve in the ranks should preferably do this in the principal towns of the urban riverain region, Wad Medani, Khartoum, Port Sudan or Atbara.[43]

Meanwhile, Political Service officers outside the riverain centre often used arguments about preserving local cultural difference to substitute a less substantial form of local training for Police School education. In 1932, R.E. Bailey, the governor of Kassala, argued that local Beja policemen would be 'likely to return from Khartoum bewildered instead of improved' whilst 'the atmosphere here is more wholesome and natural'.[44] Thus the province administration sent local policemen for a limited one-month course in Kassala town, rather than allowing them more professional training in Khartoum. Duncan Cumming, who combined the roles of DC for Kassala District and provincial police commandant, argued that the local training system was justified since 'the fact that the men work among friends and in their own environment appears to outweigh the advantages of the longer course given at the Omdurman Police Training School'.[45]

Administrative policy towards the Native Administration police

The Political Service also reduced its reliance on the regular police to deal with infringements of colonial law by delegating criminal policing to the Native Administration. This administration was formalized by a series of ordinances in the 1920s and 1930s which served the function of excluding riverain 'effendis' from provincial administration. In 1922 the government issued the *Power of the Nomad Sheikhs Ordinance*, which devolved judicial and police functions on the rulers of various nomadic 'tribes' in the north. It was followed in 1927 by the *Powers of the Sheikhs Ordinance*, which extended similar powers to the rulers of sedentary 'tribes' in the north.[46] The policy was particularly keenly applied in the regions of Darfur, Kordofan and Kassala.[47] A similar policy was also developed for the south, where after 1922 the government began to establish 'Chief's Courts' which would be endowed with similar powers to those enjoyed by the *Sheikhs* in the north.[48] In some places the creation of 'Native Authorities' simply amounted to a recognition of

[43] Note on Police by Governor-General Stewart Symes, dated 14 July 1934, NRO Civ Sec (1) 99/1/3.
[44] R.E. Bailey, Governor Kassala, 'Foreward on Mr Cumming's Police Note', 10 October 1932, SAD 989/7/89.
[45] D.C. Cumming, 'A General Note on the Kassala Police', 9 October 1932, SAD 989/7/91–93.
[46] Holt and Daly, *History of the Sudan*, 118.
[47] M.W. Daly, *Empire on the Nile: The Anglo-Egyptian Sudan, 1838–1934* (Cambridge: Cambridge University Press, 1986), 220.
[48] Daly, *History of the Sudan*, 119.

already existing local notables who had exercised de facto authority since the beginning of the Condominium and assisted the police in a similar manner in the 1910s and 1920s;[49] elsewhere, the colonial state was forced to step in and establish customary authority where it had not previously existed.[50]

The colonial state legally empowered Native Administration bodies to exercise police powers. In the Criminal Procedure Code, *Shaikhs* were granted authority to play the role of policemen in investigating and drawing up reports on suspicious deaths in their area; and they were legally bound to report the passage of suspected criminals through their village, quarter or district.[51] The colonial administration also decided that the newly empowered local potentates would need their own police forces to match their new legal powers. The new forces were known as 'chiefs' police' in the south and 'retainers' of the *Nazir* or *Shaikh* in the north. Both *Shaikhs* and their retainers had the power to arrest without warrant in cases where ordinary policemen could arrest without warrant, such as cases of homicide, bodily harm, theft, robbery and certain types of assault.[52]

Johnson argues that the Native Administration police remained supplementary to the regular police as rural courts were separate and largely subordinate to the urban courts.[53] This may have been the case, but the overstretched colonial administration afforded these police considerably more authority than in theory they should have possessed. Native Administration authority even extended into some of the major urban centres. From February 1930, the town *omda* and his Native Administration *ghaffirs* were made responsible for maintaining public security in the 'native quarter' of Fasher Town, which was understood to be the whole town except the British cantonment and Western Arab Corps lines.[54] In the same year, control of the town 'watch and ward' in Kassala was handed over to the force of 'native retainers' under the 'native bench' of the town.[55] Similar systems were operating in Tokar and Gedaref by the early 1930s.[56]

These forces were even further from meeting the professional police ideal than the government police. Often, their creation was simply a legal empowerment of already existing chiefly retinues.[57] Bell recalled that Nuba 'Chiefs'

[49] Mu'tader, *Kitab*, 31.

[50] Daly, *History of the Sudan*, 118.

[51] 1925 Code of Criminal Procedure, articles 110 and 110A, in Cecil Bennet (ed.), *Laws of Sudan Vol. 9* (London: Haycock P., 1956), 167.

[52] 1925 Code of Criminal Procedure, article 107, in Bennet, *Laws of Sudan*, 165, 230–68.

[53] Douglas H. Johnson, 'From Military to Tribal Police: Policing in Upper Nile Province of the Sudan', in Anderson and Killingray, *Policing the Empire*, 165.

[54] Governor Darfur to Civil Secretary, 5 April 1931, NRO Civ Sec (1) 1/22/64.

[55] GGAR 1930, 125.

[56] D.C. Cumming, 'A General Note on the Kassala Police', 9 October 1932, SAD 989/7/91–93.

[57] See, for instance, Justin Willis, 'Violence, Authority and the State in the Nuba Mountains of Condominium Sudan', *The Historical Journal* 46.1 (2003), 106.

Police' in the 1930s were taken to small settlements like Talodi for 'a few days' course of drill and basic police duties', but this was usually the limit of their training.[58] Barter wrote of one set of retainers in Hadendoa District that 'their activities are wide, varied and to a great extent unorganised'.[59] Thus the Political Service ensured that the Native Administration police forces were subject to even less regulation and institutionalization than the regular force.

Administrative neglect of government law codes in provincial policing

Throughout the colonial period, members of the Political Service serving in the provinces, such as governors and DCs, used their authority over the police force to enforce their own understanding of how Sudan's regions should be policed. While the Legal Department saw provincial police forces as potential vectors for the emergence of a centralized law enforcement system upholding universal principles of law, administrators frequently criticized the impracticality of attempting to use such forces to apply a modern or 'civil' system of law in the regions. The result was the development of a form of administrative policing which eschewed the use of government policemen to launch detailed criminal investigations. The lack of interest that local administrators showed in launching detailed investigations was exemplified by the DC of Nyala, who observed in 1944 that:

> Police seldom arrive to investigate a crime until some days after it has happened. As there are few fully literate police in the District and none of them are experienced in investigation, no investigation is likely to be complete or accurate.[60]

Administrators resented having to use provincial police forces to resolve offences under the Sudan Penal Code that resulted from *shaklas*, or large inter-village fights, where they believed that local methods of dispute resolution might have been more appropriate. In 1945, the governor of Darfur, Dudley Lampen, wrote to the civil secretary expressing his resentment at being required to command police investigations into every homicide case that occurred in the province. Recent homicide trials that had been conducted in Darfur involved those resulting from two *shaklas*, one between the Fur and Beni Hussein, and another between the Berti and Meidob. Lampen protested that:

> In both cases, but particularly in the first, an enormous amount of work fell on the investigating police, and the magistrates and the judge (in all three cases the District Commissioner) for a result which carried only some of those responsible. The District Commissioner had to hold down

[58] Bell, *Shadows*, 66–7.
[59] G. Barter, Hadendoa District Annual Report 1931, 15 January 1932, SAD 448/1/75.
[60] DC Nyala to Governor Darfur, 22 November 1944, NRO 2.D.1 Fasher. A. 32/1/3.

a difficult, and in one case dangerous tribal situation threatening public security, while the lengthy criminal proceedings progressed as no settlement could be effected until the processes of law were finished.[61]

Instead Lampen supported the use of Native Courts which would 'punish with an eye on the final settlement' by using 'blood money' or *dia* settlements to compensate the relatives of the deceased and thus facilitate a peace (*sulh*) between the opposing factions.[62] The collective nature of *dia* punishments, which fell on the entire kin-group from which the killer or killers came, was, in Lampen's eyes, infinitely preferable to the more retributive nature of the Westernized Sudan Penal Code. For him, the European legal practice of attributing individual guilt simply caused a greater deterioration in 'public security' by distributing punishments unevenly, rather than balancing the culpability of the respective parties for the fight. If the Legal Department wanted to impose a more decisive form of justice, Lampen believed – just like the DC in Nyala cited above – that this would require 'trained investigating police, better communications, transport to get them to the spot and a Province Judge who could relieve overworked District Commissioners'.[63] It is ironic that Lampen should have pointed this out, since elsewhere administrators would discourage the emergence of an educated and professionalized police force. The sheer persistence of the *dia* system demonstrated that the Political Service was capable of maintaining a sphere in which Sudan's professional judiciary and professional police force had little capacity to intrude.

Colonial administrators running local courts also displayed an unwillingness to be burdened by the niceties of English legal procedure with regard to *habeas corpus*. R.C. Mayall proudly recalled in his memoirs how he dealt with the case of three robbers who had attacked three merchants leaving Nahud, where he was a District Commander. Mayall suspected that the robbers had hosted the merchants in Nahud prior to their departure, and hoped that the one blind merchant who had survived the attack would be able to identify the culprits:

> I therefore sent word back to Nahud to the police officer that every man who lived in the street where the blind man had stayed was to be arrested on suspicion and questioned about the crime. I then continued my trek, but cut it short and returned to Nahud about ten days later. The blind man, I found, was better, but still in hospital and about 170 men were still detained in prison on suspicion without a charge having been laid against them. Thank goodness Habeas Corpus did not run in Nahud!!

[61] Lampen, Governor of Darfur to Civil Secretary, Legal Secretary, 28 May 1945, NRO 2.D.1 Fasher. A. 32/1/3.
[62] Ibid.
[63] Ibid.

Mayall's tyrannical behaviour did achieve results; an identity parade was later held in which the blind man claimed to have identified the murderer (presumably by his voice).[64]

The issue of *habeas corpus* provided another area of friction between provincial administrators and the lawyers in Khartoum, although it was not until later in the colonial period that the Legal Department started to challenge administrative laxity with regard to the rights of the accused. In 1950 a new Criminal Circular, No. 27, was distributed. This reminded administrators that under Section 236 of the Criminal Procedure Code the police had the power to imprison a suspect without trial for 15 days before they must be produced before a magistrate, at which point – should the prosecution not have enough evidence available – they should apply for a remand. In 1952, the governor of Darfur distributed this circular, reminding his DCs that he had recently issued a provincial order that all unconvicted prisoners should appear before a magistrate every week. However, he regretted that 'in spite of this order instances have been occurring in which local courts – who have no power to remand – send prisoners back to gaol for long periods without the magistrate apparently being aware of it'.[65] Thus even during the late colonial period the administrative sphere of arbitrary, non-professional and illegal policing persisted, unrestrained by the attempts of the Legal Department to control it.

The anti-individualistic nature of administrative justice was also apparent in DCs' continued use of collective punishment. One extremely irregular but common colonial practice was to arrest the families of criminals to convince them to turn themselves in.[66] During his time as ADC in Port Sudan in the early 1920s, J.W. Miller recalled that at one point he visited a nearby community and arrested 11 men, six women and almost 600 goats to force them to hand over a murderer.[67] In his memoirs from Upper Nile, J. Winder recalled how his predecessor as DC at Akobo, J.C. Alban, dealt with Nuer cattle thieves. He would have the Eastern Nuer Chief's police visit the suspected sections, and then 'take hostage' all the cattle and marriageable girls to force the section to hand over the culprits.[68] Hence we see a new and innovative notion of law being formed – one that was not quite like pre-colonial law and not quite the law the colonizers had claimed to introduce either. These methods stereotyped Sudanese communities as collective, de-individuated crowds. This was convenient for the colonial state, which, as seen above, usually possessed neither the resources nor local knowledge to make investigations and pinpoint individual culprits.

[64] R.C. Mayall memoirs, 1940, SAD 851/7/38.
[65] Criminal Circular Letter No 1/1950 3/2/1950 Lecture by J. Lomax on Criminal Court Circular no. 27, NRO 2.D.1. Fasher A. 32/1/3.
[66] AC-CP-249-29 KDN-Maj.Ct-41.C.49-29, SAD Hayes Box 1 File 1.
[67] J.W. Miller to his mother, 26 February 1923, SAD 968/9/5.
[68] Winder Memoirs, SAD 541/14/13.

Conclusion

The colonial state, in its persistent reluctance to bring a 'British' style of policing to Sudan, revealed its limited integrity. The British colonizers were reluctant to develop systems of policing that would exercise a thorough regulation of Sudanese society. This was partly because of the colonial administration's preoccupation with purely political policing and its focus on protecting its main strategic nodes. However, it also reflected wider ideological and political tensions within the colonial state itself. The British had become reliant on one of the riverain ethnic groups, the Shayqiyya, to man the police force at the urban riverain heartlands of the state. Whilst these officers, encouraged by British professionals, began to develop a more professional and educated outlook to meet the requirements of policing the urban riverain economy, the Political Service was not eager to employ these riverain professionals throughout the country. This was partially because agents of the Political Service feared the potential for professional policemen to act as vectors for nationalism, and partially because they preferred to assert their own outlook with regard to the policing of provincial Sudan, which eschewed modern and professional methods.

The result was that the colonial state established a bifurcated system of policing in Sudan. In this system, the administration left the specialized police professionals who were educated at the Police School to manage the major towns of the riverain area while delegating provincial policing to Native Administration bodies. Meanwhile, the Political Service used government policemen in the provinces to serve as the personal retinues of British officials. This system ensured that the administration, which often admitted to the lack of unity within the police system, did not subject the vast majority of Sudanese to the specialist, technical and individualistic forms of policing envisaged in the Sudan Penal Code and Criminal Procedure Code.

5 Policing in Hong Kong and Macau

Transformations from the colonial era to special administrative region

Lawrence Ka-Ki Ho

The 1980s saw the People's Republic of China assert and realize its territorial claims over Hong Kong and Macau as negotiations on the transfer of sovereignty from Britain and Portugal proceeded apace. Subsequent treaties with London and Lisbon prescribed a novel 'One Country, Two Systems' principle that stipulated 'a high degree of autonomy' from the Central People's Government in Beijing in virtually all policy areas except for diplomatic and military affairs and preserved some of the colonial institutions in the process. With regard to policing, Hong Kong retains an Anglo-Saxon model with a single police force anchored in common law traditions. Macau, by contrast, operates under a continental model of policing rooted in the civil law tradition, with separate judicial and administrative police bureaus.[1]

This chapter introduces key features of both territories' police forces and plots their coming-of-age from the violent leftist riots of the 1960s through the handovers of Hong Kong in 1997 and Macau in 1999, along with the latest developments in the first 'post-return' decade. It examines the evolving relationship between the police and society; the organizational differences of the two forces; and police involvement in internal security management against both general crime and social unrest. The post-colonial question has far-reaching implications. How did colonial administrations effect their authority over the majority Chinese populations? What were the characteristics, rationale and effectiveness of the policing systems they developed? What drove the police to change in these cities; and to what effect? The discussion is primarily based on interviews with veteran colonial officers and publicly accessible official archives.

Author's note: a substantial portion of the original research and analysis in this chapter was originally published in *Policing Hong Kong 1842–1969: Insiders' Stories*, ©2012 City University of Hong Kong Press, while part of the analysis on the evolution of Macau policing appeared in Lawrence K.K. Ho and Agnes I.F. Lam, 'Transformation of Macau Policing: From Portuguese Colony to China's SAR,' in Springer's *Crime, Law and Social Change* (On-line First article), 17 November 2013: http://link.springer.com/article/10.1007%2Fs10611-013-9493-3.

[1] Jeffrey T. Martin and Peter K. Manning, 'Policing the Southern Chinese Seaboards', *Crime, Law and Social Change* 61.4 (2014), 369–75.

Velvet gloves: between consent and coercion

Policing literature and analyses of formal social control systems based on Western nation-states, exercising self-determination or otherwise, tends to fall into two major categories. The first might be called 'policing by coercion', emphasizing force and control exerted by a government as it attempts to ensure peace and order. To achieve this objective, the government develops a strong law-enforcement apparatus to manage public order. The police tend to operate as a military or paramilitary force and use violence to control those who intend to disrupt the social order. The second approach is known as 'policing by consent', which emphasizes the partnership between police and citizens by positioning the police as public servants. Police do not constitute a military force but are a civic department that works closely with citizens. Violence is avoided and firearms are not considered necessary when discharging general duties.[2]

Colonial policing is usually assumed to follow the 'coercive policing' paradigm, in which both hard power (physical force) and soft power (autocratic legislation) serve to secure the metropole's interests in the colony. Some recent research is beginning to re-evaluate this perception, critically examining assertions of repressive policing with material evidence and mindful of knee-jerk reactions against colonial revisionism. Scholars such as Daniel Neep have suggested that some colonial administrators may not have been overly coercive when managing subjects, due to the absence of either the means or the need for violent force.[3] For example, some colonial authorities used 'divide and rule' tactics to avoid confrontation with local communities and maximize the effectiveness of colonial governance.[4] The cases of Hong Kong and Macau are consistent with such arguments, albeit within unique historical, political and sociological contexts.

In 1966, the police forces of Hong Kong and Macau were tested to their operational limits by an explosive mix of leftist riots (spilling over from the Cultural Revolution across the border), anti-imperialist sentiments, and general social deprivation. In the aftermath of these events, policing developed in the two territories in very different ways. The Hong Kong Police Force (HKPF) was professionalized and embarked on a series of structural, almost missionary, reforms. The British Hong Kong administration made highly public attempts to eradicate syndicated corruption in the police force and to improve relationships between the government, the police and society. After ratification of the Sino-British Joint Declaration in 1984, the HKPF reduced the number of overseas inspectorate recruits; sent aspiring officers to the UK

---

[2] Georgina Sinclair, *At the End of the Line: Colonial Policing and the Imperial Endgame 1945–80* (Manchester: Manchester University Press, 2006), 1–5.

[3] Daniel Neep, *Occupying Syria under the French Mandate: Insurgency, Space and State Formation* (Cambridge: Cambridge University Press, 2012), 179.

[4] Sinclair, *At the End of the Line*, 1–5.

for immersion and secondment;[5] commenced official liaison with the *Gong'an* (Public Security Police) of China, and introduced a 'service-oriented culture' in 1992 after the arrival of the last colonial governor, Chris Patten. These steps increased the operational capacity of the Royal Hong Kong Police Force (RHKP[6]) and gradually won the trust of the public, which came to view the force as professional and competent. By contrast, the Portuguese colonial regime in Macau further withdrew from its already limited interactions with the Cantonese-speaking population after the 12–3 incident in 1966.[7] No major police reforms were introduced until the eve of the handover to China in 1999, when there was a show of 'full cooperation with the Beijing authorities'. A lame-duck colonial government with conflicting policies suffocated Macau's policing agencies and added to public discontent and social turbulence as the clock dwindled on Portuguese rule. Interactions between police and public were mediated through corporatized 'patriotic associations' with strong connections to Beijing:[8] they had long received tacit support from the Portuguese administration through monetary support and public appointments.[9] Hampered by a lack of resources and language barriers, the force was limited in its role within a politicized civil society fuelled by the participatory aspects of corporatist colonial governance. Manes argues that Portuguese colonial leaders were not mandated to properly govern Macau in the 1990s because by then the colony had ceased to be of economic value to Portugal, and internal and external accountability was absent from Macau's policing system before 1999.[10]

---

[5]   Since the mid-1980s, Hong Kong Superintendents have been nominated for official duties in a UK force in order to expose them to the latest trends in policing.

[6]   The Hong Kong Police Force was granted the Royal Charter in 1969.

[7]   The so-called '12–3' incident took place on 3 December 1966 (in Chinese 12–3). The politically inspired Chinese leftists confronted with the Macau Police to protest against government's disapproval to the building of a 'patriotic' Communist school in Taipa. The Portuguese government deployed anti-riot police to disperse the crowd but eventually signed an extremely humiliating agreement with the 'people of Macau' after the intervention from the Beijing authorities. The agreement strictly limited the powers of the government and the control of Beijing has extended to the Macau since then. See Carmen Amado Mendes, *Portugal, China and the Macau Negotiation, 1986–1999* (Hong Kong: Hong Kong University Press, 2013), 15–16.

[8]   Eva Hung and Alex Choi, 'From Societal to State Corporatism: The Making of the "Uncivil" Society in Macau', Paper presented to the Conference 'The Dynamics of Civil Society Coalitions in Asia' (Department of Public and Social Administration, City University of Hong Kong, 10–11 February 2012), 5. See also Eva P.W. Hung, 'Guanxi Networks and Social Resources (*Guan xi wangluo yu sheshui zijyan*)', in Fanny M.C. Cheung, Siu Lun Wong, Po-san Wan and Victor Zheng (eds), *The New Face of Macao SAR: Ten Years of Development and Changes* (Hong Kong: Hong Kong Institute of Asia-Pacific Studies, Chinese University of Hong Kong, 2011), 165–97.

[9]   In 2013, 19 of 33 members in the Legislative Assembly in Macau were either appointees or elected by an electoral college, a functional constituency, with limited popular representation; the Hong Kong legislature is challenged by a similar irregularity.

[10]   See Mendes, *Portugal, China and the Macau Negotiation*.

Policing colonial Hong Kong: 'London calling'

Hong Kong was a British colony for more than 160 years from 1842 to 1997. To ensure British control over the territory, the colonial government established the HKPF in 1844 with just a few dozen European, Indian and Chinese policemen who carried out their duties under the fifth Ordinance of the Laws of Hong Kong.[11] For the better part of the next 130 years, the HKPF was perceived to be poorly disciplined, corrupt and ineffective, with one Hong Kong governor characterizing it as the worst police force amongst the British colonies.[12] By the 1970s, there were four key characteristics of the HKPF. First, it was a highly centralized and hierarchical civil force equipped with paramilitary capacity.[13] While the Metropolitan policing model restrained use of more hard-core methods in policing, the HKPF inherited via the Empire certain paramilitary features of the Irish Constabulary. The force comprised local junior Chinese officers, together with Indian and Pakistani recruits, who discharged their duties under the command of their British superiors under quasi-military, disciplinary codes.[14] Officers patrolling the streets were armed and had responsibility for protecting the ruling class and government agencies. Policing by coercion and force was liberally exercised when the government faced wider societal challenges, with a large group of mobile reserves and support from the British military garrisoned in Hong Kong in internal security management.[15]

Second, the 'policing by strangers' model was evident in 1960s with European personnel in decision-making and management positions while Indian and Chinese staff served as frontline constables and junior officers. Prior to the Second World War, policing in Hong Kong was marked by racial segregation policies that established a form of 'apartheid' in the colony.[16] Initially founded for the benefit of the European community, the HKPF was

[11] Hong Kong Police College, *Policing in Hong Kong at the Turn of the Century* (Hong Kong: Hong Kong Police College, 2007), 2.

[12] C.W. Ng, *Establishment and Early Development of Police System in Hong Kong (Xianggang jing cha zhi du de jian li he zao qi fa zhan)* (in Chinese) (Ann Arbor: UMI, 1999), 167.

[13] Michael King quoted the work of Cartwright (1995) who identified seven features of a para-military colonial police force: (1) centralized command system; (2) constables subject to a disciplinary code that required them to obey the lawful orders of their senior officers; (3) to ensure integrity, members of the force should not be deployed in districts from which they originated; (4) to enhance capability, officers should be regularly rotated between districts; (5) the force should be capable of dealing with large-scale disturbances; (6) the force was to have a mobile reserve that could be deployed anywhere in the country to deal with unrest; and (7) comprehensive training for all officers. See Michael King, 'Policing and Public Order Issues in Canada: Trends for Change', *Policing and Society* 8.1 (1997), 47–76.

[14] Tsui Yiu-kong, *The Promotion System in the Officer Cadre of the Royal Hong Kong Police Force,* unpublished M.Soc.Sci. thesis (Hong Kong: University of Hong Kong, 1982); J. Vagg, 'Policing in Hong Kong', *Policing and Society* 1.3 (1991), 235–47.

[15] Sinclair, *At the End of the Line*, 1–5; Ng, *Establishment and Early Development of Police System in Hong Kong*, 167–8.

[16] Ng, *Establishment and Early Development of Police System in Hong Kong*, 167.

supplemented by a separate District Watchmen Force in 1886 due to Chinese demand. It was paid for by Chinese community group fund-raising efforts along with some government financing. As more Chinese men in good physical health were recruited as watchmen for patrols and arrests, the administration's distrust and fears of usurpation were compounded by complaints from expatriates who found Chinese patrolmen in their segregated communities. Indian personnel were duly brought in.[17] A glass ceiling ensured that Indians and Pakistanis could not rise above the rank of inspector and ethnic Chinese could not rise above the rank of sergeant. Different ethnic recruits also underwent separate training.

Subtler ethnic divisions also marked the HKPF. In the early twentieth century, new recruits were drawn from Weihaiwei (Weihai Garrison, now the city of Weihai), a British lease in China's northern Shandong Province, since 1922.[18] By 1946, there were about 300 recruits, but most were not fluent in Cantonese and could not communicate with the vast majority of residents.[19] Post-war recruitment of local and Cantonese-speaking immigrants coincided with the promotion of some ethnic Chinese Probation Inspectors, but most command posts were still reserved for British colonial servants. Young inspectors without military or overseas exposure were also recruited from Britain and enjoyed better terms and conditions of service than their local counterparts. After the Second World War, millions of Chinese civil war and economic refugees flooded the city and most showed limited trust towards the criminal justice system, the police, and government authority in general. In the 1970s around 270 Muslim Pakistanis were employed by the Force and then brought to Hong Kong, despite having little or no knowledge of the colony or the local language.[20] There was little interaction outside of the ethnic cliques.

The third feature of the HKPF was that it consistently claimed to be politically neutral in its capacity as a law enforcement agency and to be discharging its duties in strict compliance with Hong Kong laws. These claims were severely tested during the 1956 riots between Nationalist and Communist civilians, when the administration questioned the allegiance of its largely Chinese police force and introduced a more stringent vetting exercise for potential recruits to prove that they had no political affiliations. At least two written references were required from serving civil servants and this proved to be an essential and successful step in securing police loyalty to the Crown during subsequent riots in the 1960s.[21]

---

[17] Ho and Chu, *Policing Hong Kong 1842–1969*, 18–19.
[18] Ibid., 25–9.
[19] Secretary for Chinese Affairs, 'Report of the Secretary for Chinese Affairs', in Appendix C, *Hong Kong Administrative Report 1929* (Hong Kong: Government Printer, 1930).
[20] Ho and Chu, *Policing Hong Kong 1842–1969*, 18–25.
[21] Ibid., 67–70.

Fourth, throughout its history, reforms to the HKPF – in terms of mission, structure and operations – were mostly 'events-driven' rather than internally triggered. Reforms introduced by the colonial government and police leaders clearly and consistently corresponded to social crises that undermined the force's legitimacy among the local population. Poor anti-riot action in 1956 exposed various issues: improper tactical training among officers for internal security management, outdated or insufficient police facilities and firearms, miscommunications amongst police stations and squads as well as between authorities and the citizenry. The military were called up for reinforcement and casualties resulted from the delayed and improper control of the disturbances.[22]

The following year, the HKPF sought to modernize and strengthen its paramilitary capacity to deal with large-scale disorder by setting up the Police Tactical Contingent (PTC). Four companies, each with about 170 anti-riot police officers, served three key regions. New anti-riot tactics such as platoon formations were introduced to improve PTC flexibility and effectiveness of crowd management, and the practice of delegating riot drill training to each police division was revised on account of lax adherence, with the PTC assuming responsibility for training all frontline policemen in anti-riot tactics.[23] Logistics were better coordinated across the force, from such basic amenities as accommodation and meals to processing large numbers of arrestees and keeping track of equipment and ammunition. The new Force would shortly find itself embroiled in the largest civil unrest throughout the colony's history, detailed in the coming pages. Ironically, the trigger for the deadly riots of 1967 came not only from across the Shenzhen River in China, but also across the Pearl River in a peaceful Portuguese enclave.

Policing colonial Macau: 'comfortably numb'

On 20 December 1999, the Portuguese concluded some 442 years of administration in Macau. The handover of power to the Chinese was the culmination of events dating back to the Carnation Revolution in 1974, when the fall of the Estado Novo, the authoritarian regime that had ruled Portugal since 1933, was followed by the withdrawal of the Portuguese from Africa.[24] The 'Macau Organic Law', approved by the Council of Revolution in Lisbon, came into effect in February 1976, stipulating that the territory would have a high degree of legislative, administrative, economic and financial autonomy.

---

[22] C.H.N. Lee, *Society and Policing in Hong Kong: A Study of the 1956 Riot*, unpublished thesis (University of Hong Kong, 1995).

[23] The old platoon could only break up into individual sections, and each section was equipped with only one type of riot weapon. Each officer could 'choose' whatever position he wished to take up. The new regime assigned each officer carrying a designated weapon to a fixed post.

[24] The Portuguese Constitution of 25 April 1976 stated that Macau was a 'territory under Portuguese administration'. See Mendes, *Portugal, China and the Macau Negotiation*, 28–9.

Government–society relations were remarkably harmonious for most of the time, with the exception of '12–3 Incident' in 1966 (detailed in the next section), and only limited socio-political confrontations emerged in the 1999 transition, as discussed below. While Cantonese-speaking Macanese criticized ineffective Portuguese governance and expressed distrust towards the public administration system, dissidents did not usually take overt action.[25] Occasional public demonstrations seldom attracted more than a thousand participants and grassroots political groups were relatively unpopular despite the presence of an anti-establishment movement.[26]

The seemingly uneasy truce of political disgruntlement and one-armed (or occasionally two-armed) bandits may be due to the forms of policing in Macau, along with its Chinese and continental cultures of criminal justice. An examination of Macau's colonial history reveals characteristics of its police provisions that support this interpretation. First, following a model adopted by many European countries, colonial legislation in Macau established two distinct, independent law enforcement agencies to handle internal security: the Judiciary Police (JP) and the Public Security Police (PSP). The PSP was responsible for management of law and order, immigration, customs, and even the fire services, while the JP concentrated on criminal investigation. The Secretary for Security, a position established in 1990, headed the Public Security Police, Marine Police and Immigration and Customs, whereas the Secretary for Justice presided over the Judiciary Police.[27] Both police forces reported directly to, and were appointed by, the governor, who was in turn appointed by Lisbon, which also approved his secretarial candidates. All such posts were headed by Portuguese who were drawn from military or legal professions, while the rank-and-file was composed mainly of local Chinese recruits.

Following the practice in Portugal, the PSP and JP were separately staffed and had different ranks and remuneration mechanisms. This transplantation resulted in numerous operational problems. In 1990, the administration attempted to reform the command and integrate the operations of the two police forces, with limited success given that they were set up to operate independently.[28] The schism led to inter-agency distrust, suspicion and rivalry – all

---

[25] Portuguese was the only official language in Macau prior to the 1985 Sino-Portuguese Joint Declaration, which recognized written Chinese as a second official language.

[26] Dissident groups tend not to overtly challenge SAR leadership. They avoided taking 'too radical action' to confront the SAR government after its establishment, although they disagreed with the first Chief Executive Edmund Ho's administrative philosophy. Dissident groups claimed that problems in Ho's governing strategy would be revealed over time as crises developed because the institutional setup would be unable to keep pace with economic development. See Hung and Choi, 'From Societal to State Corporatism'.

[27] K.F. Jim, 'Analysing the Restructure of Macau Police Forces', in Guomin Lu (ed.), *The Proceedings of Public Administration in Macau during the Transition Period* (in Chinese) (Macau: Macau University Press, 2000), 117.

[28] Ibid.

well-known to the public.[29] The JP, acting as the criminal investigation agency, had to submit a formal request to PSP for operational support where necessary, whereas PSP commanders could only request the support of their JP counterparts in assisting with criminal cases.[30]

Apart from the tilted staff and duty balance between PSP and JP, the ongoing struggle between the two forces can be attributed to separate recruitment and training exercises and pay mechanisms. In contrast to the PSP, the JP set relatively high entry criteria. Enrolees entered at the rank of 'Technician', a professional rank popular across the administration. The JP personnel consequently assumed an air of superiority over other security forces in Macau.[31] PSP recruitment was separately coordinated by a recruitment office under the Security Bureau. Graduates of a degree programme offered by the Public Security Tertiary Institute were automatically enrolled as Deputy Superintendents and rank-and-file junior police were publicly recruited through a mass selection exercise. To be appointed Police Constable (PC), recruits only had to have attended primary school and Portuguese language proficiency was not required. Most of these recruits had weak writing skills and little understanding of the Macanese legal system despite instruction in the Police Training School. There was no formal vetting requirement for new PSP recruits.[32] These educational and training differences brewed mutual suspicion. JP officers doubted the competence of their PSP counterparts; whereas PSP constables felt underpaid.[33]

Second, expatriate (Portuguese or ethnic Macanese[34]) commanders drawn from the military or legal professions headed both forces, while the rank-and-file was composed mainly of local ethnic Chinese and this hierarchical structure and laissez-faire policy resulted in segregation between police and citizens. The first non-military police commander was not appointed in Macau until

---

[29] Andrew Blackburn, *Police and Policing in Macau*, unpublished PhD thesis (University of Hong Kong, 1992), 1–3.
[30] The JP had only 400 personnel in 1999; this increased to 969 by 2011. There were 3,000 PSP personnel in 1999 and 4,489 in 2011. See Macau SAR Administrative and Public Service Bureau 2012, 119. Under the law of Macau, any criminal cases involving valuables worth MOP$500 or above had to be passed to the JP for subsequent investigation and prosecution. Since the size of the JP force has always been much smaller than that of the PSP, this relatively low threshold for demanding JP involvement accounts for some of the conflict that arose between the two forces.
[31] Jim, 'Analyzing the Restructure of Macau Police Forces', 129–32.
[32] The information is derived from author's personal communication with a retired Macau police officer in 2012.
[33] Newly recruited JP technicians entered at 260 points on the Macau government's civil service pay scale, but new PSP enrollees started at 190 points. In 2010, 1 point was equivalent to about MOP$60, but even before 1999, a 70-point difference meant much larger salaries for JP personnel. This discrepancy in pay scales led to the perception that even new JP recruits were 'senior' to PSP officers. Being treated as 'juniors' further demoralized PSP constables.
[34] The heavily contested demonym may variously refer to people with Portuguese ancestry, acculturation, or either creole or native speakers of Portuguese.

1996 and there was always considerable social distance between the police's non-local, military leadership and the local community. Public scepticism and avoidance thus developed towards the professionalism, capability, corruption and ethnic allegiance of frontline Cantonese-speaking officers before 1996.[35] The force became such a potent symbol of colonizing interests to the point where it was suspected of gathering intelligence for the colonial government.[36] Much of the law was never translated from Portuguese to Chinese, and an educational gap persisted without local legal professionals working in the JP or PSP who could explain the law to the general population.[37] Ethnic Chinese residents of Macau consequently resorted to informal negotiations rather than the police to resolve non-urgent disputes and sought Chinese assistance through clan associations and trade unions. Between Portuguese segregation and Chinese customs, the police force of Portuguese Macau failed to gain the trust of its population.[38]

Third, no major reform initiatives were undertaken by the colonial government and police authorities in Macau to modernize and professionalize the police until the Portuguese flag was lowered in 1999. Public demand for the maintenance of law and order was unmet, in contrast to Hong Kong, where the HKPF was granted the Royal Charter in 1969 in recognition of its success. Criticism of the Portuguese authorities intensified during the 1990s transition preparations. Because Lisbon showed no enthusiasm for reforming either the JP or the PSP, this hindered any movement towards modernization and undermined the capacity of the two forces to prevent crime during the decade.[39] Gang fights and street violence became common, and were often linked to gambling.[40] The issues of succession and localization certainly influenced Macau policing for the worse during the transitional period. The Sino-Portuguese Joint Declaration of 1986 made

[35] The information is derived from author's personal communication with a retired Macau police officer in 2012.

[36] All criminal investigations were carried out by the PSP CIDs before the JP was formed in 1960. Afterwards, the PSP and JP had some overlapping jurisdiction since they could both conduct criminal investigations.

[37] Police effectiveness was undermined by the simultaneous application of Portuguese and local Chinese laws even after the MSAR government was established. Maintaining public security was hindered by lack of progress in translating relevant legal codes from Portuguese to Chinese. The Chinese did not adopt the Codified Law and Criminal Law until 1998, even though these law codes were to become the basis for legal hearings and proceedings in the MSAR. Jim, 'Analysing the Restructure of Macau Police Forces', 130–1.

[38] The information is derived from author's personal interview with a retired Macau police officer in 2012.

[39] Mendes argues that the lack of commitment to maintaining order in Macau can partly be attributed to domestic Portuguese party politics, as the president and the prime minister had conflicting approaches towards dealing with the Sino-Portuguese relationship. See Mendes, *Portugal, China and the Macau Negotiation*, 63–8.

[40] Jim, 'Analysing the Restructure of Macau Police Forces', 129–30; Ian Scott, 'Social Stability and Economic Growth', in Lam Newman and Ian Scott (eds), *Gaming, Governance and Public Policy in Macao* (Hong Kong: Hong Kong University Press, 2011), 1–3.

references to a government composed of 'local inhabitants', but otherwise explicitly stated that persons of all nationalities 'who have previously
worked in public services (including police) in Macau can maintain their
functional links'.[41] Further stipulations in the Macau Basic Law of 1993
detailed requirements of either Chinese citizenship and/or ordinary residence periods for 15 to 20 years with principal posts.[42] This made the localization of police forces all the more urgent, as most of the commanding
officers in the PSP were Portuguese military officers, while JP heads were
principally Portuguese legal professionals trained in Lisbon. There were
only a few Macanese personnel and even fewer Macau-born ethnic Chinese
in the force: succession plans were non-existent compared to the Hong
Kong force. Up until 1999, most of the prominent positions in the colonial
government, including the police chiefs, remained occupied by Portuguese
nationals. The PSP got their first Chinese commander in March 1998; the
JP left it until December 1999.

The lack of preparation and the chaos that ensued after transition resulted
in drastic announcements during what was a sensitive time: Beijing declared
in 1999 that People's Liberation Army (PLA) troops stationed in Macau were
available to Chief Executive-elect Ho to assist in maintaining public order.[43]
By the late 1990s, police constituted nearly 1 per cent of the population,[44]
seemingly reasonable for the city, but in reality resources were stretched to
the limits.[45] No post-colonial analysis of these two cities is complete without
a discussion of the 1967 riots: the episode is a both a microcosm of China's
bloody rebirth and a case study in wide-scale police action against an ethnic
Chinese population.

Generally regarded as a spillover of the Cultural Revolution in China from
1966, rising revolutionary sentiments among leftists in Macau led to a general strike on 3 December 1966, paralysing the administration and 'liberating'
Macau for leftists as Kuomintang (Chinese National Party) members were
driven out of the colony in an attempt to eradicate Taiwanese influences. The
government agreed to implement many of the leftists' demands in a tacit sur-
render.[46] These events led leftists in Hong Kong to initiate industrial disputes

41 'Declaração Conjunta Do Governo Da República Portuguesa e Do Governo Da República
   Popular Da China Sobre a Questão De Macau', accessed 10 July 2013, http://bo.io.gov.mo/
   bo/i/88/23/dc/pt/default.asp.
42 Ibid., articles 46, 63, 57.
43 The presence of the PLA in Macau was generally perceived as a way for the Central People's
   Government in Beijing and the MSAR government to boost public confidence in the Macau
   police and thus Macau SAR governance.
44 The Macau population was around 400,000 in 1999; 3,184 people worked at the PSP (a third
   were Marine Police) and the JP had 340 established posts.
45 Jim, 'Analysing the Restructure of Macau Police Forces', 131–2.
46 Jin Yao-ru, the chief editor of pro-Beijing Hong Kong-based newspaper *Wen Wei Po* and
   member of Hong Kong and Macau Work Committee of the Chinese Communist Party
   in 1967, recalled that 'his comrades in Hong Kong's leftist organizations were encouraged
   by Macanese developments, and thought they could follow the footstep of these leftists,

to secure greater labour protections. Riots erupted from May to December 1967. During this time, the police were fully mobilized against leftist groups, principally the New China News Agency (now Xinhua, then de facto Beijing representative in Hong Kong): encounters ranged from mass protests, general strikes, cross-border shootings and urban bomb threats. At least 15 people were killed, including several police officers, and many more were wounded.[47]

Prior to May 1967, the government had doubted the reliability of the multiethnic police force, the allegiances of its officers, and whether it had sufficient strength to handle society-wide disturbances. Sit-ins escalated into street violence, which was suppressed by hard-line police actions. The general public was inclined to be sympathetic to the strikers' calls for fair treatment from employers, but the policemen eventually gained favourable public support for restoring social order.[48] As a mechanism of colonial rule, however, the force proved inadequate. Contrary to expectations, the local Guangdong and Shandong, Pakistanis and European officers were relatively united in the face of a common enemy, and their cooperation was surprisingly smooth. Instead, the administration was alarmed by the lack of communication between the citizens and the police at the beginning of the riots, and concluded that the public's low level of trust in the police was partly due to long-standing perceptions of widespread corruption. This triggered Governor David Trench to approve a series of internal reforms launched by a new Commissioner, Charlie Sutcliffe, aimed at tackling police corruption and increasing contact between the police and the public.[49]

The events of 1967 transformed policing in Hong Kong in several ways. It pushed forward the institutionalization and modernization of the policing system due to entirely pragmatic considerations. Alarmed by popular suspicions towards the unrepresentative force, the government attempted to build a more legitimate, consensual and community-based policing framework. The reform efforts included consolidating capacity for internal security protection and regularization of crowd control tactics during disturbances. All members

ultimately triggering a struggle with the British colonial government'. See Yao-ru Jin, *The Secrets of the CCP's Policy in Hong Kong (Zhonggong Xianggang zhengcemiwenshilu: Jin Yaoruwushinianxiangjiangyiwang)* (in Chinese) (Hong Kong: Tianyuan Shuwu, 1998), 85–90.

[47] According to official colonial government accounts, the 1967 riots should be understood as unfolding in three stages: (1) demonstrations to gain public support; (2) stoppages of work to paralyse the colony's economy; and (3) urban terrorism to undermine citizens' morale. See Hong Kong Police, *Annual Departmental Report, 1967* (Hong Kong: Government Printer, 1967). On the strengths of leftist organizations in Hong Kong, see C.Y. Wong, *The Communist-Inspired Riots in Hong Kong, 1967: A Multi-Actors Approach*, unpublished M.Phil thesis (University of Hong Kong, 2001).

[48] Lawrence K.K. Ho, *Policing the 1967 Riots in Hong Kong: Strategies, Rationales and Implications*, unpublished PhD thesis (University of Hong Kong, 2009), 189–90.

[49] Ibid., 189. See also Kevin Sinclair, *Royal Hong Kong Police: 150 Anniversary Commemorative Publication, 1884–1994* (Hong Kong: Police Public Relations Branch, Royal Hong Kong Police, 1994).

of the force were taught the key procedures for handling the public order events. Following the stringent test of its anti-riot capacity, the Police Tactical Unit (PTU) was expanded into a squad specifically set up for internal security management from the former PTC and made use of new public order control tactics developed from the 1967 riots with an emphasis on reconciliation over enforcement. The shift to a less confrontational strategy in public order policing was characterized by the use of fewer lethal weapons like baton rounds and plastic bullets. The military kept an increasingly low profile and its involvement in policing was gradually reduced to a limited role as an external cordon and its profile.[50]

The police also underwent a structural transformation after the riots, with the publicized objective of devolving authority and responsibility to the lowest practical level.[51] One key feature of the structural reform was the relocation of an independent line of command of the Criminal Investigation Division (CID) from the Police Headquarters to the Police Districts. Before this reform, there were very few non-local officers in the CID, and most of the CID detectives were locals. The heads of CID were Chinese Staff Sergeants who were not accountable to the expatriate District or Regional heads. The independent command structure developed a distinctive type of collegiality within the CID, and it also inadvertently empowered the Chinese Staff Sergeants who headed teams of CID subordinates in all Police Districts. Somewhat unfortunately, the mechanism also disabled the District Commander of each district from supervising the performance of CID members in his jurisdiction.[52]

Under the new structural organization, the CID was no longer an individual unit directly accountable to the Regional Headquarters. The boundary between the uniformed and the plain clothes divisions was removed and CID was placed under the command of the Station Commanders, parallel in status to the uniformed division. The new arrangement substantially cut down on the autonomy of the CID officers, and facilitated the Station/District Commanders acquiring supervisory power over the potential inappropriate behaviour of their plain clothes subordinates.[53] The police never explained the reasons for these reforms. However, it was quite clear that the structural reorganization might target the eradication of traditional and powerful conglomerates inside the CID, which were often borderline-corrupt syndicates. These developments could not be effectively controlled by the police

---

[50] Ibid., 194–7.

[51] Carol Jones and J. Vagg, *Criminal Justice in Hong Kong* (London: Routledge-Cavendish, 2007), 435–47.

[52] Ho and Chu, *Policing Hong Kong 1842–1969*, 89–91.

[53] Ho, *Policing the 1967 Riots*. Meanwhile another structural transformation wrought by the Commissioner of Police, Charlie Sutcliffe, was the abandonment of the old rank of Staff Sergeant. The holders of this rank were either promoted to officer grade as Probationary Inspector (PI), or re-titled as Station Sergeant (SS). At the same time, a large number of Sergeants were also promoted to SS.

commanders in the headquarters, and this significantly de-legitimized the police authority.[54]

The 1967 riots also taught the colonial government in Hong Kong the importance of public support in legitimizing its authority. In the following years, the government became more responsible and responsive by canvassing public support and providing channels for the public to air their grievances about the administration. The Government Information Service (GIS) was established in 1971, 'The Secretariat of Chinese Affairs' became 'the Home Affairs Department' in all government documents, and the term 'colony' was replaced by 'territory'. City district officers were also created to organize ceremonies honouring local dignitaries, and a crime-fighting campaign was held annually. Advisory and consultative committees were also established and some well-known Chinese social elites were appointed as members. As Scott argued, this inclusion strategy aimed to improve the government's capacity to rule via 'administrative absorption' of politics, along with other proactive and inclusive approaches by the formerly aloof state.[55] The government publicized the force's role as maintaining law and order and safeguarding the property of the citizens, for example, and in the 1980s it sought to narrow the communications gap between the police and society by launching community-policing programmes. A City District Officers Scheme, a 'fight crime' committee, the police community relations officer scheme, Junior Police Call, and neighbourhood policing units were among the many initiatives launched.[56]

One country, two crimes: new cross-border regimes

The integration of Hong Kong and Macau into the Chinese mainland brought human mobility and increased cross-border economic activity, partly due to trade agreements; cross-border crime also flourished as three separate law enforcement agencies established new legal and policing interfaces. The Hong Kong Special Administrative Region (SAR) remains a highly urbanized free port with a mature economy since the handover, maintaining a separate customs entity with constitutional freedom of movement. However, the introduction of the Closer Economic Partnership Agreement (CEPA) with Beijing in 2003, right upon the heels of the Asian Financial Crisis and SARS epidemic, has shifted the political and socio-economic terrain.

Under the CEPA, provincial immigration authorities may issue Chinese citizens with visas for personal visits to Hong Kong. CEPA aimed to further integrate the economy of Hong Kong and mainland China, but at the time of ratification Hong Kong saw it as a shot of adrenaline to the retail and tourism

---

[54] Ho and Chu, *Policing Hong Kong 1842–1969*, 89–91.
[55] Ian Scott, *Political Change and the Crisis of Legitimacy in Hong Kong* (Hong Kong: Oxford University Press, 1989).
[56] Jones and Vagg, *Criminal Justice in Hong Kong*, 430–5.

heart of its flagging economy. Gradual economic recovery was accompanied by rising white-collar crime in the form of commodity smuggling, money laundering, prostitution, gambling, drug trafficking, counterfeit circulation, and sham marriages. Jarring discrepancies in disparate legal systems have also become a pressing and controversial aspect of Hong Kong policing since 1997. When the colonial government launched a series of 'draconian legislation' outlawing 'unauthorized public assemblies' after the 1967 riots, the citizens themselves often exhibited political apathy. Mass demonstrations and gatherings were infrequent until a series of administration scandals in the public sector, such as the arrest of Superintendent of Police Peter Godber on corruption charges; the chiselling scandal of Golden Jubilee Secondary School, and the patriotic students' protest against Japan's seizure of Diaoyu (Senkaku) Islands. In 1989, over one million citizens assembled in Hong Kong Island to stand with the student movement in Beijing and witnessed the Tiananmen Incident.

Since the handover, there has been an increase in the frequency of mass demonstrations, rallies and gatherings mobilized by different civil groups to protest against the Chinese government, the Hong Kong administration, and often specific policy decisions. In fact, as the Chinese flag was raised, a large rally was organized outside the ceremony hall to oppose Beijing's infractions against its promises of 'One Country, Two Systems'. The SARS epidemic in 2003 cemented handover day as a general protest event.

The government reported that there were about 7,500 public processions in Hong Kong in 2012.[57] The figure may be variously attributed to the glacial pace of development in attaining political rights and extending the suffrage, economic inequality and controversial social policies implemented by the local government. While protests are generally a matter of airing grievances, they serve as a canary in a coal mine with regard to promises made by Beijing. Police actions in protest management are under heavy public scrutiny as political overtones are projected into every interpersonal interaction between officers and protesters in Chinese Hong Kong. Any interference from the authorities, especially restrictions imposed by the police during protests, are often reinterpreted as the thin end of a Communist wedge threatening long-held freedoms in the city.[58]

The average public procession in Hong Kong is small in scale, with usually less than a hundred participants and often involving marching, demonstrations, sit-ins, and the encircling and occupation of public sites. A

---

[57] S. Cheung, 'Tech Crimes Surge But Cases Prove Tough To Crack', *South China Morning Post*, CITY1, 30 January 2013.

[58] The manner in which the Hong Kong Police manage protest activities in the Hong Kong SAR is often highlighted by local politicians, researchers and even diplomats as it shows the degree to which the Hong Kong SAR government tolerates opposition under the PRC sovereignty. Police actions have also been widely regarded as indicators of Beijing leaders' respect towards freedom of speech, assembly and expression under the One Country, Two Systems principle that has operated in Hong Kong since reunification with China in 1997.

number of protests have mobilized in excess of 10,000 people, though police and organizers' estimates are often at odds. The responsibility for keeping order in public processions and public gatherings is in the hands of the HKPF. Extensive media coverage of such events is widely available, and civic-libertarian groups often file complaints or otherwise accuse law enforcers of using excessive and unnecessary violence when maintaining order at these events. Public discourse on Hong Kong policing occasionally focuses on the exercise, infringement or suppression of human rights, but in response to criticisms from civil rights groups, authorities usually emphasize the legal foundations for the police's actions; praise the 'excellent performance' of the frontline officers, claim that they have displayed 'maximum restraint', and used 'minimum force' in their operations; and refer to favourable public approval ratings of the police. Their defence also invariably includes claims that accusations of civil rights infringements are ungrounded and exaggerated, and that some officers were humiliated when exercising their duties.

Policing the New Vegas

Macau's biggest leap forward, to paraphrase Mao Zedong, may lie in a single policy decision: de-franchising legal casino operations. An explosion of economic activities and tourism, the localization of leadership in both of Macau's policing forces, and the prevalence of violent and syndicated crime associated with the gambling industry all exerted structural pressures on police reform during the late colonial period. Internal social conflict rose to the fore as growing public demand for transparency and accountability, the presence of more critical local and overseas media, and the emergence of social activists unwilling to compromise with the new social order all put policing efforts under more intense scrutiny than ever before. These changes are likely to trigger waves of reform in the organization, staffing and management philosophy of Macau police agencies.

When Chief Executive Edmund Ho decided to de-franchise gambling licences in 2002, Macau's existing reputation as the sole Chinese gambling resort rapidly translated into income inequality, high inflation and public dissatisfaction with governance. New challenges to police authorities were compounded by large annual demonstrations on Labour Day and Macau SAR Establishment Day, but the Macau police had little previous experience with crowd management and control. When a scuffle broke out between protestors and police on Labour Day in 2007, a detective fired a warning shot to 'ensure law and order'.[59] The ensuing chaos attracted international media to

---

[59] M.C. Cheng and C.K. Ng, 'The May-First Rally: Organized by Newly Emerged Civic Groups Composed of Low Skilled Labor', *Hong Kong Economic Times*, 2 May 2007, A21, Social News (in Chinese).

Macau and a public debate on police strategies during demonstrations began in earnest.[60]

The Ho administration won the approval of the public and Beijing for its remarkable economic achievements during its first term from 1999 to 2004 and these continued throughout the rest of the decade. The Free Individual Travel (FIT) scheme for mainland Chinese tourists has boosted arrivals by 1.9 per cent each year since 2003, with 2,382,156 tourists recorded in the year to April 2012. The winding-down of the *Sociedade de Turismo e Diversões de Macau* (Macau Tourism and Entertainment Company, STDM), which had exercised a 40-year monopoly over the gaming industry, immediately drew two Nevadan entrants to the sector: Las Vegas Sands Corporation and Wynn Resorts.[61]

The unprecedented economic boom in Macau – real terms growth reached an annual rate of 18.4 per cent by the first quarter of 2012 – has benefitted the tourist sector but left low-income families struggling to cope with inflation rates above 5 per cent.[62] Hiring at twice the going rate, casinos have also adversely affected local small and medium enterprises whose wages are low by comparison and have reported difficulties in attracting new staff as a result.[63] In turn, as Macau's spectacular economic growth has eroded the quality of life among low- and middle-income earners, it has threatened to de-legitimize the nascent administration. The police are therefore presented with novel challenges as they confront newly discontented civilians and the emergence of autonomous interest groups.

Participation in civil society activities and associations remains quite weak in Macau, and centuries of peace mean that most are inclined to support their government. Civic groups generally establish a collaborative relationship with the government and seldom overtly challenge public policies.[64] While dissident groups do exist in Macau, their voices – much like those of

---

[60] In a press release issued by the Macau Special Administrative Region Government Information Bureau, the government declared its intolerance towards 'any act [intended] to wreck the rule of law and Macau's stable development' and its determination to 'trace responsibility for any attempts to do so'.

[61] The total revenue from gaming activities grew from MOP$42,306 million in 2004 to a whopping MOP$55,884 million by the end of 2006. Taxes on gaming activities supplied 47 per cent of the government budget in 1999; by 2006 it accounted for 76 per cent. See Statistics and Census Service, Government of Macao Special Administrative Region, 2007, in *DSEC* website, accessed 10 July 2013, www.dsec.gov.mo/e_index.html. By 2011, the Gross Domestic Product (GDP) had reached MOP$2,921 billion, with unemployment at just 2.6 per cent. See Macau SAR Government Statistics and Census Service, 2011.

[62] In 2006, the inflation rate reached 5.15 per cent and it has consistently been over 5 per cent since 2011. Chi-leung Ng and Hao Yu-fan (eds), *Blue Book of Macau: Annual Report on Economy and Society of Macau, 2012–13* (in Chinese) (Beijing: Social Sciences Academic Press, 2013); Macau SAR Government Statistics and Census Services, 2007.

[63] SME employees' monthly wages range from MOP$6,000–8,000. By contrast, a croupier working in a casino earns double that, from MOP$12,000–14,000 a month. See Ng and Hao, *Blue Book*.

[64] See Hung and Choi, 'From Societal to State Corporatism'.

the general electorate – are weak and under-represented in the legislature. Yet the relatively harmonious corporatist partnership between the government and civil groups has started to fray in recent years. New autonomous interest groups have, however, emerged since the transition and more than 50 were registered in the first half of 2007.[65] These new groups are mostly comprised of low skilled workers who have been marginalized from the labour market and unlike their old counterparts they tend to take a more aggressive approach, adopting street-level strategies such as demonstrations and intervening in certain policy debates. The 2007 Labour Day Rally, for example, revealed that organizers could not rely on self-policing to maintain the peace, because protestors came from a heterogeneous background of different civic groups. The main organizer was powerless to control more vocal participants in the rally simply because they were not among its members.

Traditionally, the media in Macau lacked independence from the government and refrained from criticizing its policies. The government owns *Teledifusao de Macau*, the only television station in MSAR. The two biggest newspapers, the *Macau Daily News* and *Journal Va Kio*, both have pro-Beijing owners who are sympathetic to the MSAR government.[66] The relationship between the government and media was strained by the 2007 demonstration, however, and since then Macau's media has become more critical of government policies. Complaints that the government has failed to protect Macau workers from external competition for jobs now appear frequently in local media, and there are calls for the suppression of illegal labour, restrictions on non-residents' access to certain jobs, the imposition of taxes on imported labour, and the establishment of a minimum wage.[67] The administration reacted to these events with a mix of appeasement and condemnation, denouncing 'the minority among the protestors' who had tried to use violence for political ends.[68] The warning shot incident was defended in statements saying that the police had taken appropriate measures to maintain public order, and that the

---

[65] Eilo Wing Yat Yu, 'Executive-Legislature Relationships and the Development of Public Policy', in Lam Newman and Ian Scott (eds), *Gaming, Governance and Public Policy in Macao* (Hong Kong: Hong Kong University Press, 2011), 57–64.

[66] Fox Yi Hu, 'Protesters Reprimanded in Macau', *South China Morning Post*, 3 May 2007, EDT 1.

[67] Macau media became a lot more outspoken about criticizing the police following the incidents at the 2007 Labour Day Rally. Riot police blocked demonstrators attempting to march into the central business district. The confrontation escalated to clashes between the two groups. One policeman attempted to disperse the crowd by firing five times into the air, but hit a passer-by with a stray bullet. The rally ended with the arrest of ten marchers and the hospitalization of 21 police officers. See *South China Morning Post*, 2 May 2007. The performance of the police in trying to control the crowd exposed the weakness and unprofessionalism of the police agencies in the new MSAR.

[68] Macau SAR Government Information Bureau, 'MSAR Government Denounces Violation of Law during Demonstration', in *Government Information Bureau of the Macau SAR website*, 2 May 2007, accessed 9 July 2007, www.gcs.gov.mo/showNews.php?PageLang=C&DataUcn=25274.

gunshots were necessary in the emergency.[69] Parliamentary queries on possible tactical errors and the appropriateness of firing shots near a crowd were tabled.[70] Many civic groups posted newspaper advertisements censuring the 'unlawful and violent crowd' that had failed to comply with police instructions on the rally route, suggesting that it was a deliberate attempt to trigger chaos and disrupt Macau's stable development.[71]

The confrontation drew attention from international media which had seldom covered Macau politics, and the incident was televised and photographed overseas soon after the demonstration.[72] The presence of local and overseas reporters did not prevent the police from taking relatively coercive action to disperse and arrest the protestors. The widespread debate about the shooting incident and the level of police professionalism in Macau society contributed to calls for reform that are still being petitioned at the time of writing.

Conclusion: the universality of policing

The accidents of history have made contemporary Hong Kong and Macau places where Chinese populations and European institutions carve out a postcolonial existence under the spectre of China. Two observations stand out in the convoluted history of these territories' policing. First, law enforcement institutions, while all too often used as an instrument of authority in the last millennium, can become a force for good when suitably administered in developing economies and emerging democracies. While historical circumstances prevent straightforward comparisons between the Hong Kong and Macau models, it seems safe to say that a proactive approach to *earn* legitimacy paid off handsomely for Hong Kong. Despite frequent challenges, the Hong Kong Police has been rewarded with a level of popular trust rarely rivalled in East Asia or in many mature economies. Second, all policing efforts face an unceasing demand for renewal insofar as society itself is progressing, and the rule of law is still very much a work in progress across the whole of China. Whether police forces make use of their ability to communicate this universal value may well influence future political developments in both cities, and with that, the rest of the emergent Chinese state.

---

[69] Ibid.

[70] Legislative Councilor Jose Pereira Coutinho made verbal inquiries to the government on the crowd control arrangements planned by the police for that Labour Day. He issued three substantive questions to the security authorities concerning excessive use of police force. See Macau Legislative Council Document No.*286/III/2007*, accessed 8 July 2007, www.al.gov.mo/interpelacao_oral/2006/07-286c.pdf.

[71] 'The Underlying Reasons for the Outbreak of May-First Incident', *Journal San Wa Ou*, 28 June 2007 (in Chinese), 3.

[72] Ibid.

6 "A holy panic"

Race, surveillance and the origins of the war on drugs in Britain, 1915–1918

Sascha Auerbach

The relationship of twentieth-century democracies to the explicit employment of fear and intimidation within their own national borders was an ambivalent one. On the one hand, police and judicial officials, responding to perceived public outcry or the insistence of higher decision-makers, have not been slow to adopt heavy-handed tactics to restore "law and order" in times of serious internal disruption. On the other hand, frequent or excessive use of violence, mass arrests, or other extreme measures carries with it the danger of provoking a public backlash, fostering even more concerted resistance, or prompting the condemnation of the media, public interest groups and rival political groups.[1] There are two circumstances, however, where the police and judiciary of liberal Western democracies, far from being restrained, have instead been encouraged by policy-makers to adopt draconian measures and to not shy away from instilling fear into their putative targets. The first is during wartime. The second is when those in authority have declared that a particular threat poses a fundamental danger to the social, physical, political and/or moral foundations of the nation.

In recent decades, governments in the United States and United Kingdom in particular, have conflated the two situations, declaring "war" on dangers that allegedly pervade both internally and externally, and threaten the integrity of the nation from within and without. The first target of these "wars" was against "drugs," and the second, against "terror."[2] The rhetorical presentation of these police, judicial and military assaults as "wars" justifies the internal deployment of a level of force generally reserved for foreign enemies – these are "wars," and therefore this cannoning up is proclaimed to be just

---

[1] For a general discussion of how such power is expressed through more pervasive and subtle means, see Michel Foucault, *Discipline and Punish: The Birth of the Prison* (1975; 2nd edition, New York: Vintage, 1995). For how the instruments of surveillance and control developed, specifically in the British context, see V.A.C. Gatrell, "Crime, Authority, and the Policeman-State," in F.M.L. Thompson (ed.), *The Cambridge Social History of Britain, 1750–1950 v. 3: Social Agencies and Institutions* (Cambridge: Cambridge University Press, 1990), 243–310.

[2] For essays on the application of Foucault's thought to the former, see Michael Dillon and Andrew W. Neal (eds), *Foucault on Politics, Security and War* (Basingstoke: Palgrave Macmillan, 2011).

and necessary.[3] This rhetorical escalation also disguises the direction of force against the true targets: those groups or individuals designated for subdual or even annihilation.[4] A state of "war," be it against internal or external threats, simplifies the moral equation and discourages any understanding of, investigation into, or sympathizing with those designated as enemies.

In Britain from 1914 to 1918, the two circumstances under which it became permissible to ignore the ordinary restrictions on deploying state force and regimes of surveillance against internal targets coalesced. The objects of the state's campaign, directed at the national level and waged at the local, were Chinese immigrants suspected by police of involvement in the opium trade. Between 1916 and 1918, police in Liverpool arrested approximately 10 per cent of the small, resident Chinese population for the possession or processing of opium. Several dozen of those arrested were deported without trial under the powers granted to local officials by the Defence of the Realm Act (DORA), Regulation 40b, in 1916, and the authority granted to the Home Office by the Aliens Restriction Act 1914.[5] Dozens more were intimidated into leaving the city, or even the country altogether, by police and local magistrates. "If a few innocents are caught in the web," one official commented, "little is to be lost by clearing the whole lot out."[6] Another highly-placed Home Office official expressed considerable satisfaction that the campaign of mass arrests and summary deportations had spread a "holy panic" among the Chinese population of Liverpool.[7]

In London, by contrast, there was not a single deportation for opium during the entire course of the war, though several deportation orders were imposed for other crimes. The initial focus of the London anti-vice campaigns in Limehouse Chinatown was on night clubs and gambling houses, and their allegedly pernicious effect on the morality and physical health of soldiers. Newspapers and other forms of popular literature had connected Chinatown and its residents with gambling for decades prior to the war, and the rising concern of metropolitan police authorities quickly focused there. They

---

[3] For the long history of such mechanisms, and the role of observation in disciplining its targets, see Foucault, *Discipline and Punish*; David Wood, "Foucault and Panopticism Revisited," *Surveillance & Society* 1.3 (2003), 234–9.

[4] For a discussion of the genocidal component of the US-led hostilities against Iraq in the last two decades, see Edward S. Herman and David Peterson, *The Politics of Genocide* (New York: Monthly Review Press, 2010), 29–38.

[5] The parent legislation, the Defence of the Realm Act 1914, was passed on 8 August, shortly after the commencement of the First World War.

[6] "Raids on Chinese Opium Dens in Liverpool on 9th June 1917," Home Office: Registered Papers 45/24683/311604/28 (hereafter HO 45) (originally registered under two subjects: Dangerous Drugs and Poisons: Deportation of Chinese opium smugglers (1916–1920) [Former Reference: 311604] and Aliens: Deportation of Chinese opium smugglers (1916–1920) [Former Reference: 311604]).

[7] "Opium Smugglers at Liverpool," HO 45/11. This comment was signed by Sidney West Harrison, who was the private secretary to the Permanent Under-Secretary of State, so it is unclear whether it was Harrison's comment or that of the Under-Secretary himself.

conducted a series of raids against Chinese gambling houses in June 1916. Whether these were done at the specific insistence of Police Commissioner Sir Edward Henry and the commanding officer of the London Division, or whether they arose from local initiative on the part of the Police Division Superintendent, a man named Boxall, is not clear. What is clear, however, is that Boxall himself did not have a favourable opinion of the Chinese residents of his division. His public statements replicated many of the tropes common in earlier, sensationalized reportage and literary depictions of the neighbourhood. In justifying the raids, Boxall exaggerated the number of Chinese living in London, highlighted their propensity for serious violence, and argued that they had a tendency to be disruptive and that their violence posed a threat to the social order of the district. He further emphasized the prevalence of interracial sexuality. Articles and editorials in local newspapers such as the *East London Advertiser* were in accord.[8] As had often been the case in previous reportage of disturbances in Chinatown, however, the supposed "threat" of violence far outweighed its actual occurrence, and one newspaper article or editorial even blamed a violent counter-demonstration that had followed Boxall's raids on local white miscreants rather than Chinese residents.[9]

In the midst of this growing public anxiety over Chinese "vice," the British state substantially increased its powers to monitor and control the domestic population. The year 1916 was a watershed in more ways than one. In January, the passing of the Military Services Act introduced military conscription to Britain. The same year also witnessed the introduction of limited prohibition on narcotics and the inauguration of a nationwide campaign to completely eradicate opium importation, exportation and use among the Chinese residents of Britain. The primary legal tool for this campaign was Regulation 40b of the Defence of the Realm Act (DORA), introduced in the summer of 1916, which criminalized the possession or sale of cocaine or opium by anyone besides licensed professionals.[10] As had been the case with gambling, the initial justification for the wartime anti-drug campaign arose from concerns over vice, immorality and physical degeneration among

[8] *East London Advertiser*, 27 June 1916.

[9] *East End News* [London], 27 June 1916.

[10] Virginia Berridge, "East End Opium Dens and Narcotic Use in Britain," *London Journal* 4.1 (1978), 16; Marek Kohn, *Dope Girls: The Birth of the British Drug Underground* (London: Lawrence & Wishart, 1992), 44. The parent legislation, the Defence of the Realm Act, had been passed on 8 August 1914. Initially intended as a means of safeguarding the secrecy of military operations and communications, it eventually became the basis for much of the government's control over the civilian population. The regulations passed under the auspices of DORA in the years following its inception allowed for the censorship of anti-war publications, imprisonment without trial, the requisition of property and resources for government use, limiting hours of opening for public houses and, starting in 1918, the rationing of certain foodstuffs. DORA applied to Great Britain, but not beyond or to the colonies (though Australia passed the War Precautions Act 1914, which was modelled on DORA, and Canada had much sterner legal controls on opium, which dated to 1908).

white men and women, and from the threat that drug-use posed to military efficiency. The framers of DORA 40b, however, viewed cocaine, a drug that appeared to have little connection to Britain's Chinese communities, as posing a far greater threat than opium did.

The campaign to eradicate illegal cocaine sale and use in Britain began in earnest in February 1916, following the conviction of a British man and woman for selling cocaine to Canadian soldiers in Folkestone. The defendants were sentenced to six months' imprisonment with hard labour. In the course of the evidence against them, it was stated that the "there were 40 cases of the drug habit in one camp."[11] This initial case was rapidly followed by a slew of reports, trials and attestations from medical experts, all contributing to a public scandal over cocaine use and its supposedly devastating effect on the health and sanity of its users. In a lead article that appeared in the London *Times* just one day after its coverage of the Folkestone verdict, the medical correspondent claimed that use of the drug led almost inevitably to paranoia, insanity, and eventually to death. The author also explicitly linked the spread of cocaine use to a disastrous decline in military effectiveness, since the drug, by offering temporary energy and solace to soldiers who were under severe physical and emotional strain, could become almost irresistible. Readers were advised, "Cocaine, once used, must become a terrible temptation, it will, for the hour, charm away his trouble, his fatigue, his anxiety … but it will also, in the end, render him worthless as a soldier and a man."[12] The *Times* correspondent asserted that the drug was largely an American vice, but that it was rapidly becoming a serious issue in Asia as well. It had already spread to India "some years ago … perhaps as one of the results of the restrictions on the opium traffic." So great was the demand there, he wrote, "that cocaine dens were opened in all the big cities." "The cocaine habit has also been met lately in China," he added, and further emphasized the threat of cocaine to Britain and the Empire by asserting that the drug trade in India was being conducted by Britain's national enemies. Cocaine arrived in India, "chiefly in Austrian steamers," whose crews "found it a lucrative business to bring the drug to India with them."[13]

The first major London cocaine case broke a few months after the Folkestone incident. In this case, William Charles Johnson, a Soho porter, was charged before the Magistrate John Campbell of the Bow-Street Police Court. Herbert Muskett, who had earlier represented the London Commissioner of Police in

---

[11] *Times*, 11 February 1916, 3. For a more detailed discussion of the Folkestone case, see Kohn, *Dope Girls*, 34.

[12] *Times*, 12 February 1916, 3.

[13] A correspondent who wrote to the *Times* in July similarly emphasized the sinister foreign involvement in the drug trade, claiming, after a witnessing the prevalence of the cocaine habit in Delhi, "that its importation was nearly always conducted through German agents." Using this vague, but alarming, supposition as evidence, the author suggested that the rapid growth of the traffic might be due in part to "an effort of our diabolically ingenious enemies to destroy the moral [*sic*] and physique of the races of the Empire." See *Times*, 22 July 1916, 7.

the West End gambling prosecutions, appeared for the State. As he had with gambling, Muskett insisted that cocaine use posed a dire threat to the moral and physical health of soldiers in London. One main vector by which this vice was being transmitted, he asserted, was prostitutes. Muskett claimed that the traffic was spreading rapidly in the West End and called for the speedy expansion of legal authority to deal with "what had become a serious social evil."[14] However, Magistrate Campbell regretfully dismissed the case due to insufficient evidence, but in the process of doing so, he echoed Muskett's sentiments and declared his sincere hope "that the result of this case would lead to a speedy and drastic alteration of the law." Muskett concluded his arguments with the suggestion that the most appropriate and effective way to deal with the cocaine traffic would be through "some addition to the regulations under the Defense of the Realm Act." Muskett and Campbell got their wish when the Army introduced DORA 40b on 12 May 1916, whereby it became a criminal offence to provide a member of the armed forces with cocaine or any other narcotic. On 28 July, the prohibition was extended to include sales to civilians as well.[15] DORA 40b forbade the possession, preparation and sale of cocaine and opium by anyone except qualified doctors and chemists, and prohibited the importation of the raw products by anyone not holding a Home Office licence permitting them to do so. The possession of prepared opium, which, unlike morphine, had no recognized medical use, was proscribed altogether.[16]

The anti-drug regulations, like the anti-gambling campaign, arose out of concerns for the moral and physical well-being of British and Commonwealth soldiers in the capital and out of heightened anxiety among government officials over the declining general state of the nation's morality during wartime. Anxiety that was articulated by Home Office officials, magistrates, police and journalists in constant reference to race and gender. Nevertheless, Chinese men in London, although they had long been identified in journalism, literature, public discourse and judicial and police statements as an "immoral" cohort and as users of opium, were not directly implicated in the initial discussions of the drug trade or drug use. The focus of the initial campaign was on white men and women and cocaine, not on Chinese men and opium. However, even though the primary aim of DORA 40b was to halt the spread

14 *Times*, 12 May 1916, 5.
15 Terry Parssinen, *Secret Passions, Secret Remedies, Narcotic Drugs in British Society, 1820–1930* (Philadelphia: Institute for the Study of Human Issues, 1983), 132.
16 Ibid., 133. Although extracted from the same source, the poppy plant, the preparation of opium, which results in a soft resin suitable for smoking in a pipe, is a relatively simple process requiring only basic equipment. Producing morphine, in contrast, is a much more complicated process requiring specialized equipment and knowledge of organic chemistry. The result of the latter was a highly potent, purified liquid that was generally administered via hypodermic injection. My thanks to Dr Colin S. Burns, Department of Chemistry, University of East Carolina, for sharing his expertise on these topics. Dr Burns has no known connections to international narcotics trafficking.

of the cocaine traffic in London, a traffic never associated with Chinese men, its consequences would have a significant impact on Chinese residents nation-wide from 1916. By outlawing the possession of prepared opium, DORA 40b criminalized a practice which had been commonplace among a significant minority of the resident Chinese population for decades and which was even more popular among the transient population of Chinese seamen, a group that had seen significant expansion in the war years due to the increasing demand for their labour.[17]

It is worth noting that the portrayal of opium as an evil, degenerating force for white English men and women in literature was concurrent with its asso-ciation with Chinese men and opium "dens" in the 1860s and 1870s.[18] By the late nineteenth century, opium was explicitly associated with the Chinese population of Limehouse, while cocaine was not, and broader concerns about Chinese immorality were essential considerations to the Home Office officials, magistrates and police that implemented the drug prohibition regime which was introduced in 1916 and expanded afterwards. Both cocaine and opium had been regulated as "poisons" under the stipulations of the Pharmacy Act 1908 and both were considered to be dangerous "narcotics" by government officials and therefore meriting regulation, but beyond this there was very lit-tle explicit connection made between opium use and the "serious social evil" of cocaine as the two habits were publicly discussed in 1916.[19]

Despite international pressure and decades of avid campaigning by the British Society for the Suppression of the Opium Trade, the literary represen-tations of opium and its attendant evils in Britain remained far more preva-lent than the legal restrictions against its use or possession, and the expression of those restrictions before 1916 was rarer still.[20] One *Times* correspondent, writing on the abuse of prescriptions, had subsumed both opium and cocaine under the umbrella term of "dope."[21] The article's author also emphasized the prevalence of "drug habits" among the women of London. "Cocaine and opium have far more women victims than is imagined," he wrote, "and the stress and anxiety caused by the war aggravate the evil." Unlike cocaine, how-ever, opium had yet to be connected to the corruption of soldiers. Popular cocaine abuse was a relatively new phenomenon in wartime London, intro-duced, according to press reports, by Canadian soldiers. But it was a habit that, according to alarmed commentators, was spreading rapidly in the West End. Opium, on the other hand, had been present in the metropolis for decades. Its illicit use was still confined largely to the East End, and it

[17] Kohn, *Dope Girls*, 65–6.
[18] Parssinen, *Secret Passions, Secret Remedies*, 61–3; Barry Milligan, *Pleasures and Pains: Opium and the Orient in Nineteenth-Century British Culture* (Charlottesville and London: University Press of Virginia, 1995), 86–94.
[19] Berridge, "East End Opium Dens," 16.
[20] Parssinen, *Secret Passions, Secret Remedies*, 130.
[21] *Times*, 13 May 1916, 3.

was associated primarily with Chinese residents, though literary and journalistic depictions also attributed the habit to some working-class white East Enders and increasingly associated it with Bohemian, West End thrill-seekers as well.[22]

The Chinese residents of London were not targeted, initially, by Britain's wartime drug prohibition laws. The extant regulations concerning aliens in Britain made the power of DORA 40b unnecessary in most cases anyway. The Aliens Restriction Act 1914, in conjunction with the Aliens Restriction (Consolidation) Order 1916, authorized the Home Office to deport without trial *any* alien whose presence was considered deleterious to the good of the nation.[23] The anti-opium campaign in Britain took place concurrently with the anti-cocaine hysteria, but its initiation preceded the passage of DORA 40b by several weeks and, in its initial phases, it relied on the laws governing aliens, not on those governing narcotics. The focus of the officials that conducted the campaign at the national level, moreover, was on the opium *traffic* not on opium use. "The ban on cocaine is also applied to opium," a *Times* story on the new regulation explained, "but for different reasons. The opium habit is not greatly practiced in this country, but the powers taken by the Government will help the authorities to stop the extensive smuggling of opium to China and America."[24] Nonetheless, by the beginning of the anti-opium campaign in the summer of 1916, the legal battle against internal vice, prominently connected in official policy and public discourse to Chinese residents and the drug traffic in which they were portrayed as central actors, had become a matter of dire national urgency.

Much of the initiative behind the wartime anti-narcotics campaign originated with Sir Malcolm Delevingne, an under-secretary of state for the Home Office who was deeply committed to halting the drug trade. He was especially concerned with opium.[25] In the years following the conclusion of the First World War, Delevingne would travel the globe advocating measures to combat the international drug trade. He represented Great Britain on the League of Nation's advisory committee on the opium trade from 1921 to 1934, and continued to serve as the nation's representative to international opium conferences even after his retirement.[26] The Home Office's authority and the anti-opium campaign that Delevingne orchestrated were national, but its execution depended upon the initiative of local officials. Local police and judiciary officials, although demonstrating some antipathy to opium, were equally concerned with Chinese vice and immorality generally, and even more so with the

[22] Parsinnen, *Secret Passions, Secret Remedies*, 115–26.
[23] Ann Dummett and Andrew Nicol, *Subjects, Citizens, Aliens and Others: Nationality and Immigration Law* (Chicago: Northwestern University Press, 1990), 107.
[24] *Times*, 29 July 1916, 5.
[25] Kohn, *Dope Girls*, 42–4.
[26] *Times*, 1 November 1932, 14; 1 December 1950, 8; P.W.J. Bartrip, "Delevingne, Sir Malcolm (1868–1950)," *Oxford Dictionary of National Biography* (Oxford: Oxford University Press, 2004), accessed 22 December 2013, www.oxforddnb.com/view/article/32774.

alleged prevalence of gambling and interracial sexuality in their communities. This general antipathy towards Chinese residents was evident in Liverpool, the locale of the most concerted of the wartime anti-opium campaigns.

By July 1917, the Criminal Investigation Department of the Liverpool Police, working in close communication with the Home Office, had arrested 133 individuals involved in the illegal importation, processing, distribution, exportation and use of opium.[27] This dramatic campaign against the opium traffic in Liverpool stemmed not from any violent or disruptive activity on the part of the city's Chinese population, but from the dogged commitment of local police to suppress Chinese vice and immorality in their city. The entire opium smuggling operation there might have gone unnoticed had it not been for the tremendously increased authority granted to the police during wartime to investigate the movement and activity of all aliens, enemy or otherwise.

However, the Liverpool anti-opium campaign that culminated in the raids and mass arrests of 1916 and 1917 began in December 1915 – well before the initiation of the anti-cocaine campaign in London or the anti-opium campaign orchestrated by Delevingne – with the arrest of a Chinese man, Ko Yin Chan (aka Ko Foo Kee), and a Chinese woman, Wong Mee, for selling liquor without a licence.[28] The police suspected that the boarding house where they had been arrested was "in reality a Chinese gambling house and [was used] for the illicit sale of intoxicating liquor and opium."[29] The suspicions of Detective Burgess of the Liverpool Criminal Investigation Division subsequently fell on Ivan Francis Liang, the manager of the boarding house, whom Burgess believed was using false registration papers in violation of the Aliens Restriction Act 1914.[30] Burgess's suspicions were further sharpened when Liang took up residence in the home of a former opium-smuggler who had recently left Liverpool for the United States. In this new location, Burgess reported, Liang cohabitated with an Englishwoman who paid his rent.[31]

At this point, Burgess had no conclusive evidence to charge Liang with any particular crime, a fact he readily admitted to in his reports. But the combination of Liang's association with two convicted sellers of liquor, his relocation to the home of a former opium-smuggler and Burgess's suspicions that he had been allowing another Chinese man to use his registration papers were enough to prompt further action. Without obtaining a warrant, which the wartime emergency powers made unnecessary in any case, Burgess and a police constable "visited" Liang's place of residence on 14 April 1916. They found not only 1,680 lbs of raw opium, but six furnaces and two boilers for its preparation and a large store of tins for the storage of the finished product.

[27] "Raids 9th June 1917," HO 45/28.

[28] HO 45/1.

[29] Ibid.

[30] All resident aliens were required to register their presence and place of residence with the local police, and to update such information whenever they moved.

[31] HO 45/1.

Burgess estimated that the entire cache, as is, was worth £2,000, but he further estimated that had those arrested succeeded in smuggling it for sale abroad, they could have made ten times that amount. Information provided by Liang's white female cohabitant, whom Burgess reported was "very afraid of him [Liang]," along with further investigation into the records of the local Thomas Cook's travel agency, revealed how the business was conducted: Liang was in charge of the smuggling operation in Liverpool, but the principle manager conducted business from Hong Kong. In order to move the finished product to the point of sale there, Liang had "booked about 100 separate passages for Chinamen to travel to China ... he also smuggles large quantities [of opium] through the agency of seamen other than Chinamen."[32] Further investigation uncovered another related set of traffickers, who "managed to smuggle [opium] out of the country by means of Chinese firemen and well-dressed Europeans."[33] On the premises belonging to these suspects, Burgess found another 200 lbs of opium in various stages of preparation and paperwork that recorded thousands of pounds' worth of bank transactions.[34]

Delevingne, not surprisingly, was mortified by Burgess's discoveries. He argued that, in addition to being an egregious violation of the wartime prohibitions on opium, the operation being run by Liang and the other Chinese men, posed a serious threat to the efficiency of Britain's wartime transportation network. "The men are engaged in a nefarious and illegal trade which has recently grown enormously," Delevingne wrote to his superiors in the Home Office, "and their operations are causing severe difficulties and delays to the shipping companies on whose vessels the opium is smuggled."[35] He recommended the immediate expulsion of all those involved, and their return to China. "Deportation of any Chinese found to be engaged in the trade," he declared, "would help very much towards [the traffic's] suppression."[36]

But here, Delevingne and Burgess encountered a legal obstacle. Although all the officials involved in the case believed that the Chinese nationals who had been arrested "prepare opium for exportation to the British colonies and America," they had not been arrested in the actual act of importation or exportation. In the period before DORA 40b came into force, still several months in the future, the mere possession of opium, even enormous quantities of it, was not even a crime, let alone one serious enough to legally merit deportation.[37]

---

[32] Ibid.
[33] "Exportation of Opium and Deportation of Those Connected Therewith," HO 45/3.
[34] Ibid.
[35] Shipping companies faced heavy fines if opium was discovered aboard their ships upon their arrival in foreign ports. One of the catalysts of Delevingne's campaign had been a memorandum addressed to the Colonial Office from operators of the Blue Funnel line expressing concern over the use of their ships for the smuggling of opium, morphine and cocaine to India, Japan and China (Kohn, *Dope Girls*, 43).
[36] Ibid.
[37] The unlicensed importation or exportation of opium was made illegal by the Prohibition of Exportation Opium Order. The strongest law on the books at the time with regard to the

It was at this point that the broad wartime powers granted to the Home Office to deal with "undesirable" aliens came into play. In May, Herbert Samuel, Secretary of State for the Home Office, simply used his authority under the Aliens Restriction Act 1914 and the Aliens Restriction (Consolidation) Order 1916 to order the summary deportation of those arrested in Burgess's raids. This was precisely the course advocated by Liverpool's Assistant Head Constable of the CID, who had written to Delevingne in late April, to advise that such summary deportation "would be a more effectual method of stopping the evil than a prosecution, even if the latter were practicable, but no offence in law is disclosed as far as the opium is concerned."[38]

The dramatic discovery of the Liverpool opium-smuggling enterprise brought Chinese men into the harsh spotlight of official attention as a vector by which vice and immorality were transmitted from the imperial periphery to Britain itself. Even so, in the Liverpool case, the relationship between empire and metropole was more complex because the goal of the operation run by Liang and his associates was not to market the opium in Britain itself, where the demand was very small, but rather to export it to China and North America and redistribute it there. Ironically, by following such a pattern, the Liverpool operation mirrored Britain's own imperial economic organization wherein raw materials were imported from the Empire, processed into the finished product in Britain, and then re-exported back to the Empire to be sold at a tremendous profit. The entire exchange was conducted via the same British merchant shipping network that formed the backbone of imperial trade and was facilitated by British shipowners' desire to take advantage of the availability of cheap Chinese maritime labour – itself a product of imperial political and economic power structures.

Thus, the DORA campaign to suppress the use of narcotics and the efforts of Delevingne, Burgess and other Home Office and police officials to identify, arrest and deport opium traffickers shared a common thread in their identification of Chinese men associated with opium as being intrinsically threatening to the social fabric of wartime Britain, and particularly to white women and the health of the nation's soldiery. But those who conducted them did so in the context of two very different discourses on the nature of this threat, the role of Chinese immigrants in British economic and social structures, and how the powers of the state should be employed. In the case of narcotics *use* the effort to constrain the cultural identity of Chinese labourers and force them to abandon their customary practices to work within Western models and expectations was a pattern that extended from merchant shipping

---

possession of opium remained the Pharmacy Act of 1908, which made unlicensed possession of opium a misdemeanour punishable by a fine. The act had been supplemented by local ordinances in some cases, such as the 1909 London County Council regulation that made the presence of opium in a lodging house grounds for the revocation of the owner's business licence.

[38] Letter from R. Everett, Asst. Head Constable, Liverpool CID to the Home Office, 22 April 1916, HO 45/119/609/113.

to the gold mines of South Africa to the trenches of the First World War.[39] In the latter, Chinese labourers recruited from their home regions would be shaved, deloused and even stripped of their clothing prior to being outfitted in Western style and shipped out to Flanders.[40] The "internationalization" of labour was conducted by British authorities on British terms, and the effacement of workers' cultural identity, opium-smoking being just one of many examples, was part and parcel of a process that had begun many decades prior to the outbreak of war.

Official efforts to stamp out the opium traffic conducted by Chinese residents, on the other hand, were much more specific to the changing attitudes towards race, immigration, foreign influence and the security of Britain's vital commercial networks during wartime. This was an acute, as opposed to perennial, concern. Its impetus came from the explicit complaints made by shipping companies about smuggling, Delevingne's dedication to opium interdiction, and a more widespread antipathy among him and local police officials to Chinese "troublemakers" in the immigrant enclaves of Britain's port cities. The encouragement and commendation offered down the chains of police administration encouraged further zeal on the part of individual inspectors and Head Constables. This zeal was not always shared by local magistrates, who showed much less inclination to forcefully execute regulations so recent in adoption and so contrary to prior practice. Regardless of judicial recalcitrance, Home Office officials and the police of Liverpool became determined to stamp out the smuggling of opium to and from England by any means necessary and did not hesitate to use all of the considerable powers granted them by wartime emergency measures. Their efforts were leant further impetus by Inspector Burgess's suggestion that at least some of the principals conducting the illicit traffic might be involved in espionage. "If this man is not an active agent in the smuggling of opium," Burgess wrote of George Kentwell, a Hong Kong-born British subject, "then the suspicion arises that he visits here for espionage. He is certainly a dangerous man and, besides visiting Liverpool, he makes frequent journeys to other ports and does not follow any regular employment."[41] Arrests and deportations continued through 1916 and early 1917 in London, Liverpool and other cities where Chinese immigrants formed distinct, though invariably small, communities.

Nevertheless, despite all the commitment to stamping out the traffic that was demonstrated by these campaigns, correspondence between Burgess and the Home Office revealed the prominent role played by reports of general vice and immorality among Chinese men, or even just the suspicion of

---

[39] Gary Kynoch, "Controlling the Coolies: Chinese Mineworkers and the Struggle for Labor in South Africa, 1904–1910," *The International Journal of African Historical Studies* 36.2 (2003), 309–29.

[40] Brian Fawcett, "The Chinese Labour Corps in France 1917–1922," *Journal of the Royal Asiatic Society, Hong Kong Branch* 40 (2000), 33–111.

[41] HO 45/11.

them, in the investigations of smuggling suspects. Reports usually based on hearsay and rumour, for example, of one suspect's immoral sexual behaviour with white women, were sometimes central features of the discussions over whether or not a person should be deported. "Wong Tip is a very undesirable person," Burgess wrote of one suspect, "he seduced a young woman some four years ago and then left her."[42] "He is a man of unscrupulous principles," he explained in another report, "and even now, although married, he would not hesitate to spend a large sum of money on a young woman to get her to sacrifice herself for his lust."[43] A suspect's involvement in illegal gambling or his past convictions for other offences also figured prominently in Burgess's justifications for deportation. In both Liverpool and Glasgow, just the suspicion that Chinese residents were involved in the traffic, even if they had never been convicted on possession charges, was enough to merit such a recommendation.[44]

As long as the opium traffic was stopped, Home Office officials seemed unconcerned whether or not the individuals who were deported without trial, or who had been coerced into leaving the country, were necessarily central to smuggling operations. In response to Burgess's June 1916 recommendations for the deportation of nine Liverpool Chinese men and one Japanese man, one high-ranking Home Office official admitted that the "[Home Office] has no means of checking [Burgess's] reports."[45] "And in making deportation orders without trial for definite offenses," the official continued, "there is some risk of hitting individuals who are not specially [*sic*] guilty. But all the Chinese in the opium business seem to stick very close together and there can be very little harm done by clearing out whole parties of them (including one Japanese). It seems a thoroughly proper use of the emergency powers of deportation."[46]

When even the rudimentary grounds necessary for deportation without trial were absent, Home Office officials and police resorted to threats and intimidation instead. In a Glasgow case where the circumstances made it difficult to obtain deportation orders for a group of smuggling suspects because a single individual had claimed responsibility for the entire operation, the Home Office simply instructed the local police to coerce the remaining suspects into leaving the country voluntarily. "Police can tell the [other suspects] that they will be advised to leave the UK also," one Home Office official wrote to the Chief Constable of the Glasgow City Police, "as on the next occasion when they come into the hands of the Police they will not be treated so leniently."[47] Such strong-arm tactics were an integral aspect of the anti-opium campaign

[42] Ibid.
[43] Ibid.
[44] HO 45/11 and 19.
[45] HO 45/11.
[46] Ibid.
[47] HO 45/24683/311604/19.

waged by the Home Office and local police forces, and those who supervised it expressed satisfaction at the terror sown among Chinese residents as a result. In June 1916, the Permanent Under-Secretary of State praised Burgess's efforts in Liverpool. "The prompt execution of the [deportation] orders has spread a holy panic throughout Liverpool," he wrote approvingly, "and cast a feeling of terrible insecurity among the Chinese population."[48]

The Chinese residents of Liverpool did not remain passive in the face of pressure from the police and their Home Office superiors. Employing a well-established tactic in the hope that the likelihood of deportation would be reduced, those arrested often claimed Hong Kong residency (i.e. that they were subjects of the Crown and therefore entitled to commensurate legal rights). But officials were wary of what was by then a standard claim made by Chinese men in their encounters with state authorities. Such officials often responded by insisting that the accused produce documentation to verify their nationality, but few of those accused possessed such documents. The men accused of involvement in the trade also frequently hired solicitors, although the Home Office's employment of emergency powers to deport them without trial undermined this strategy. As a result, in the absence of a trial and with no higher authority to which an appeal could be submitted, the best a solicitor could do in most cases was to plead for a delay in the enforcement of the order so that the deportee would have time to put his personal affairs in order. Ironically, a suspect's engagement of legal representation could actually work against him, since the correspondence between clients and their solicitors could be used as evidence. For example, on two previous occasions, Liang had engaged a Liverpool firm of solicitors to sue for the recovery of opium illegally seized by customs officials or ships' captains. One suit, filed in January 1915, well before the initiation of the anti-opium campaign and the passage of DORA 40b, had been successful.[49] In May 1916, Burgess seized Liang's correspondence from these cases and employed it as proof of the accused's history of involvement in the opium trade. Liang's past conduct of a perfectly legal suit for the recovery of private property thus became evidence to support his subsequent deportation without trial.

Following a massive raid on Chinese shops and boarding-houses by Liverpool police in June 1917 that netted a further seventy-three suspects, the anti-opium campaign in the city began to wind down, largely because Inspector Burgess believed that there were so few traffickers left to arrest. "The illicit exportation of opium from this port as far as I can discover," he wrote in his report, "has now almost ceased and we are not receiving any complaints from the shipping companies. I have the matter well in hand, and

---

48 HO 45/24683/311604/11.
49 Ibid. The successful suit, brought by the Liverpool firm of Messrs. R. Killey and Stewart Lloyd, had been initiated by Liang on behalf of Cheong Lung, another suspected opium smuggler, against the seizure of opium on the *S.S. Den of Ogil* by HM Custom's inspectors on 16 January 1915.

I do not anticipate much more trouble."[50] This turned out to be an overly optimistic assessment, as a raid in November 1919, which resulted in nine more deportation orders for "habitual traffickers," would later prove. But by mid-1917, the Home Office and the Liverpool Police seemed, at least for the time being, to be satisfied that the traffic and those who conducted it had been driven from the city. Although the absence of reliable population figures makes the overall impact of the campaign difficult to assess, the 133 men arrested in Liverpool between May 1916 and June 1917 certainly represented a substantial portion of the Chinese population there – as much as 10–15 per cent, by one estimate.[51]

In London, according to the popular author Thomas Burke, the results of DORA and wartime prohibition had been similarly dramatic. "The word 'Chinatown,' which once carried a perfume of delight [is] now empty of meaning save as indicating a district of London where Chinamen live," he wrote, describing the Limehouse district in 1917.[52] "To-day Limehouse is without salt or savour; flat and unprofitable; and of all that it once held of colour and mystery and the macabre, one must write in the past tense. The missionaries and the Defence of the Realm Act have together stripped it of all that furtive adventure that formerly held such lure for the Westerner." The East London district was still ethnically diverse as "the streets and lodging-houses were thronged with Arabs, Malays, Hindoos, South Sea Islanders, and East Africans," Burke claimed, "and the Asiatics' Home for Destitute Orientals was having the time of its life."[53] Casual interracial socialization was still a visible element as well, and the author described finding "the usual crowd of Chinks and white girls" at one Pennyfields public house, and another restaurant "crowded with yellow boys and a few white girls" nearby. But "stern policing" had suppressed the former violence, drama and vice of the district, and "Thames Police Court had become almost as suave and seemly as Rumpelmayer's."[54] Opium in particular, Burke wrote, had largely disappeared from public view, and was now "secretly hoarded … fetching £30 per pound." By comparison, opium had been sold over the shop counter in 1914 at 18s. 6d. for a four-ounce tin and sold wholesale in that portion for 12s. 6d.[55]

The judicial and police assault on Chinese residents suspected of involvement in the opium trade had been quick to develop, but it would be slow to abate. Once thought of as an exotic and degrading vice, by the end of the First World War, opium importation and use had been elevated by police, politicians and press to represent a dire threat to Britain, its white residents, and

[50] "Raids on Opium Dens in Liverpool on 9th June 1917," HO 45/24683/311604/28
[51] In a letter written to the *Liverpool Courier*, a group of concerned Chinese residents put the Chinese population of Liverpool at "about 1000." *Liverpool Courier*, 15 September 1916.
[52] Thomas Burke, *Out and About London* (London: Holt, 1919), 85.
[53] Ibid., 86. Rumpelmayer's was a famous upscale London tea-shop.
[54] Ibid., 86–7.
[55] Annie Lai, Bob Little and Pippa Litte, "Chinatown Annie: The East End Opium Trade 1920–1935: The Story of a Woman Opium Dealer," *Oral History Journal* 14.1 (1986), 21–2.

its imperial commerce. As such, according to Delevingne and others in the Home Office, those involved deserved to feel the full force of the state's newly-expanded powers to investigate, arrest, imprison and deport without trial. Of all the emergency powers passed under the umbrella of the Defence of the Realm Act, only those concerning narcotics would survive almost undiluted into the interwar period, and would even be strengthened further. In Britain, the "war on drugs" had claimed its first casualties, though far from its last.

Part II
Punishment

7   Austria's penal colonies

Facts and visions[1]

Stephan Steiner

In the late 1970s a group of historians confronted Michel Foucault with the question of whether he was not "inclined to overstate the importance of the prison in penal history, given that [in the nineteenth century] other quite distinct modes of punishment (the death penalty, the penal colonies, deportation) remained in effect too." Despite his lengthy answer, in which he was very concerned to position himself as a philosopher and not a historian, Foucault elegantly circumvented the question and slipped into the terrain of methodological considerations. While he rightly claimed that there had been "studies of prisons as institutions, but very few of imprisonment as a general punitive practice in our societies," he was at a loss in the face of the question as to why this remark would only apply to the prison universe and not also to various forms of coerced migration and convict labour that were primarily practised in the colonies or peripheries of major European powers.[2]

This chapter will argue that, with the exception of the English transportation system, the European deportation practices of the early modern period and the nineteenth century have been significantly understudied and deserve greater scholarly attention. The case of the Habsburg Empire will serve as an example of a significant European player in world affairs, whose ambitions for deportation are virtually unknown in current historiogaphy or at least have been highly underestimated. From the nineteenth century onwards, historians argued that the Habsburg Empire had pursued a policy of "no colonies – no deportations," and generations of historians built on this myth of a state that had no ambitions to govern and police its population by means of forceful relocations. In light of documented evidence that forms the basis of the present study, however, this approach is entirely untenable; on the contrary, the Habsburg Empire has played an integral part in the European deportation

---

[1] For discussing and editing this chapter I am deeply indebted to Pelin Tünaydın. A previous version of it was presented at the 9th European Social Science History Conference, Glasgow, 11–14 September 2012.
[2] Michel Foucault, "Questions of Method: An Interview with Michel Foucault," in Kenneth Baynes, James Bohman and Thomas McCarthy (eds) *After Philosophy: End or Transformation* (Cambridge, MA: MIT Press, 2008), 100–3. The interview was "distilled" from round table commentaries by Michel Foucault, which were later extensively recast by him.

system of the modern period. In the period 1700 to 1760, for example, which serves as a useful basis for international comparison, the total number of men and women who were forcibly relocated in the Habsburg realm came close to 8,000. During exactly the same time period, the figures for other European states were: England 37,720 deportees, Portugal 11,750, Spain 5,875 and France 5,400.[3] Thus deportations in the Habsburg realm were, at least in these decades, comparable to other European powers.

Penal colonies in modern European history

The term "penal colony," in popular European conceptions, quite often evokes associations of islands, far-off in the Pacific or Indian Oceans, tropical heat, hardcore criminals and back-breaking chain gang labour. Whereas such depictions might be true for the most brutal overseas penal colonies, such as the British Norfolk Island in the Pacific Ocean or Devil's Island off the coast of French Guiana, it does not apply to the many "colony-like" penal institutions *within* the borders of Europe, that were built on the concept of an *internal colonialism*, according to which early modern states made use of the fringes of their "motherland" territory in a purely colonial manner.[4] Workhouse inmates, delinquents in labour battalions, and forced workers in fortresses, were among the victims of such schemes, and more often than not they were guilty of no actual crime and nor were they involved in settling any particularly grim or distant location.

In the early modern period such "internal penal colonies", as one might call them, were places of confinement, reserved for delinquents as well as those with unblemished records who were nonetheless deemed to pose a present or future threat to the public or state authorities. Selected groups of a population were forcibly transferred from Location A to Location B on foot, by horses and carts or on boats, but always under military escort. People transferred in this manner, under pain of severe punishment, were not permitted to leave their target Location B, usually for the rest of their lives. Forced labour was not always a part of such deportations, yet – with socially marginalized groups of deportees and with outright criminals – it was a significant additional element of the punishment. Internal penal colonies were segregated from "normal life," but they were not necessarily restricted to extremely remote places. Fortress detention or workhouse labour, for instance, quite often took place next to free people's dwellings.

---

[3] David Eltis, "Free and Coerced Migrations from the Old World to the New," in David Eltis (ed.), *Coerced and Free Migration: Global Perspectives* (Stanford: Stanford University Press, 2002), 74.

[4] Michael Hechter, *Internal Colonialism: The Celtic Fringe in British National Development, 1536–1966* (Berkeley and Los Angeles: University of California Press, 1975); Mark Netzloff, *England's Internal Colonies: Class, Capital, and the Literature of Early Modern English Colonialism* (New York and Basingstoke: Palgrave Macmillan, 2003).

Penal colonies, coerced labour and deportation had existed since the beginning of overseas exploration and colonial settlement from the fifteenth century onwards. As early as 1415, at the very start of European colonialism, Portugal sent convicts to the recently conquered Ceuta along the coast of Northern Africa, and Columbus is said to have taken a few delinquents on his third voyage to the Americas.[5] In France, in 1540, Jacques Cartier got approval from the monarchy to take fifty criminals on board for his third voyage.[6] Despite this long tradition of deportation, however, broader public debate over the practice only started in the eighteenth century and finally peaked in the second half of the nineteenth century. During these decades the book market was laden with historical synopses and juridical treatises as polemical pamphlets both for and against the implementation of deportation and penal colonies circulated among scholars as well as aspiring intellectuals.[7] Both advocates and opponents of these measures gathered at numerous conferences, resolutions were signed, and recommendations forwarded to the respective rulers of states. Countries such as Britain and France with long colonial histories had, without much theoretical consideration, engaged in deportation for centuries already; others like Germany and Belgium adopted deportation much later, and, perhaps as a result, engaged more fervently in theoretical deliberations on the issue. The experiences of the Habsburg Empire,

[5] Jean-Paul Lehners, "Die Anfänge der portugiesischen Expansion," in Peter Feldbauer, Gottfried Liedl and John Morrissey (eds), *Vom Mittelmeer zum Atlantik. Die mittelalterlichen Anfänge der europäischen Expansion* (Vienna: Verlag für Geschichte und Politik/Oldenbourg, 2001), 126–47; Kirkpatrick Sale, *Christopher Columbus and the Conquest of Paradise*, 2nd edn (London and New York: Tauris Parke, 2006), 169.

[6] The related document has been published by Ramsay Cook in *The Voyages of Jacques Cartier* (Toronto: University of Toronto Press, 1993), 139–40.

[7] A good bibliographical overview can be found in Franz von Holtzendorff, *Die Deportation als Strafmittel in alter und neuer Zeit und die Verbrecher-Colonien der Engländer und Franzosen in ihrer geschichtlichen Entwickelung und criminalpolitischen Bedeutung* (Leipzig: Barth, 1859), 573–6. See also N[icolas] D'Alfaro, *Observations sur le système pénitentiaire* (Paris: Balitout, 1864); [Ernest Poret] De Blosseville, *Histoire de la colonisation pénale et des établissements de l'Angleterre en Australie* (Évreux: Hérissey, 1859); Felix Friedrich Bruck, *Fort mit den Zuchthäusern!* (Breslau: Koebner, 1894); Felix Friedrich Bruck, *Neudeutschland und seine Pioniere: Ein Beitrag zur Lösung der sozialen Frage* (Breslau: Koebner, 1896); Felix Friedrich Bruck, *Die gesetzliche Einführung der Deportation im Deutschen Reich* (Breslau: Marcus, 1897); Ivan Foïnitski and Georges Bonet-Maury, *La transportation russe et anglaise avec une étude historique sur la transportation* (Paris: Lecène, Oudin & Cie, 1895); Arthur Girault, "La Colonisation pénale," in *Congrès international colonial: Rapports, mémoires & procès-verbaux des séances* (Paris: H. Roberge, 1901), 139–55; George Kennan, *Siberia and the Exile System*, 2 vols (London: Osgood, McIlvaine & Co., 1891); D[avid] Levat, "Utilisation de la Main-d'Œuvre Pénale aux colonies," in *Congrès international colonial*, 589–623; Paul Mimande, *Criminopolis* (Paris: Calmann Lévy, 1897); Maurice Pain, *Contribution à l'étude des questions colonials. Colonisation pénale* (Paris: Societé d'Editions Scientifiques, 1898); G. Pierret, *Transportation et colonisation pénale* (Paris: Tribune des Colonies et des Protectorats, 1892); Édouard Teisseire, *La transportation pénale et la relégation d'après les Lois des 30 mai 1854 et 27 mai 1885: Étude historique, juridique et critique accompagnée d'un long aperçu sur le régime des forçats et des relégués dans nos possessions d'outre-mer* (Paris: Larose, 1893).

however, due to its lack of overseas colonies, offer a different perspective that complicates both conceptions of and practices surrounding penal colonies and the deportation of criminals and political undesirables.

The case of the Habsburg Empire

Over the course of the early modern period the various territories ruled by the Habsburgs transformed into an empire. The Austrian countries, already under Habsburg command in the late Middle Ages, were in 1526 decisively expanded by the incorporation of Bohemia and Hungary, inherited after the death of King Louis II at the battle of Mohács. Heavily contested by the Ottomans during the two centuries that followed, the eighteenth century finally saw the Habsburg Empire become a major player in European affairs, but despite this newly acquired important role on the continent, it remained without any overseas territories for almost the entire duration of its history, which ended with defeat in the First World War in 1918. Nevertheless the Habsburgs did have experience of *internal colonialism* that was put into practice in Southeastern Europe. There, shortly after the reconquest from the Ottomans during the eighteenth century, Transylvania and especially the Banat of Timişoara were transformed into laboratories where all sorts of population policies could be tested.[8] Both the widely remembered *voluntary* recruitment of new settlers and the completely forgotten *forceful* displacement of whole groups of delinquents, deviants and dissenters were priorities for state representatives as well as the political elites.[9] In the course of the eighteenth century, deportations included the removal of miners, farmers, craftsmen and artisans who continued to adhere to their forbidden Protestant beliefs; other religious dissenters, such as the extremely sectarian *Bohemian Deists*; pensioners of Spanish origin, who were viewed as a drain on the government's pocket; groups of political insurgents stubbornly fighting to retain their privileges (or the "old rights") in the face of bureaucratic reform; and those petty criminals, poachers, drunkards or prostitutes who exhibited all sorts of deviant behaviour or whose lifestyles invited condemnation from officials.[10]

---

[8] Konrad Schünemann, *Österreichs Bevölkerungspolitik unter Maria Theresia* (Berlin: Deutsche Rundschau, 1935). Albeit deeply influenced by Nazi ideology, the book is still worth reading thanks to its rich archival materials, which in some aspects are still unsurpassed.

[9] Márta Fata, "Einwanderung und Ansiedlung der Deutschen (1686–1790)," in Günter Schödl (ed.), *Land an der Donau* (Berlin: Siedler, 1995), 89–196; Stephan Steiner, *Rückkehr unerwünscht. Deportationen in der Habsburgermonarchie der Frühen Neuzeit und ihr europäischer Kontext* (Vienna, Cologne and Weimar: Böhlau, 2014), 155–494. For a very brief outline in English, see Stephan Steiner, "'An Austrian Cayenne': Convict Labour and Deportation in the Habsburg Empire of the Early Modern Period," in Christian G. De Vito and Alex Lichtenstein (eds), *Global Convict Labour* (Leiden and Boston: Brill 2015), 219–46.

[10] Erich Buchinger, *Die "Landler" in Siebenbürgen: Vorgeschichte, Durchführung und Ergebnis einer Zwangsumsiedlung im 18. Jahrhundert* (Munich: Oldenbourg, 1980); Stephan Steiner, *Reisen ohne Wiederkehr: Die Deportation von Protestanten aus Kärnten 1734–1736* (Vienna and Munich:

Over the course of the second half of the eighteenth century the penal system in the Habsburg Empire underwent radical change. In 1768, Empress Maria Theresa (r. 1740–1780) published the *Constitutio Criminalis Theresiana*, which unified the many different regional practices that were in place across the Habsburg countries, although the new policy did not apply to Hungary. The *Theresiana* reflected new ideas about the rehabilitative function of punishment, but also clung to conventional measures of deterrence. Maria Theresa's son and co-regent for more than a decade, Emperor Joseph II (r. 1765–1790), who was deeply influenced by the principles of natural law, became a driving force in the abolition of torture in 1776 and the suspension of the death penalty in 1781, which finally led to its abrogation in 1787 (except under martial law). After some early experimentation in the first half of the eighteenth century, the triad of "punishment, discipline and betterment" which governed practice in the penitentiaries and workhouses (*Zucht- und Arbeitshäuser*) in the Austrian hereditary lands spread all over the Habsburg countries from the 1750s onwards.[11]

The triumph of enlightened approaches in bureaucracy, politics and intellectual discourse brought many of the aforementioned kinds of deportations to a halt, and Emperor Joseph II was occasionally at the forefront of these abolition movements.[12] In some cases he was even willing to run the risk of escalating conflict with his mother and co-regent Maria Theresa. At the end

---

Oldenbourg, 2007); Stephan Steiner, "Transmigration. Ansichten einer Zwangsgemeinschaft," in Rudolf Leeb, Martin Scheutz and Dietmar Weikl (eds), *Geheimprotestantismus und evangelische Kirchen in der Habsburgermonarchie und im Erzstift Salzburg (17. / 18. Jahrhundert)* (Vienna and Munich: Böhlau-Oldenbourg, 2009), 331–60; Reinhold Joseph Wolny, *Die josephinische Toleranz unter besonderer Berücksichtigung ihres geistlichen Wegbereiters Johann Leopold Hay* (Munich: Lerche, 1973); Stephan Steiner, "Der Schwarmgeist der Intoleranz. Deisten und Israeliten im Böhmen des späten 18. Jahrhunderts," *Schweizerische Zeitschrift für Religions- und Kirchengeschichte* 102 (2008): 59–79; Rudolf Till, "Die Ansiedlung spanischer Pensionisten von Wien im Banat im Jahre 1736 / 37," *Wiener Geschichtsblätter* 2.2–3 (1947), 25–31; Agustí Alcoberro, "L'exili austriacista i la Nova Barcelona del Banat de Temesvar: teoria i pràctica," *Boletín de la Real Academia de Buenas Letras de Barcelona* 48 (2002), 93–112; Karl-Peter Krauss, "Deportation und Rückkehr des Hauensteiner Aufständischen Jakob Fridolin Albiez / Deportarea şi reîntoarcerea lui Jakob Fridolin Albiez, răsculat fin Hauenstein," in Annemarie Roeder (ed.), *Dan hier ist beser zu leben als in dem Schwaben land. Vom deutschen Südwesten in das Banat und nach Siebenbürgen / Pentru că aici este mai bine de trăit decât în ţara şvabilor. Din sudvestul Germaniei în Banat şi Transilvania* (Stuttgart: Haus der Heimat, 2002), 195–216; Stephan Steiner, "Wien – Temesvar und retour: Der Wasserschub unter Maria Theresia," in Martin Scheutz and Vlasta Valeš (eds), *Wien und seine WienerInnen. Ein historischer Streifzug durch Wien über die Jahrhunderte: Festschrift für Karl Vocelka zum 60. Geburtstag* (Vienna, Cologne and Weimar: Böhlau, 2008), 203–19.

[11] Gerhard Ammerer and Alfred Stefan Weiß (eds), *Strafe, Disziplin und Besserung. Österreichische Zucht- und Arbeitshäuser von 1750 bis 1850* (Frankfurt a.M., Berlin, Bern, Bruxelles, New York, Oxford and Wien: Peter Lang, 2006).

[12] See, for instance, the fervent abolitionist opinions Emperor Joseph II presented to the *Staatsrat*, the highest council in the Habsburg government: Vienna, Österreichisches Staatsarchiv, Haus-Hof- und Staatsarchiv, Habsburg-Lothringisches Familienarchiv, Hofreisen, Karton 2, fol. 269v–284r.

of his rule, deportation schemes had changed dramatically: Protestant dissenters, who at times accounted for almost half of the deportees, were now
tolerated in the whole Empire and consequently they were no longer subjected
to relocation; the same applied to all those "misfits" of society like prostitutes
or small-time crooks, who were not considered a threat to the security of the
state. According to this policy, however, one field of state intervention in the
form of deportation was left untouched by both Maria Theresa and Joseph
II: political insurrection still called for a punishment by deportation.

Despite these changes in general policies over the course of the eighteenth century, in 1799, following the Austrian takeover of Venice, 130 of the
local adherents of the French Revolution, who were rightfully considered
insurgents, were deported to Croatia by the Habsburgs.[13] Among them was
Francesco Apostoli, a well-known author in his time, who wrote a report on
his forced removal immediately after his return to Italy.[14] Apart from a diary by
Zaccaria Carpi, this is one of very few detailed personal accounts of deportation that survive from that period.[15] Apostoli was deported to Fort Šibenik
on the Croatian coast of the Adriatic Sea, which he described as nothing less
than a penal colony, comparable to Botany Bay in Australia – which he likely
learned of through the pamphlets circulating in Europe about the new British
transportation policies in the aftermath of James Cook's explorations – in its
lack of basic hygiene, shortage of food, total control, and the mental torment
suffered by those who were transported there.[16]

The *Deportati Anstalt* in Szeged

In the first two decades of the nineteenth century, the Habsburg bureaucracy
was very interested initially in the Dalmatian coastline as a deportation
location. Osor on the island of Cres was surveyed to see whether it might

13 Attilio Butti, "I deportati del 1799," *Archivio storico lombardo* 7 (1907), 379–427; Luigi Rava,
    *Le prime persecuzioni austriache in Italia: I deportati politici Cisalpini del Dipartimento del
    Rubicone ai lavori forzati in Ungheria e alle tombe di Sebenico, 1799–1800* (Bologna: Zanichelli,
    1916); Steiner, *Rückkehr unerwünscht*, 23–8 and 531.
14 Francesco Apostoli, *Lettere sirmiensi per servire alla storia der deportazione dercittadini cis-
    alpini in Dalmazia ed Ungheria* (Milan: AXR, 1801). Apostoli and all of his surviving com-
    rades were released in 1801 as a side effect of the peace treaty of Lunéville signed between
    France and Austria. In Bergamo he was received with a victory parade and became a local
    hero. He was appointed the official representative of San Marino in Paris and later on he
    returned to Venice as a playwright and clerk. After the Austrians regained Venice, Apostoli
    was dismissed immediately and died of hunger in 1816.
15 Zaccaria Carpi, *I deportati cisalpini: Diario del deportato Zaccaria Carpi di Revere. 11 giugno
    1800–12 aprile 1801* (Mantua: Mondovi, 1903); Francesco Lemmi, "Per la storia della depor-
    tazione nella Dalmazia e nell'Ungheria," *Archivio storico italiano* 40 (1907), 310–48.
16 The oldest pamphlet of this kind, a satirical broadside called *Botany Bay Song, sung at the
    Anacreontic Society* (kept in the collections of the British Library) presented politicians as fit
    candidates for transportation, see also Nathan Garvey, "'Folkalising' Convicts: a 'Botany Bay'
    Ballad and its Cultural Contexts," *Journal of Australian Studies* 38.1 (2014), 32–51.

be suitable for accommodating a *Deportati Anstalt*, probably best translated as an institution specializing in detaining deportees.[17] However, interest in Dalmatia as a host for penal colonies diminished as soon as Habsburg authorities became aware of the untapped potential of well-constructed forts in Hungary that could easily be substitutes for the fully-fledged overseas penal settlements that other European nations had established. From 1831 onwards, a total of around 800 so-called *precettati* – a special type of offender convicted of crimes against the state, consisting of insurgents, barraters and deviants of a wide range of social strata – were brought to Hungarian fortresses from the Lombardo-Venetian parts of the Habsburg Empire. The *precettati*'s freedom of movement was severely restricted even before their transfer to Hungary, first to Fort Arad (in present-day Romania) and then to Fort Szeged, an abandoned citadel reopened exclusively for these convicts.[18]

The stated aim of the *Deportati Anstalt* (Deportation Institute) in Szeged was the "moral betterment" of its convicts and ultimately – visionary as it was – their reintegration into society. Inmates were tasked with labour based on their former occupations, and if they did not have a profession they were trained in spinning wool. The workhouse was run along military lines, with hours of labour from 6 to 11 in the morning and from 1 to 4 or 7 in the evening depending on the sunset at different times of the year. Inmates laboured in silence and talking was only allowed during the two hours of rest at noon. From the point of view of the wardens, Szeged, with its "ramshackle walls," was little more than a convenient place to hold potential runaways who were notorious for their "cat-like" skills in climbing, a remark that clearly indicates that escapes must have occurred.[19]

Although in theory obedient delinquents could be discharged after three years, this was never executed and most of the detainees remained locked up for almost two decades until, in the course of the revolutionary movement of 1848, the scandal was revealed in the newspapers. Until then, Austrian rulers had avoided the term "political prisoners," and had preferred to allude to some supposed "deviant moral conduct" of the detainees. In a cynical response to such concepts, an insurgent of the 1848 revolution remarked: "Their deviant moral conduct was nothing else but hate against the [Habsburg] dynasty, an offence for which now in 1849 half of the monarchy would have to be put in irons."[20] Calls for the immediate release of these inmates were finally success-

[17] Alberto Gianola, *Deportati lombardo-veneti in Ungheria dal 1831 al 1848* (Modena: Società Tipografica Modenese, 1934), 3–4.
[18] Steven C. Hughes, *Crime, Disorder, and the Risorgimento: The Politics of Policing in Bologna* (Cambridge, New York and Melbourne: Cambridge University Press, 1994).
[19] Károly Vajna, *Hazai régi büntetések: Irta és a magyar királyi igazságügyminisztérium támogatásával kiadja*, vol. 2 (Budapest: Lőrintz János Univers, 1907), 473–8. This quotation and the following ones from German are the author's translation.
[20] [Ferdinand Daniel] Fenner von Fenneberg, *Geschichte der Wiener Oktobertage. Geschildert und mit allen Aktenstücken belegt*, vol. 1 (Leipzig: Verlagsbureau, 1849), VII–VIII.

ful and the *Deportati Anstalt* came to an end with the return transport of the former deportees under guard to Italy.[21]

The *Novara* Expedition and its aftermath

Whereas such measures as the transportation of 1799 or the *Deportati Anstalt* were of a purely practical nature, theoretical debates about penal colonies in Austria did not emerge until a later period and were first triggered by the *Novara* Expedition. The *Novara* was a frigate and its closely observed circumnavigation of the globe between 1857 and 1859 has been widely acknowledged solely for its scientific achievements, which included the improvement of nautical skills, the expansion of geographical knowledge and the enhancement of botanical, zoological and anthropological findings in the footsteps of Darwin. Only quite recently have researchers begun to scrutinize the colonial background of the mission.[22]

Archduke Ferdinand Max (1832–1867), the brother of Emperor Franz Joseph I, and from 1864 on Maximilian I of Mexico, was an eager follower of ideas about penal colonies. However, after the failure to establish penal colonies in the Indian Ocean or the Red Sea, he became a vehement promoter of the *Novara* adventure instead.[23] The two-faced nature of this undertaking is evidenced by the list of participants, which on the one hand included Captain Bernhard von Wüllerstorf-Urbair (1816–1883), a vice admiral and in his later life Austrian Imperial Minister of Trade, and on the other hand a crew of scientists, headed by eminent Viennese naturalist Georg von Frauenfeld (1807–1873). The archduke expected the expedition's prospective travelogues and their impact on future readers to trigger a revival of the colonial ambitions of the eighteenth century that would amalgamate with current visions about deportation, punishment and coerced labour. Indeed, referring to Austria's short-term overseas seizure of the Nicobar Islands in the Bay of Bengal in the eighteenth century, the acquisition of the exact same territory was proposed in the official report of the *Novara*'s voyage.[24]

---

[21] Parts of the back story for this final decision can be found in Vienna, Österreichisches Staatsarchiv, Haus- Hof- und Staatsarchiv, Länderabteilungen, Österreichischer Reichstag 1848–1849, Karton 85 VIII. Interpellationen, fol. 177–188. Partly published in N.N., "Oesterreichische Monarchie," *Allgemeine Zeitung* (Munich), 10 September 1848.

[22] David G.L. Weiss and Gerd Schilddorfer, *Die Novara: Österreichs Traum von der Weltmacht* (Vienna: Amalthea, 2010).

[23] The following paragraphs owe greatly to the pioneering study by Ilse Reiter, "Strafkolonien für die Habsburgermonarchie? Zur Deportationsfrage in der zweiten Hälfte des 19. Jahrhunderts," in Ulrike Aichhorn and Alfred Rinnerthaler (eds), *Scientia iuris et historia: Festschrift für Peter Putzer zum 65. Geburtstag. Vol. 2* (Egling: Kovar, 2004), 779–821.

[24] Karl von Scherzer, *Reise der Österreichischen Fregatte Novara um die Erde, in den Jahren 1857, 1858, 1859, unter den Befehlen des Commodore B. von Wüllerstorf-Urbair*, vol. 2 (Vienna: Gerold, 1866), 277–90; Bernhard von Wüllerstorf-Urbair, *Vermischte Schriften des k. k. Vice-Admirals Bernhard Freih. v. Wüllerstorf-Urbair*, ed. by his widow (Graz: self-published by the author, 1889), 178–207.

Through the rest of the nineteenth century and until the beginning of the First World War, debates about the deportation of delinquents under the Habsburg monarchy remained commonplace. For example, politicians such as Georg von Schönerer (1842–1921), who is otherwise remembered as one of the trailblazers for anti-Semitism in Austria, campaigned for the annexation of Bosnia-Herzegovina in part with the aim of establishing penal colonies there.[25] His party, the *Deutschnationalen* (German Nationalists), also included a specific demand for penal colonies in its manifesto from 1883. Use of more distant destinations for deportation, including the Congo and islands off the coast of Equatorial Guinea, were also debated in the Imperial Assembly.[26] Deliberations about Habsburg penal colonies changed markedly, however, when Germany seized its first colonial possessions in 1884 and 1885, including German Southwest Africa (present-day Namibia), German West Africa (chiefly consisting of today's Togo and Cameroon), German East Africa (including modern-day Tanzania, Burundi and Rwanda); and German New Guinea, which held protectorate status. Austria almost immediately started thinking about capitalizing on those developments. In search of convincing arguments to persuade Germany's ruling elite to enter into a joint venture to establish penal colonies, Austrian advocates of a common future transportation strategy were not lost for words. Penal reformers as well as journalists promoted the benefits of shared colonies, but also highlighted the potential negative outcomes that could result if a common policy was not developed. They made the case, for example, that unless deportation was adopted as a form of criminal punishment in both Austria and Germany, criminals could find sanctuary simply by crossing the border between the two nations, and they called for immediate action to address this concern. As one of the leading advocates of Austrian–German collaboration on penal colonies explained:

> We cannot foresee what an impression deportation will make on the population … but we can be sure that, if deportation will be restricted to just one of the two countries … an alternating move of exactly the most dubious parts of it will take place. This argument by itself should be reason enough for Germany to share with Austria the blessings of this new juridical practice … Let's bring about an agreement with Germany as soon as possible, before the value of colonial property will be so unaffordable … that this big issue cannot be solved any more.[27]

[25] Herwig [Eduard Pichl], *Georg Schönerer und die Entwicklung des Alldeutschtums in der Ostmark*, vol. 1 (Vienna: Berger, 1912), 149.

[26] Reiter, "Strafkolonien," 803–14.

[27] Hans Gross, "Zur Deportationsfrage," in Hans Gross (ed.), *Gesammelte kriminalistische Aufsätze* (Leipzig: Vogel, 1902), 70–1. All following quotes have been translated from the German by the author of this chapter.

Furthermore, Germany was advised to rent out small pieces of its colonial soil to Austrians, thus giving them a chance to develop their own deportation strategies in close connection with their neighbours.

The Gross–Hoegel debate

Efforts to develop a common deportation policy with Germany came to nothing, but they certainly encouraged a remorseless discourse against "habitual" criminals and against the "refusal to work." Towards the end of the nineteenth century, two highly influential Austrian penologists, who represented the two main factions in juridical discourse at the time, engaged in a bitter debate over the policy of deportation that had limited practical consequences but generated some extraordinarily polemical writing. Hans Gross (1847–1915), an influential proponent of the "Graz School of Criminology" initiated the debate on 18 September 1896 in an article for the *Allgemeine Österreichische Gerichtszeitung* (Austrian General Court Gazette).[28] He pleaded for the introduction of life-long deportation as a punishment for offenders considered to be especially dangerous to the public: namely so-called "incorrigible" law-breakers and "work-shy" youngsters with previous convictions or long-term sentences. He vividly depicted his vision about the purifying function of such deportations:

> [T]he most important aspect is that the whole deportation issue should be transformed into a work of culture. The aim of deportation is by no means to dispose of the rabble, but to avoid breeding such rabble between dungeon walls in the first place. Deportees will turn into decent people; foreign countries will thereby gain real pioneers.[29]

Hugo Hoegel (1854–1921), a jurist known for his propensity for dissent against mainstream penological thought and the political establishment, immediately reacted to Gross's article with a brilliantly formulated polemic in which he sardonically stated:

> Haven't we all known a stage of life that was full of ideas about deport-ation, just as most criminologists have not always been totally free from a certain romance for corporal punishments? But conversion was inevitable in the end … As far as I am concerned, the former predilection for the Dalmatian Islands as a dump site for criminals leaves me today with the impression of a juvenile Robinson-Crusoe-like enthusiasm … It could be that I have become too much of a sceptic over the years, but Gross has definitely retained too much idealism and imagination … The mere fact that an old question is brought into debate again and again, without ever

[28] Ibid., 64–71.
[29] Ibid., 71.

granting it some rest, does not necessarily mean that it is worth posing it
... Jurisprudents simply run out of new things to write about sometimes
and then turn to old, already dismissed subjects instead.[30]

From Hoegel's point of view the whole issue had resolved itself: compulsory
methods of colonization had proved useless; transforming deserts into an
"Eldorado of Civilization" had already turned out to be nothing more than
wishful thinking. Drawing on Russia, England and France's unfavourable
experiences with deportation, he succinctly stated his opposition to Austria
pursuing a similar course: "In the absence of its own colonies, Austria is
hopefully not in danger of falling into the trap of deportation, only to learn
its mistake later on."[31]

We do not know so far whether – aside from such juridical controversies –
more concrete plans for establishing penal colonies were ever developed by the
Austrian government or penologists. Nevertheless, there is sporadic evidence
to suggest that the matter was under official consideration. In the mid-1880s
for instance, the British government was reportedly troubled by Austria's suspected intentions to use New Guinea as an "open gaol."[32] It also seems as if
the Italian example of the so-called *domicilio coatto*, in the course of which
delinquents were brought to islands and were forced to work for their living
there, aroused the interest of the Austrian penal system.[33]

Philosopher Ralf Rother has pointed out that the jurisdictional aspects
of the deportation debate in Austria were increasingly replaced by arguments of a more "hygienic" nature: "While at first only the so-called habitual
criminals, repeat offenders, hoboes, beggars and traitors were intended for
deportation, later on the so-called 'degenerated' as well as socialists, anar-
chists, homosexuals and Gypsies were included in the scheme."[34] Indeed, the
emphasis on the amalgamation of the discourses of fighting crime and of
promoting public health was a specifically Austrian contribution to the whole
debate. "Inferiority" and "degeneration" were – decades before the euthan-
asia programmes of the Nazis – already seen as phenomena virtually ask-
ing for selection via deportation. In the eyes of Hans Gross, for instance, all
forms of deviance such as vagrancy, gambling addiction, work-shyness, sex-

---

[30] Hugo Hoegel, *Straffälligkeit und Strafzumessung* (Vienna: Perles, 1897), 171–2.

[31] Hugo Hoegel, *Die Straffälligkeit wegen Arbeitsscheu in Österreich* (Wien: Hölder, 1899), 213.

[32] Stephen Nicholas and Peter R. Shergold, "Transportation as Global Migration," in Stephen
Nicholas (ed.), *Convict Workers: Reinterpreting Australia's Past* (Cambridge, New York and
Melbourne: Cambridge University Press, 1989), 36.

[33] William Tallack, *Penological and Preventive Principles, with Special Reference to Europe and
America; and to the Diminution of Crime, Pauperism, and Intemperance; to Prisons and their
Substitutes, Habitual Offenders, Sentences, Neglected Youth, Education, Police, Statistics, etc.*
(London: Wertheimer, Lea & Co., 1889), 194.

[34] Ralf Rother, *Gewalt und Strafe. Dekonstruktionen zum Recht auf Gewalt* (Würzburg:
Königshausen & Neumann, 2007), 60.

ual perversion, general discontent or rebellion were perfectly viable reasons for establishing penal colonies.[35]

Kafka's response to the debate

Interestingly enough, one of Gross's students made an international career in a field completely different from jurisprudence. Franz Kafka, arguably the most influential Austrian novelist of the twentieth century, attended some of Gross's lectures in Prague and they could very well have been the initial spark for his long-lasting interest in the topic of deportation, which culminated in the novella *In der Strafkolonie* (In the Penal Colony), published in 1919.[36]

One of the books Kafka's text incorporated was the richly illustrated report *Meine Reise nach den Strafkolonien* (My Travel to the Penal Colonies), published in 1913 by the young Bavarian lawyer Robert Heindl (1883–1958).[37] This work deeply influenced the debate on penal colonies and ultimately brought an end to both German and Austrian ambitions. Having visited French and English penal institutions, Heindl summarized his eyewitness impressions and his appraisal was devastating to all deportation enthusiasts. Not even drawing on humanitarian or juridical arguments, Heindl dismissed deportation for purely practical reasons: based on his direct observations of the system, deportation brought no economic benefits and did nothing at all towards the moral reform or betterment of delinquents.

With this radical paradigm shift, the Habsburg monarchy abandoned its aspirations for participating in overseas penal colonies. What had started out as a population experiment based on an *internal colonialism* in the eighteenth century, evolved in the first half of the nineteenth century into plans for convict settlements on islands and forced labour in fortresses, but by the turn of the twentieth century these ambitions had dissipated to just visions of a parasitic participation in imperial colonialism that due to the disinterest of Germany were never carried into effect. By the time of the First World War, plans for Austrian penal colonies were abandoned as new and much more urgent questions about the end of Empire confronted Austrian politicians, columnists, agitators and jurisprudents.

---

[35] Hans Gross, "Degeneration und Deportation," in *Gesammelte kriminalistische Aufsätze*, vol. 2 (Leipzig: Vogel, 1908), 70–7.

[36] Franz Kafka, *In der Strafkolonie* (Leipzig: Wolff, 1919); Ralf Rother, "Die Damen in der Strafkolonie. Zu Hans Gross und Franz Kafka," *Tumult* 27 (2003), 33–49.

[37] Robert Heindl, *Meine Reise nach den Strafkolonien* (Berlin and Vienna: Ullstein, 1913).

8   Punishment and parade

The cultural form of penal exile in Russia

Laura Piacentini

The theme of this edited collection, *Transnational Penal Cultures*, examines representations of culture in punishment forms. The interpretations of penal histories presented in this collection challenge conventional Foucauldian analyses of punishment that view penality as an instrumental form of power-knowledge and body regulation. The challenge presented to the contributors was to look beyond Foucault, and therefore beyond the power-knowledge dichotomy as the object of study, to a cultural account where idealisms and historical meanings are emphasised in penality's unfolding. This chapter trains attention on Russia's culture of punishment and demonstrates that this exceptional penal form is marked – indeed scarred – by a penal style involving exile and banishment.[1] I argue that Russia's culture of punishment reproduces specific cultural and penal-historical tropes that are appropriated from experiences of imprisonment that date back to the nineteenth century. The historical discourse of 'in exile imprisonment' presented in this chapter cannot be separated from present-day experiences of incarceration in Russia because it plays an essential role in understanding penality today amongst the general public and the prison population in that country. William Sewell's *cultural schema*[2] will form the basis of the analysis of how in Russia, a distinctive cultural knowledge of punishment (in which exile endures as a punitive response) and a particular action (the use of geographical displacement suggests that penal power continues to migrate from the centre to the margins) makes for a certain kind of 'common sense'. The cultural schema of 'in exile imprisonment' is recognisable to Russians because it allows for a common understanding of the punishment process, however so defined.

   This chapter will first introduce what I understand to be a cultural understanding of penality against a Foucauldian account of penal change before

[1] Some of the ideas presented in this chapter are drawn from the ESRC-funded study in women's imprisonment in Russia titled: 'Women in the Russian Penal System: The Role of Distance in the Theory and Practice of Imprisonment in Late Soviet and Post-Soviet Russia', RES-062-023-0026, 2006–2010.

[2] William H. Sewell, 'The Concept (s) of Culture', in V.E. Bonell and C. Hunt (eds), *Beyond the Cultural Turn: New Directions in the Study of Society and Culture* (Berkeley: University of California Press, 1999), 35–61.

presenting a brief history of exile in Russia. I then examine how memory-making in Russia's penal spaces, and the cultural trope of exile, have created, to paraphrase Garland, *penal place*, *penal purpose* and *penal culture*.[3] A point of note is that I do not set out to endorse a cultural account of punishment over a Foucauldian account. Rather, my argument is that Russian imprisonment has evolved against a cultural panorama of using the geographical peripheries of the Tsarist empire and Soviet and post-Soviet nation-state(s), and an exceptional spatial exclusion, to anchor penal and political power. Moreover, whilst the popular tropes of 'exile' and 'camps' are fashioned from remembering, creating a repertoire of penal narratives and symbolic framing that are familiar, it is also the case that contemporary penality in Russia is highly politicised around what I call a 'moral-nationalism' that sustains these historical narratives. As evidenced in the Pussy Riot, Khodorkovsky and the Greenpeace imprisonment cases, there is currently in Russia a moral and pragmatic discourse circulating in civil society about impropriety, illegality and so-called malevolence that requires the state to exercise removal as an expression of penal power.[4] More seriously then, this chapter seeks to offer a new and more developed theorisation for understanding penality in contemporary Russia that may helpfully move prison sociology forward towards considering two things: first, how all forms of incarceration might be experienced as exile, and second, a renewed sense of understanding how historical discourse shapes the fates of those punished.

Punishment and culture

Foucault's contribution to the study of punishment was immense and in quite fundamental ways he has shaped consensus on how subjects come to be disciplined. It would not be an understatement to say that he has produced a new carceral imaginary; in particular his startling analyses of madness, and the birth of the prison and the clinic, have reversed conventional historical understandings and, at the same time, forged new epistemological challenges on how to map power onto knowledge. His legacy on the study of history itself, and on the study of the subjects of power, is profound, with notable effects on how prison and punishment have structural counterparts in other forms of social relations. In Foucault's thesis the prison, rather than being seen as a remnant of pre-Enlightenment brutality, is part of a matrix of modern governmental social structures and, therefore, merely reproduces, with a little more emphasis, all the structures that are to be found in the social body.[5]

---

[3] David Garland, *Punishment and Modern Society: A Study in Social Theory* (Oxford: Clarendon Press, 1990), 211.

[4] Laura Piacentini and Judith Pallot, '"In Exile Imprisonment" in Russia', *The British Journal of Criminology*, 54.1 (2014), 20–37.

[5] Michel Foucault, *Discipline and Punish: The Birth of the Prison* (1977; trans. Alan Sheridan, London: Penguin/Peregrine Books, 1979).

In assembling and interpreting a new social history of punishment, Foucault's reading of history, and how it intersects with the discourse of power, has been met with much opposition. Writing in 1999, Willem Frijhoff argues that historians have responded in the past somewhat uneasily to the historical validity of Foucault's work, casting him at one time as an outcast. This is partly because Foucault challenged historians to introduce the principle of power onto bodies and into hospitals, prisons, clinics, asylums in order to cultivate new constructions of social life and, moreover, a new way of recording history, which had the effect of undermining conventional historical approaches as exclusionary and limiting.[6] Sociologists and philosophers have gone further in their criticisms. Fred Alford points out:

> My criticism of Foucault is not new. It has been made by a number of criminologists, who argue that Foucault mistakes the utopian discourse of prison reform for its practice. I repeat the criticism only to emphasize that Foucault is mistaken about more than the details of prison life. He has systematically mistaken an ideology for a practice. This affects not just his view of prison, but of power.[7]

Alford describes Foucault as missing the point insofar as his conceptualisation of the iconic, but not-realised, Panopticon, was not so much about discipline or finding big meanings in the smallest of symbols. Rather, the point of punishment in modern societies is to produce, through the form of incarceration, a spectacle or performance. That punishment is about saying rather than doing, about style rather than bureaucratic or instrumentalist tendencies,[8] is picked up and given shape by Phillip Smith who in commenting on Foucault's thesis, states: 'There remains no affect or passion, no symbolism and no culturally specified imperatives other than those relating to domination.'[9] In other words, what is missing from Foucault's analysis is punishment's capacity to express culture. Smith's position is 'radically anti-Foucauldian', instead developing a neo-Durkheimian approach to how punishment is styled and discussed in popular culture.[10]

[6] Willem Frijhoff, 'Foucault Reforms by Certeau: Historical Strategies of Discipline and Everyday Tactics of Appropriation', in John Neubauer (ed.), *Cultural History After Foucault* (New York: Walter De. Gruyter, Inc., 1999), 84.
[7] C. Fred Alford, 'What Would it Matter if Everything Foucault Said About Prison Were Wrong? *Discipline and Punish* After Twenty Years', *Theory and Society*, 29.1 (2000), 134.
[8] Ibid.
[9] Phillip Smith, *Punishment and Culture* (Chicago and London: The University of Chicago Press, 2008), 11.
[10] Ibid., 11–16. The historical-social and cultural development of punishment in Western jurisdictions is also discussed in Dario Melossi and Massimo Pavarini, *The Prison and the Factory: The Origins of the Penitentiary* (London: Macmillan, 1981); David Garland *Punishment and Welfare: A History of Penal Strategies* (Ashgate: Gower Publishing, 1987); David Downes, *Contrasts in Tolerance: Post-War Penal Policy in the Netherlands and in England and Wales*

Smith maps out a cultural terrain of punishment as an object of dread, of amusement and of fetishism and, importantly, marked by one important contingency – cultural accomplishment. This is a significant and fascinating sketch of punishment forms that provides clues as to how state punishment requires ridding society of the polluted in order to re-narrate to civil society how it *accomplishes* crime and civic control and, ultimately, purity. He adds: 'the building of a penitentiary system was generally acclaimed as a sign of progress for humanity'.[11] This invites us to explore the role of 'experience' and 'expression' in a framework of punishment in which habits of speech, gestures and feelings come to have influence on punitive activity and its modernisation, so defined. Foucault's modernity is one of classification, regulation, discipline and monitoring. Yet, in his concern with regulation, he overlooks the cultural representations of punishment as meaningful, styled and communicative and a response to sin, taboo, evil and profanity.

Over the last 15 years or so, Phillip Smith, David Garland and John Pratt have each separately analysed, with great depth and quality, the conditions of culture that have produced social meanings in penal spaces. Culture is not only a social product but it is integral to the social. Expressions of culture can be found in the forms punishment takes, from the guillotine, to the electric chair, to the Supermax, and each punishment form has its own symbolic logic and cultural expression. However, it must also be said that where prison sociologists have intended to show how culture can be explained, and hence interpreted, the tendency has been to isolate factors that may be co-variant with some cultural phenomenon.[12] And in this (limiting) understanding of culture – as that which is 'embedded' in penal control – the effect, argues Garland, has been to produce narrow terms for understanding penality. Testing and measuring culture in carceral settings is also fraught with epistemological difficulties when the theoretical status of culture is considered. As Roger Friedland and John Mohr identify: 'The implication is that the social is the domain of materiality, of hardness, thingness, objects and objectivity.'[13] Indeed, the kinds of intellectual problems that excite sociologists of the prison remain of the type where human relationships and power dynamics unfold in the 'thing' of the prison. A resultant problem then becomes how to utilise empirical work to measure and test for the presence of culture in prisons, where the commanding power of control can be fluid and hidden but also

---

(Oxford: Oxford University Press, 1993); Garland, *Punishment and Modern Society*; Michael Tonry, *Punishment and Politics – Evidence and Emulation in the Making of English Penal Policy* (Cullompton: Willan, 2004); John Pratt, *Punishment and Civilization: Penal Tolerance and Intolerance in Modern Society* (London: Sage Publications Limited, 2002).

[11]   Smith, *Punishment and Culture*, 113.

[12]   David Garland, 'A Culturalist Theory of Punishment?' [Book Review of Philip Smith *Punishment and Culture* (2008)], *Punishment and Society,* 11.2 (2009), 259–68.

[13]   Roger Friedland and John Mohr, 'The Cultural Turn in American Sociology', in Roger Friedland and John Mohr (eds), *Matters of Culture: Cultural Sociology in Practice* (Cambridge: Cambridge University Press, 2004), 6.

complexly coterminus with state discipline. Hence, there remains a quite fundamental split, a worrying 'either/or', in prison sociology between the social versus the cultural; as though social things are separate from interpretive cultural artefacts.[14] Consequently, there is still much intellectual work to be done on how, or indeed if, a culturalist account coheres with a Foucauldian power/knowledge theorisation.

The Russian prison case study offers new ways to understand penality and to break down the social versus cultural duopoly dominating prison sociology. As will be shown, a quite profound cultural process is happening when Russia punishes its convicted offenders and sends them to jail. The dense cultural meaning of exile does not stand in *opposition* to penal discipline but instead *combines* discipline with display, punishment with 'parade'. I would describe today's carceral punishment system in Russia as 'in exile imprisonment'. In Sewell's path-breaking thesis on culture and structure, this real cultural value and common-sense need are referred to as *cultural schema*, which can be understood as an analytical set of conventions present in a variety of institutions, spheres and discourses. Cultural schema are things we take for granted and are relatively unconscious.[15] Sonya Rose suggests:

> This formulation while appealing, because it seems to suggest that particular cultural forms endure because they are deep, in the end relies on circular reasoning. If a cultural form or practice endures, it is deep. It is deep because it is part of common sense and it is pervasive. It is part of common sense and pervasive because it is structured in a particular way.[16]

It is helpful to consider punishment in Russia as a cultural schema that uncovers a mentality and a wider belief system embodying two aspects of Russia-Soviet culture. First, 'in exile imprisonment' exists in *common sense* in the minds of Russian prisoners and the Russian publics at large. To internal appearances (at least) it is a straightforward response to crime. Second, it is *real* in the history of punishment because penal exile existed in the world of resource development (to populate Russia's far-off lands). The ways in which culture has been presented, indeed paraded, in Russian penal spaces throughout history is explored in the next part of this chapter, while the third part seeks to analyse and reflect on memory-making through the cultural schema of exile.

---

[14] Garland, 'A Culturalist Theory', 262.

[15] Sewell, 'The Concept (s) of Culture', 35–61.

[16] Sonya O. Rose, 'Cultural Analysis and Moral Discourse: Episodes, Continuities and Transformations', in V.E. Bonnell and C. Hunt (eds), *Beyond the Cultural Turn: New Directions in the Study of Society and Culture* (Berkeley and Los Angeles: University of California Press, 1999), 226.

A brief history of exile in Russian penal culture

A full appraisal of exile in Russia is beyond the scope of this chapter, but suffice it to say that it is a historical postulate that the cycles of purge, exile and confinement that occurred throughout Russian-Soviet history have constituted major challenges to advancing a fuller account of penal development up to the present day. It comes as no surprise, therefore, that criminologists and prison sociologists working in the field of Russian incarceration are few.

Moreover, it remains the case that whilst social historians and area studies specialists are now reconstructing prison scholarship to include in their analysis careful attention to values, sentiments and norms, the analysis does not incorporate a discussion of punishment in Russia as either a cultural artefact or a cultural form, embodying a sensibility that is quite exceptional in the history of penal systems.[17] To better understand the cultural schema of Russian prisons requires a careful understanding of how Russia comes to terms with its past, how the country internalises transformation and how things are remembered. In other words, how culture is defined and, hence, expressed. In its configuration, ideology, rules and laws, the traces of the past were targeted to move the penal system into a modern (if Western) form.[18] Yet, whilst there was reform of all the parts of the criminal justice apparatus from around 1991, certain traces or echoes were left behind, namely, the practice of 'in exile imprisonment'. The carceral punishment form of exile is not presented here solely as a legal response. Instead, it continues to produce a specific set of historical, *disciplinary mythologies and meanings* about penal ideology in twenty-first century Russia.

Prisoner exile has been used in Russia since the sixteenth century.[19] In the period up to the early eighteenth century, expulsion – exile (*ssylka*) and banishment (*izganie*) – were not so much punishments in and of themselves but the consequences of punishment, since the political and religious dissidents and criminals to which they were applied had already been tortured, mutilated and interned and subjected to 'civil death'.[20] Administrative changes meant

---

[17] See, for example, Steven A. Barnes, *Death and Redemption: The Gulag and the Shaping of Soviet Society* (Princeton: Princeton University Press, 2011) and Daniel Beer, 'Decembrists, Rebels and Martyrs in Siberian Exile: The "Zerentui Conspiracy" of 1828 and the Fashioning of a Revolutionary Genealogy', *Slavic Review*, 72.3 (2013), 528–51.

[18] See Bill Bowring and Valeriy Savitsky (eds), *Prava Cheloveka i Sude bniy Kontrol* [Human Rights and Judicial Review] (Moscow: Human Rights Publishers, 1996), and Laura Piacentini, *Surviving Russian Prisons: Punishment, Economy and Politics in Transition* (Cullompton: Willan Publishing Ltd, 2004).

[19] See Beer, 'Decembrists, Rebels, and Martyrs'; Andrew A. Gentes, 'Katorga: Penal Labour and Tsarist Russia', in Eva-Maria Stolberg (ed.), *The Siberian Saga: A History of Russia's Wild East* (Oxford: Peter Lang, 2005); Andrew A. Gentes, 'Vagabond and the Tsarist Siberian Exile System: Power and Resistance in the Penal Landscape System', *Central Asia Quarterly*, 30.3–4 (September–December 2011), 407–21; A. Solzhenitsyn, *The Gulag Archipelago, 1918–1956: An Experiment in Literary Investigation* (London: Harvill Press, 1976).

[20] See Piacentini and Pallot, '"In Exile Imprisonment" in Russia'.

that exile powers were granted to serf owners and village and civilian authorities in the mid-eighteenth century and over the 90-year period from 1807 to
1917 nearly one-and-a-half million subjects were forcibly removed to Siberia.[21]
The significance of this period is the normalisation of exiling large numbers
of Russian citizens. Not all of these exiles were criminals and according to
Gentes' study of vagabond culture and exile, most 'were simply unwilling to
engage in farming and therefore resorted to begging, prostitution and petty
thievery to survive'.[22] The exile of vagrants, *brodiagi*, accounted for the highest
cohort of exiles between the years 1827 and 1846 (30.4 per cent), although this
number dropped after serf emancipation at the end of the Crimean War.[23] The
vastness of Siberia as a sparsely populated but fertile land was a discourse that
ran through Russian culture centuries earlier. In effect, Russia came to possess
a penal colony in the form of Siberia – the country's Far East – and it is notable that this development occurred at the same time as Western Europe and
the United States were acting to eradicate vagrancy through other disciplinary
mechanisms including prisons. This is significant because it is the period that
marks the moment when a line can be drawn to distinguish between what we
now refer to as Western penality and Eastern European penality. Russia was
colonizing itself through exile and forced labour whilst Western Europe was
considering using confinement with restraint.

The various categories of exile created a ladder of punishments that were
applied inconsistently in Tsarist Russia due to a lack of sentencing guidelines, and which contributed, in part, to a later characterisation of exile as
'unreasonable and an anomaly'.[24] The *brodiagi* were not alone in this exile
persecution. The exile of the Decembrists (army officers who revolted against
the Tsarist regime in the nineteenth century and who were sent to Siberia
for 'exile-resettlement') in the early nineteenth century was also an iconic
example of exile. Some Decembrists were imprisoned as well as exiled and
once *katorga* (penal servitude/labour) was introduced, exiles were imprisoned.
We see here Russia moving, in part, towards Western penal methods such as
imprisonment. The Decembrist uprising illustrates how, through exile, the state
responded to challenges to its sovereign power, and the role of the autocrat in
promoting an extreme punitive response. In Tsarist Russia it was the aristocratic elite who faced expulsion and who brought with them to Siberia reform
plans and a commonly-held rights discourse. Hence, libraries, schools, hospitals and settlements, alongside hard labour, came to be established as a consequence of exile. Families joined the exiled Decembrists and their introduction

---

[21] Gentes, 'Vagabond and the Tsarist Siberian Exile System', 407–21.
[22] Ibid., 407. Gentes outlines how Russian vagrancy laws, like those in Western Europe and the
   United States, were sufficiently opaque to enable the persecution of a range of individuals who
   did not meet the strict criteria of homeless or deviant. The *brodiagi* – the vagrants – would be
   assigned to public works and labour when previously, they would have been assigned to military service.
[23] Gentes, 'Vagabondage and the Tsarist Siberian Exile System', 409.
[24] Ibid., 411.

of innovative agricultural techniques to Siberia earned them an iconic status that was shared by the wives of the exiled (the *Dekrabistki*). Today in Russia the archetypal good wife model is still the *Dekrabistki*.[25] It would appear that by the late nineteenth century, a cultural practice of follow-the-exile had been established. Exile volunteers, the *dobrovol'nye*, were the wives and families who 'voluntarily' followed their male convict relatives into exile.[26]

Furthermore, exile as a state response to so-called malevolence also produced additional complex responses from resistance to engagement, thus creating a kind of cultural spectacle of othering and an embedded social and penal response to criminality. In a fascinating ethnographic analysis of the pseudonyms used by exiles in the late nineteenth century, Sergei V. Maksimov claimed that exiles would adopt boastful names reflecting the Siberian landscape such as *Dubrovin* (Oak), *Brilliantov* (Gemstone), *Sokolov* (Falcon) and *Koronev* (Root).[27] Deeply institutionalised through this punishment form in one sense, the exile system can be simultaneously understood here as being almost culturally romantic and profound.

The Soviet era marked a turning point in Russia's penal culture. Cleansing the metropolitan centres of 'undesirable elements' was intended to assist the early Soviet regime in mobilising its power, funnelling resources to Siberia, and promoting cultural expansion of the Soviet utopia. Exile *as* punishment was used most notoriously in the mass deportations for the whole period from 1930 to Stalin's death in May 1953, including the deportation of kulaks during the collectivization drive, the 'mass operations' in 1937–8, and the deportation of ethnic groups and 'criminals' in the 1930s and 1940s.[28] In Tsarist Russia, penal exile occurred primarily as a by-product of a badly administered and chaotic penal system, but in Soviet Russia exile was a mainstream – indeed primary – mode of punishment. The distinction between exile and imprisonment in the USSR also flows through Solzhenitsyn's *Gulag Archipelago*; the introduction of *katorga*, for Solzhenitsyn, degraded the Imperial Russian system of exile. The best of the recent scholarship has gone a long way towards deconstructing the boundary between exile and imprisonment. We now understand that camp inmates who earned non-convoy status could spend long periods outside the confines of the camp, whilst the degree of power-and-control exercised over their lives meant exiles shared many of the experiences of the camps.[29] In his analysis of the Gulag in Kazakhstan,

[25] See David Saunders, *Russia in the Age of Reaction and Reform, 1801–1881* (Routledge: Longman Publishing, 1992); Piacentini and Pallot '"In Exile Imprisonment" in Russia', 30–3.

[26] Gentes, 'Vagabondage and the Tsarist Siberian Exile System', 423.

[27] Maksimov cited in Vladimir Doroshevich, *Russia's Penal Colony in the Far East: A Translation of Vlad Doroshevich's 'Sakhalin'* (trans. Andrew A. Gentes, New York: Anthem Press, 2009), 446.

[28] Gentes, 'Katorga'; Beer, 'Decembrists, Rebels, and Martyrs', 528–51.

[29] For an excellent review of research on special settlements, see O. Klimkova, 'Special Settlements in Soviet Russia in the 1930s-50s', *Kritika*, 8.1 (2007), 105–39. For a discussion of non-convoy prisoners, see W.T. Bell, 'Was the Gulag an Archipelago? An Examination of De-convoyed

Steven Barnes treats camps, colonies, prisons and internal exile as a single punishment system, whilst for Kate Brown evidence in Gulag histories of the merging of camps and special settlements reinforces her view of the USSR as made up of a spectrum of incarcerated space.[30] All these works make clear that the treatment of people expelled to the peripheries did not necessarily map neatly onto their legal status, and vice versa.

By the 1950s, exile had become normalised as a legal category of imprisonment. When fused with the mythic landscape of Russia, particularly during Stalinism, it was revealed as iconic and dominant. According to Gentes (2011) embodying the exile experience is the modification of the self into new places. Yet, there is staticity in exile in that once the destination is reached the prospect of return seems overwhelming and improbable. Exile, is, therefore, a liminal space of leaving and becoming. Or more precisely, 'in exile imprisonment' marks a rebirth of one's identity as s/he develops a sense of connectedness to a new land following fluid, fractured and frail coerced mobilisation. As a cultural schema, 'in exile imprisonment' articulates the boundaries of tolerance of deviancy and produces an exceptional cultural memory ingrained in the national psyche. In Gulag testimonies, there are thick descriptions of 'night blindness' in prison ships, and how the 'purplish hills' called to mind the giant roofless prison of penal exile.[31] Soviet dissidents from the 1980s talk about exile across Russia as 'moving with the breeze', the 'brilliance of the stars' seen through transportation to colonies and re-creating traffic noises in their heads to make associations with home. Solzhenitsyn writes of how he came to loathe forests.[32]

As exile became one of the main repertoires of penal discipline in Russia, so too is it the case that the place of exile becomes an environment of torment and we see this in today's testimonials from women prisoners, which are discussed towards the end of the chapter. Coupled with resource development, which was insistently pursued in the criminal justice sphere, 'in exile imprisonment' was not only a particular style of punishment, but also, a particular style of *moral-nationalism*. Criminals were wreckers and contaminators of the Soviet utopia. If imprisonment served the purpose of political correction, ultimately ideological perfection would follow. Penality, therefore, did not solely function to promote discipline. In expanding the ideological parameters of what constituted criminality, the regime could create the capacity for

Prisoners in Western Siberia', paper presented at the Conference on the History and Legacy of the Gulag, Harvard University, 2–5 November 2006.
[30] Steven A. Barnes, *Death and Redemption: The Gulag and the Shaping of Soviet Society* (Princeton: Princeton University Press, 2011); Kate Brown, 'Out of Solitary Confinement: History of the Gulag', *Kritika*, 8.1 (2007), 67–103. Nick Baron also emphasises the Gulag's spatiality in his exploration of the Gulag, see Nick Baron, *Soviet Karelia* (New York: Routledge, 2007).
[31] Nataliya Ginzburg, *Into the Whirlwind* (San Diego: Harcourt, 1967).
[32] Aleksandr Solzhenitsyn, *The Gulag Archipelago, 1918–1956: An Experiment in Literary Investigation*, Vols I–III (Glasgow: Harvill Collins, 1974).

resource expansion and economic development by exiling so-called criminals to the frontiers not yet reached. The evolution and trajectory of penal norms was cyclical but the framework remained the same: exile linked to a particular theory of the social and geographical structure of Russia and, therefore, social change that linked cultural ideals to penal institutional development in a sometimes systematic way and placed, at the centre, a very distinctive tradition of social thought that was sometimes Tsarist, sometimes Marxist and later Stalinist. Gentes posits that in perpetuating the Tsarist penal exile system, '[the] Bolsheviks merely perfected the teachings of their predecessors for their own ends. Contemporary Russia's treatment of its convicts suggests the lingering influence of this ancient and destructive catechism'.[33] Thus, through metaphors of territorial border and periphery, a prisoner's identity, as an offender of Soviet ideals, came to be formed as they were absorbed fully into new sites and lands.[34]

'In exile imprisonment' became embedded in the conventional penal apparatus that remained after the dismantling of the Gulag despite periods of reform such as under Nikita Khrushchev.[35] Prisoners in Russia lived and worked (and indeed many died) under a giant universe of ideas about culture, crime and political expansion so that, by the 1980s, rehabilitation (political correction) and repression co-existed as the inevitable outcomes of Russia's culture of punishment. Exile was another cultural category that ran through all of Soviet-Russian life in its entirety.[36] So in the 1930s, we see the criminologist F.P. Miliutin establish the principle that serious offenders should not be confined in the 'home provinces' or those with a clement climate, but should be shipped east where the climate itself 'will assist in hastening re-education'.[37] This principle was reasserted in 1961 when strict regime colonies were statutorily required to be located far from population centres.[38] And the same is true today with the exemption of prisoners sentenced to special and strict regimes colonies (and of women also) from the provision in the criminal correction code that convicted offenders should be imprisoned in their own

---

[33] Stolberg, *The Siberian Saga*, 84.

[34] See Edith W. Clowes, *Russia on the Edge: Imagined Geographies and Post-Soviet Identity* (Ithaca and London: Cornell University Press, 2011).

[35] Miriam Dobson, *Khrushchev's Cold Summer: Gulag Returnees, Crime, and the Fate of Reform after Stalin* (Ithaca and London: Cornell University Press, 2009); Jeffrey S. Hardy, 'A Camp is not a Resort: The Campaign against Privileges in the Soviet Gulag, 1957–1961', *Kritika*, 13.1 (2012), 89–122.

[36] One of the more celebrated exiles was Nobel Prize winner, Andrei Sakharov, who was sent into internal exile in Gorky, 250 miles east of Moscow, for his opposition to the Soviet invasion of Afghanistan. Another exile, but this time abroad, was Aleksandr Solzhenitsyn, expelled from the USSR in 1974. Apart from such high profile political oppositionists, criminal offenders could be excluded from major cities after their release or debarred from large metropolitan centres as punishment.

[37] See Piacentini and Pallot, '"In Exile Imprisonment" in Russia', 28.

[38] Hardy, '"The Camp is not a Resort"'.

region (*oblast*).[39] By the 1990s, prisoners were still corralled onto trains and prison trucks (*avotzeki*) so that once exiled, they became the relentless symbols of how the 'imprisoned body' generated more socialism, more economic advancements through forced labour, better alignment to culture, stronger political allegiance – all of which contributed to a cultural, political and economic utopia.[40]

In summary, Russia has used an elaborate and complex system of exile for centuries to create a unique and exceptional penal landscape that extended across the country. Exile of prisoners in Russia had a communicative power, and was folded into a structural design that ensured that the Soviet regime's message was unequivocal: that at the centre of the Soviet Union's ideology was an incontestable collective conscience and national identity. From urban centres, to the peripheries, regardless of climate and extremity, the regime created penal place, penal culture and penal purpose.

Exile today

There are numerous traces of exile that have passed down through Russian culture, including the prison chansons which equate imprisonment to exile linguistically, and the use of the vocabulary of exile to refer to contemporary prison infrastructure: *etap* (or group of prisoners being transported) and *etapirovanie* (or the process of being transported) were the names given in the seventeenth century to the marching of prisoners to exile and the overnight stopping points. Transit prisons in Russia are also described today as *peressylnie tyurmi* ('prisons on the exile route') and the phrase '*mesta ne stol' ordalennie*' – a place not so very far away – is used in its literal translation to describe anything with a lock on it from the lavatory to a prison (the actual phrase was used in law to distinguish places of exile in West Siberia from those in East Siberia and the Far East). Furthermore, whilst popular poems are sung, like *Milenka ty moi*, about a Siberian exile leaving his Siberian lover for his wife in European Russia, the Decembrist trope – *Dekabristki* – is also used to describe the relatives of prisoners from the nineteenth century right up to the present day.

The geography of modern Russian exile imprisonment provides a further example of how the traces of the country's exile history resonate in the present. As was the case in the Soviet period, the *donor* regions, characterised by substantial urban metropolitan populations, hold the majority of remand prisons and the fewest penal colonies, while the *recipient* regions to the East and North, where the general population is more sparsely populated, contain the most prisoners.[41] Prisoners are exported from Russia's European centre to

---

[39] Piacentini and Pallot, '"In Exile Imprisonment" in Russia'.

[40] See Barnes, *Death and Redemption*.

[41] See Judith Pallot and Laura Piacentini *Gender, Geography and Punishment: The Experience of Women in Carceral Russia* (Oxford: Oxford University Press, 2012), 57.

the east and to the north. Moscow exports prisoners to other parts of Russia from its ten remand prisons (Moscow city has just one small correctional colony located on the city's edge which is 'reserved' for prisoners 'with connections'). Komi Republic, on the other hand, is in the far north and is one of the original islands of the Gulag. It has 33 correctional colonies and three remand prisons. The consequence of this for prisoners is the realistic probability of transportation to a remote place with the probability increasing with the severity of the sentence.

The prison service does not publish statistics on the distances that prisoners are sent from their place of arrest or home when they are incarcerated in their home *oblast* but what is known is that just 15–20 per cent of prisoners of all categories serve their sentences in their home *raion* (or county).[42] Even if imprisoned in their home region, the distances that prisoners are transported can be considerable, especially in the Urals, the North and Siberia where regions can be equivalent in area to a whole country in Europe. There are other factors that distinguish certain groups of prisoners and it is important to note that these differences do have a determining effect on where prisoners are sent. For example, there is a critical difference in where sentences are served between male and female prisons. The law in Russia states that prisoners should serve their sentences in their home region, which suggests that, officially, there is an awareness that sending prisoners 'out of region' can produce many different types of exclusions. Yet, there are exceptions for women and juveniles as well as men serving life sentences in prisons, and those suffering from infectious diseases like tuberculosis. This reflects the fact that there are fewer colonies for each of these groups.

Moreover, such categorisation of minority groups, and the impact on sentencing to the peripheries, reveals Russian penality's communicative power: that in being 'sent away', the distance travelled is read as exile for prisoners. The following is a statement from a prisoner's relative returning from a visit to the large penal complex that houses 14,000 prisoners in the heart of the Mordovian forest in 2004 and is a further example of the traces of Russia's exile past:[43]

> to get to Leplei is another 25 'taiga' [that is through the coniferous forest] kilometres … There is nothing but colonies. If you are going there for the

---

[42] These figures are extracted from the census of prisoners conducted under the auspices of the Federal Penal Service and are taken from Valerii I. Seliverstov (ed.), *Osuzhdennye po materialam spetsial'noi perepisi osuzhdennykh i lits, soderzhashchikhsia pod strazhei 12–19th noiabria 2009 g* [Prisoners According to the Special Census of People under Detention on 12–19 November 2009], vols 1–9 (Moscow: Iurisprudentsiia, 2009). For the distribution of different categories of penal facilities, see 'Mapping the Gulags', www.gulagmaps.org, specifically series 5 and 6.

[43] This was posted on a now defunct ARESTANT website that supported prisoners' relatives. This site and various examples of the postings are discussed in Judith Pallot, '"Gde muzh, tam zhena" ["Where the Husband Is, So Is the Wife"], Space and Gender in Post-Soviet Patterns of Penality', *Environment and Planning, A*, 39 (2007), 570–89.

first time, I advise you to prepare yourself; the place is, of course, creepy. Have a read of Solzhenitsyn's *Gulag Archipelago*. It's just the same today. Nothing has changed.[44]

Prisoners' talk today contains many, mostly unconscious, references to exile. The following is from a woman serving a 12-year sentence when interviewed in 2010, responding to a question about distance:

> It's just that it's emotionally easier if you are in prison in a familiar place. You know, they bring transports with women who don't even know where [this town] is. We have women here from A– and B–. They can't even imagine where they are and what sort of place this is. They know it's somewhere way up in the north, but they have no idea of where precisely. Yes, for them, it is very difficult, they don't understand anything, and it's as if they've arrived in a foreign country … they think they are in a strange land.[45]

Interviews with prisoners conducted for an earlier ESRC project confirm that sending them 'out of region' has historical and penological meanings. Some interviewees, without prompting, translated their imprisonment as exile. The time taken on the transportations (*etap*) that can take circuitous routes and involve the suspension of all communication with home creates in prisoners a sense of estrangement that underlines their physical separation from all that is familiar. It also creates an impaired sense of geography. Prisoners talk about arriving at the 'edge of the world'.[46] As was the case during the Stalinist period, a large number of penal colonies are simply inaccessible. In her work on prisoners in India who were expelled by the British Empire to the Andamans, Clare Anderson outlines the fear, confusion and isolation that were acutely felt in the process of exile.[47] The attribute of expulsion was particularly evident from the Russian interviews conducted in 2010. One prisoner told us:

> I don't know how to explain it; it's just that you are taken out of society and transplanted to who-knows-where. I deserve it, though three years would be enough. Throughout my sentence I've had one foot here and the other – there. In other words, I don't actually 'live' here.

---

[44] The research is drawn from the ESRC study referred to earlier ('Women in the Russian Penal System'). The research included 119 interviews conducted by three different research teams between 2006 and 2010. In addition, 30 interviews with juvenile young women offenders were conducted in 2007.

[45] Interviewee who participated in the ESRC study 'Women in the Russian Penal System'.

[46] Pallot, '"Gde muzh, tam zhena"', 576.

[47] Clare Anderson, *Convicts in the Indian Ocean: Transportation from South Asia to Mauritius 1815–53* (Basingstoke: Macmillan, 2000).

Further evidence of the normalization of understanding imprisonment as exile
is the self- and societal representations of prisoners' relatives as *Dekabristki*,
the symbol of the good wife, but also a potent and enduring symbol of penal
culture. In the twenty-first century, the Decembrist trope has crossed the class
and family status divide, so that it is used as an appellation by anyone who
has a relative in prison:

> It seems to me there is no difference [between us and the Decembrist
> wives] … it's possible to say that because the wives of the Decembrists –
> they followed them to Siberia, into the cold wastes. And we, in essence,
> are tied by the same chains … we can be compared yes.[48]
>
> I will do what I want, let them say what they want … We are indeed
> wives – *Dekabristki* – where the husband goes so does the wife.[49]
>
> There is some truth in it [the Decembrist appellation]. Yes, many leave
> everything behind but I will say of myself, I won't go.[50]

These excerpts from the families of prisoners in the twenty-first century echo
the observation made by Evgenia Ginzburg nearly 80 years earlier when
she was sent as a prisoner to Kolyma in the 1930s: 'I always thought the
Decembrists endured the most frightful sufferings, but listen to this: "of the
wondrous built so firm, so fast the carriage" … they ought to have tried one
of Stolypin's coaches'.[51]

In all the extracts above, the point is not how the historical stereotype is
being used, but that it is used at all to describe twenty-first century imprisonment. Olga Romanova, the wife of a financier held in Butyrka in St Petersburg,
affirms that the need to travel great distances as a demonstration of wifely
duty, defines the modern-day Decembrist wife:

> And when you without thinking fill bags with food and trudge through
> the snow field to prison or camp – is that not a Dekabristka, and is it not
> a heroic feat? And here I think; for me to get to the prison is ten minutes
> on the metro but women come from the auls, leave children at stations,
> almost don't speak Russian, know nothing and don't understand but
> make their way to this Devil's prison and try there, by hook or by crook,
> to find out anything about husbands but all of them are interrogated,
> humiliated – go and talk to them about extraordinary love and a high
> sense of duty.[52]

48 Interview with a prisoner's wife, 2010, Mordovia Russia.
49 'Всё о жизни в тюрьме (Everything you need to know about life in prisons)', accessed 25 July
2013, http://forumtyurem.net/lofiversion/index.php/t86-100.html.
50 Interview with Olga, prisoner's daughter, Mordovia, 2010.
51 Ginzburg, *Into the Whirlwind*, 205.
52 *Novaya Gazeta*, accessed 25 July 2012, www.novayagazeta.ru/data/2011/044/00.html?print=
201103070927.

When prisoners talk about being sent 'to another country' or to *katorga*, or that women from the Far North are 'in exile' in colonies to the south, or when prisoners' relatives compare their experiences with those of the *Dekabristki*, they are translating punishment as exile through historicising penal processes. Indeed one of the members of Pussy Riot, Maria Alyekhina, says of her period of imprisonment in a Perm penal colony in the Urals region:

> The transit was difficult. I got to see several cities before I got here. But this prison ... Shalamov was exiled here. It's as if this place keeps some kind of memories ... But I dislike the methods. I don't like that human rights here are a phrase used on a par with something like 'toilet mop'. That's what I don't like.[53]

In summary, in Russia, there is a sense of abject displacement inscribed in the penal experience because, like the exile, many prisoners simply do not know where they are going. Returning to Sewell's *cultural schema*, remembrances are incomplete but do, nonetheless, produce 'fictions' that enable memories to survive, endure and, importantly, to have an everlasting presence. For prisoners, because these remembrances are memories of historical events that they did not experience, but learnt about, they form a circular reasoning. The memories are still alive and are therefore contemporary traces of a distant past that have continued significance amongst ordinary people. In online forums, prisoner families discussed being sent thousands of miles 'as not so far away'. Indeed one visitor to the online prisoner websites stated in response to a question about where a prisoner was going: 'it's best not to find out where'.[54]

In conclusion, the theorisation of penal culture in Russia as rooted in exile reveals something else about Russia's cultural attachment to punishment. In recent years, the Russian government has shown inertia on the issue of penal exile, which has thrived as an institutional form, and as a cultural practice, because it articulates a specific political and social message and is associated with the exclusion of dissent. 'In exile imprisonment' reinforces a moral nationalism that intensifies a disciplinary myth that dissent requires expulsion. In the Putin era, there are ongoing political struggles between activists, human rights groups and international monitors; thus, the power of the prison to affirm state values has never been as potent as it is now. To internal audiences, the disproportionate sentences handed down in recent high-profile cases in Russia (Mikhael Khodorkovsky (2004, 2008), Pussy Riot (2012) and

---

[53] Varlam Shalamov was the famous Russian writer, poet and Gulag survivor whose *Kolyma Tales* of life in Soviet forced labour camps is considered to be one of the great Russian collections of short stories of the twentieth century. See the Official Free Pussy Riot Online Campaigning website, accessed November 2013, http://web.archive.org/web/20140326172138/http://freepussyriot.org/content/translations-interviews-masha-and-nadia-january-2013.
[54] 'Колонии России ГУФСИН Пермского края (Penal Colonies of Russia: Perm Region)', accessed November 2013, www.uznik.info/guin-perm.php.

the Arctic 30 Greenpeace Group (2013)) are presented as the cultural accomplishments of a regime insistently pursuing re-invigorated nationalism.[55] That this *parading of punishment* is now at its most visible in Russia is particularly ironic when one considers that for centuries Russia's culture of carceralism was hidden and excessive. Yet, imprisonment in Russia has always served the purpose of connecting 'the people' with the advancing interests of the state. Hence, in translating Russian's penal culture, it is in exile where we find the gestures and meanings and also the cultural, historical and criminological associations and experiences. The ways in which 'in exile imprisonment' is read today are contingent and problematic, and leave traces on today's penal culture where it continues to be conventionally understood as a normal penal practice even though it is no longer a legal sanction.

Where the subject of exile makes a contribution to the prison sociology field more generally is in how exile and imprisonment share common features (rupture, connection, estrangement, a necessary othering and a connection to power and social capital). Yet both are studied as two concepts that have distinguishable characteristics.[56] Exile is a mobile exclusion, a process of moving backwards and forwards, whilst imprisonment is a fixed exclusion. Thus, both imprisonment and exile share dialectical forms, yet they continue to be understood, as Foucault asserts in *A History of Madness* (2006), as moving apart.[57] So too can imprisonment seem like an endless journey towards a form of intended purification.[58] Exclusion is one way of distinguishing between the pure and the contaminated and of symbolically performing a cleansing function and simultaneously reassuring the (allegedly) righteous.

In *The Culture of Control* Garland argues that imprisonment as a subject of sociological inquiry is full of historical ironies.[59] Pain, pleasure, vengeance and reform have become both normalised discourse and mobilised into prisons with effects on social values about crime and appropriate punishments, but, importantly, mediated by the political classes. Whilst Gready likens exile to a prison without borders, exile *to* a prison redefines the contours of confinement to include dimensions of landscape and place.[60] The prison, to

---

[55] In December 2013 all of the above individuals listed were released from prison penal colonies under a Christmas Amnesty.

[56] F. Egon Kinz, 'Exile and Re-settlement: Refugee Theory', *International Migration Review,* 15.1/2 (spring – summer, 1981), 42–51; Jorge Barudy, 'A Programme of Mental Health for Political Refugees: Dealing with the Invisible Pain of Political Exile', *Social Science and Medicine,* 28.7 (1989), 715–27; Stephen Castles and Alistair Davidson, *Citizenship and Migration: Globalization and the Politics of Belonging* (New York: Routledge, 2004); Sofia A. McClennen, *The Dialetics of Exile: Nation, Time, Language, and Space in Hispanic Literatures* (West Lafayette: Purdue University Press, 2004)

[57] Michel Foucault, *A History of Madness* (New York: Routledge, 2004), 12.

[58] See Smith, *Punishment and Culture.*

[59] David Garland, *The Culture of Control: Crime and Social Order in Contemporary Society* (Oxford and New York: Oxford University Press, 2001).

[60] Paul Gready, *Writing as Resistance: Life Stories of Imprisonment, Exile and Homecoming from Apartheid South Africa* (Maryland: Lexington Books, 2003).

paraphrase Crewe, becomes a distinctive social destination and punishment place when exile is considered.[61] A further point is that prison sociology scholarship reveals that imprisonment is acutely painful, its 'innards obscured' but with specific non-obscured public effects.[62] If a society of prisoner exiles is then considered the practice of exile as a political or cultural corrective, a territorial strategy of social control and a technique of political power, it can be understood as a distinctive pain of imprisonment. Thus, if exiles become the subject of a distinctive form of politics, then the imprisoned exile may require a new terminology or conceptual framework to understand more fully the interconnections between exile, culture and confinement. If such a framework were to be considered in the context of Russia, Foucault's disciplined bodies of punishment meet and mesh with historical cultural tropes to create the *disciplinary mythologies and meanings* referred to in the introduction. There is disciplinary intervention but there are also embodied traditions.

Does 'in exile imprisonment' imply there can be no return? Or does it imply that where there is physical return, a former prisoner's identity is bound up in geographical displacement and so-called civil death? In that case exile has something in common with an indeterminate sentence or life without parole. Indeed very long sentences may be experienced as permanent exile by some prisoners as the date of release is so far into the future as to be unimaginable, while the revolving door of short sentence recidivists may be experienced as a different form of exclusion. The obvious question for the study of imprisonment in Russia, where prisoner exile really embodies a whole history, culture and political sensibility, is what are its effects on today's culture of punishment? It is instructive to respond to this question with a comment on the Pussy Riot case. The unfolding internal and external debate about the jailed artists being 'sent to labour camps'[63] and 'shipped off to faraway prison camps'[64] has pushed Russia's still-hidden penal system onto a world stage where a specific pre-Soviet and Soviet penal norm and practice is shown to have a distinctively modern face: the prison exile. The treatment of the women of Pussy Riot was not unusual for Russia – since exile remained in the criminal justice code as a category of punishment until as recently as 1993 – yet, the influence of this cultural practice of exile lingers and remains a problematic term and concept for penal policy-makers in Russia today.

[61] Ben Crewe, *The Prisoner Society: Power, Adaptation and Social Life in an English Prison* (Oxford: Oxford University Press, 2009).

[62] Ibid., 1.

[63] Amnesty International's Summer Action Campaign 2013, accessed June 2013, http://action.amnesty.org.uk/ea-action/action?ea.client.id=1194&ea.campaign.id=16482&utm_source=aiuk&utm_medium=Homepage&utm_campaign=IAR&utm_content=PR_nib.

[64] 'Pussy Riot's Yekaterina Samutsevich Speaks Out,' *The Daily Beast*, accessed 12 May 2013, http://www.thedailybeast.com/articles/2012/11/30/pussy-riot-s-yekaterina-samutsevich-speaks-out.html.

9 "A perfect hell of misery"

Real and imagined prison lives in an "American Siberia"

Vivien Miller

In 1891 *The American Siberia: Fourteen Years' Experience in a Southern Convict Camp* by J.C. Powell, who identified himself as "Captain of the Florida Convict Camp," was published by H.J. Smith & Company of Chicago. Powell's memoir detailed the terrible conditions of life and labour endured by convicts in Florida from 1876 to 1890 as convict leasing became the principal penal arrangement for both state (felon) and county (misdemeanant) prisoners.[1] Even though Powell's "frank recital" was not wholly accurate, and separating the faithful from the rhetorical and embellished descriptions is not straightforward, it provides a rare first-hand detailed account of an emerging leasing system.[2] Powell's memoir also contained some explicit comparisons between conditions in late nineteenth-century Florida convict camps and Russo-Siberian cellhouses that were garnered from a series of essays by George Kennan, published in *Century Magazine*, and Kennan's two-volume *Siberia and the Exile System*, also published in 1891. Despite Kennan's more nuanced portrait, to many late nineteenth-century Americans, "Siberia" was both a place and a metaphor for particularly degrading and brutal punishments (including the chaining of inmates to wheelbarrows), sanctioned by a despotic imperial regime whereby state criminals were practically enslaved, compelled to labour in unsafe underground mines and struggled constantly against unremitting hardship and misery.[3] The appropriation of "Siberia" to denounce southern, and in this case, Florida, prison conditions and the mistreatment of prisoners could offer powerfully emotive ammunition for critics of specific state systems

---

[1] Originally published by H.J. Smith & Company in 1891, the following citations are from a later reprint: J.C. Powell, *The American Siberia or Fourteen Years' Experience in a Southern Convict Camp* (Chicago: W.B. Conkey Company, 1893).

[2] Powell, *American Siberia*, 355. A later exposé by former Florida convict guard "E.G.B." was published as "White Slavery in Florida," (*NY) Evening Post*, 12 February 1898.

[3] George Kennan, *Siberia and the Exile System*, Vol. 2 (Forgotten Books, 2012; London: James R. Osgood, McIlvaine & Co., 1891), 178. See also Fyodor Dostoyevsky, *The House of the Dead or Prison Life in Siberia* (London: J. M. Dent & Sons, Ltd., 1911). "American Siberia" was also used as a descriptor for northern states such as Minnesota, and in relation to a short-lived plan to make Alaska (recently acquired by the United States from Russia) into a penal colony. See Edmund Noble, "Peonage in the South," Arlington *Independent*, 9 July 1903, 1616–18.

and southern penal practices generally. *American Siberia* was a powerful political tract for anti-convict leasing campaigners in the late nineteenth- and early twentieth-century United States and has influenced studies of Florida leasing and post-Civil War southern punishments.[4]

This chapter provides a brief overview of Kennan's critique of prison conditions in late nineteenth-century Siberia, examines the nascent leasing system in Florida in the 1870s and 1880s described by Powell – of vermin-infested convicts in communal barracks, clad in distinct uniforms and leg irons, and guarded by armed "Cracker" or rural poor white guards – and considers the rhetorical linking of the two, and the ways in which borrowed ideas, images and forms framed real and imagined penal experiences. There were of course numerous differences between the two exposés, not least because Kennan was an external observer of a foreign carceral system while Powell was employed in a domestic state system and had been directly responsible for the disciplining and punishment of state prisoners. Kennan's tone was frequently of outrage and condemnation while Powell's was critical but often defensive, particularly in relation to his own conduct.

An American in Siberia

Kennan's observations on the Siberian penal system were based on first-hand research carried out over a sixteen-month period in 1885 and 1886 with Boston artist George A. Frost.[5] Kennan's earlier writings on Siberia had countered US views that it was an unproductive, semi-civilised and backward arctic wasteland, but this fourth expedition from European Russia to Eastern Siberia was undertaken specifically to provide "a truthful description of the country, the prisons and the mines" that housed political exiles and common criminals.[6] Kennan was particularly keen to understand the system of exile

---

[4] For example, Blake McKelvey, "Penal Slavery and Southern Reconstruction," *Journal of Negro History* 20.2 (1935), 159: Christopher R. Adamson: "Punishment After Slavery: Southern State Penal Systems, 1865–1890," *Social Problems* 30.5 (1983), 555–69; Jeffrey A. Drobney, "'Where Palm and Pine Are Blowing': Convict Labor in the North Florida Turpentine Industry, 1877–1923," *Florida Historical Quarterly* 72.4 (1994), 414–15; Matthew J. Mancini, *One Dies, Get Another: Convict Leasing in the American South, 1866–1928* (Columbia: University of South Carolina Press, 1996), 33, 186, 193; Paul Ortiz, *Emancipation Betrayed: The Hidden History of Black Organizing and White Violence in Florida from Reconstruction to the Bloody Election of 1920* (Berkeley: University of California Press, 2005), 53, 266, n.135.

[5] Kennan, *Siberia and the Exile System*, 2: 429.

[6] George Kennan, *Siberia and the Exile System* Vol. 1 (2012; New York: The Century Co. 1891), 2. Following the publication of *Tent Life in Siberia* in 1868, respected journalist and writer George Kennan had become a US expert on the Russian Empire but was criticised for his benign portraits of Imperial Russia, particularly of the exile system. See for example, George Kennan, "Siberia, The Exile's Abode," *Journal of the American Geographical Society of New York* 14 (1882), 13–68. What Kennan witnessed first-hand during the 1885 trip to Siberia led to a complete change of his views on political exile and imperial mistreatment of prisoners, but he was also deeply influenced by Siberian patriot and exile critic, Nicholas Mikhailovich Iadrintsev. Kennan's articles in *Century Magazine* and his two-volume study

and to meet with political exiles, including those denounced by Russian authorities as "nihilists."[7] Thus, Kennan and Frost followed the usual exile route through Moscow, the temporary annual market and fair-city of Nízhni Novgorod, the cultural and commercial centre of Ekaterínburg, and Tiumén which contained "the most important exile forwarding prison in Siberia" along with the *Prikáz o Sílnikh* or Chief Bureau of Exile Administration, and on to settlements such as Ulbínsk and Ust Kamenogorsk.[8]

They visited a range of penal establishments during the 5,000-mile journey, including city and forwarding prisons, prison mines and *etapes* (exile station-houses for the shelter of travelling parties of exiles and convicts at night).[9] Common features were elevated sleeping benches or *nári* without any bedding, overcrowded and vermin-infested *kámeras* (communal cells) with large wooden overflowing *paráshas* (excrement buckets), and rundown structures. Crowds of prisoners in leg-fetters and wearing grey coats with diamond-shaped patches of black or yellow cloth sewn on the back were guarded by armed Cossacks.[10] At Tiumén, Kennan recalled, "The air in the corridors and cells, particularly in the second story, was indescribably and unimaginably foul .... fetid odors from diseased human lungs and unclean human bodies, and the stench arising from unemptied excrement buckets at the ends of the corridors" was intolerable and extended also to the hospital wards – which Kennan later referred to as a "perfect hell of misery." Along with the annual autumn epidemics of typhus fever, typhoid, acute bronchitis and rheumatism, scurvy and syphilis were common complaints.[11]

By 1889, up to 13,000 persons journeyed into Siberian exile every year, as *Kátorzhniki* or hard labour convicts; *Poselentsi* or penal colonists; *Sílni* or persons simply banished; and *Dobrovolni* or women and children that voluntarily accompanied their exiled husbands or parents. Political offenders were to be found in each category.[12] Kennan also offered a remarkably compassionate portrait of the political exiles as generally honourable, intelligent and cultured people eager to discuss US literature, institutions and history.[13] As their expedition continued eastward to the Trans-Baikal mining district,

---

of the exile system had a profound effect on American public opinion. See Helen Hundley, "George Kennan and the Russian Empire: How America's Conscience Became an Enemy of Tsarism," *Kennan Institute Occasional Papers* 277 (2000), International Relations and Security Network, accessed 30 November 2013, www.isn.ethz.ch/Digital-Library/Publications/Detail/?lng=en&id=18782.

[7] Kennan, *Siberia and the Exile System,* 1: 75, 76, 258, 328; 2: 21, 25, 29–31, 128–9, 206.

[8] Ibid., 1: 6, 19, 31, 35, 49, 52, 71, 83, 251; 2: 357–8.

[9] Ibid., 1: 69; 2: 37. I have retained Kennan's Russian spellings throughout this chapter.

[10] Ibid., 2: 296, 350.

[11] Ibid., 1: 84–97; 2: 121–4.

[12] Ibid., 1: 79, 81, 82, 458–9. Vagrants comprised another group of offenders sent to Siberia as punishment. All felons were deprived of all civil rights, forfeited all their property and were to sever all family relations, unless their family voluntarily accompanied them into exile.

[13] Ibid., 1: 185–6, 189; 2: 129.

Kennan and Frost found several state criminals chained to wheelbarrows among the 1,800 hard labour convicts assigned to the chain of seven prisons, gold mines and convict settlements that stretched along the Kara River for some twenty miles.[14] Similarly harrowing conditions were found in prisons at the Nérchinsk silver-mining district.[15] However, Kennan concluded that the "worst feature of penal servitude in Siberia" was the condition of the prisons rather than "hard labor in the mines."[16]

Kennan countered the views of his critics that US prisons were as forbidding as those he had encountered in Siberia by declaring that "when an American says that [US prisons] are as bad as the Tiumen forwarding prison, he does not know, or does not appreciate, the state of affairs in the latter."[17] Drawing heavily on George Washington Cable's recent exposé of convict leasing in ten US states, Kennan made explicit reference to southern practices to show that while morality rates in Mississippi, Louisiana, North Carolina and Tennessee were "shocking and shameful," they compared somewhat favourably to that of Tiumén's 44.1 per cent in 1879 (against 11.5 per cent in North Carolina that same year).[18] Yet, mortality rates for southern convict leasing systems could be just as high; for example, 45 per cent for the railroad construction gangs in South Carolina in the period 1877–1880.[19]

Convict leasing was a penal system associated with the post-Civil War US southern states, in which a predominately black chained convict labour force (some of whom were attached to fifty-pound iron balls) was effectively enslaved by private contractors in a vicious and degrading system. The leasing of convicts to private railroad companies, naval stores and turpentine operators, farmers, and coal and later phosphate mining companies quickly became embedded in the penal and disciplinary apparatus, as well as the political economies, of most late nineteenth-century southern states. As a consequence, the spectacle of hard labour in public, and the use of corporal and physical punishments continued in the South well into the twentieth century. Early exposés of convict leasing often highlighted the importance of race and climate to explain the peculiarities of "backward" southern penal practices; later studies have emphasised the similarities between antebellum slavery and convict leasing, and linked the emergence of the lease

---

[14] Ibid., 1: 157, 228, 235, 240–2, 348, 351; 2: 27, 138–50 [quote on 140], 283–317.

[15] Ibid., 2: 270

[16] Ibid., 2: 307.

[17] Ibid., 1: 99–100.

[18] See George Washington Cable, *The Silent South, together with The Freedman's Case in Equity and The Convict Lease System* (Montclair: Patterson Smith, [1885] 1969). The Siberian figures quoted by Kennan included extraordinarily high child and infant mortality rates associated with forwarding prisons and exile parties. See Kennan, *Siberia and the Exile System*, 1: 101, 299.

[19] See William Cohen, "Negro Involuntary Servitude in the South, 1865–1940," *Journal of Southern History* 42.1 (1976), 56.

to post-Emancipation racial control, while others (myself included) have connected convict leasing (and later chain gang road construction) and labour subordination more explicitly to the emerging extractive industries and industrial sector of the late nineteenth-century South. Thus, more than just a functional replacement for antebellum slavery, the convict lease was one important cog in a wider network of unfree labour systems that enabled southern governments and entrepreneurs to embrace industrial transformation and infrastructural modernisation at minimal cost while perpetuating white supremacy and ensuring black and lower-class white labour subordination.[20]

Fifteen years ago, I argued that convict leasing in Progressive-era Florida provided a crucial bridge between an older agricultural economy and a nascent industrial one, in which both racial control and labour subordination were crucial elements. I argued also that it was difficult to reconcile Foucault's conception of Western penality with the timetable and conditions associated with the implementation and expansion of southern convict leasing, and suggested that it was the great exception in this framework because of the durability of an older model of punishment that centred on physical punishment to the body and exhibited scant concern for the soul.[21] Revisiting Powell's memoir and other state documentation for the earlier post-Reconstruction leasing period has reinforced this, but when viewed through a more comparative transnational lens, it is clear that that southern convict leasing was just one of many exceptions.

---

[20] For example, W.E.B. DuBois, "The Spawn of Slavery: The Convict-lease System in the South (1901)," reprinted in Shaun L. Gabbidon (ed.), *W. E. B. DuBois on Crime and Justice* (Aldershot: Ashgate, 2007), 117–24; Fred Cubberly, "Peonage in the South," (Arlington) *Independent*, July 9, 1903, 1616–18; Richard Barry, "Slavery in the South To-Day," *Cosmopolitan Magazine* 42/5 (1907), 481–91; Mary Church Terrell, "Peonage in the United States: The Convict Lease System and the Chain Gangs," *Nineteenth Century* 62 (1907), 306–22; Frank Tannenbaum, *Darker Phases of the South* (New York and London: G. Putnam & Sons, 1924); C. Vann Woodward, *Origins of the New South* (Baton Rouge: Louisiana State University Press, 1951); Edward L. Ayers, *Vengeance & Justice: Crime and Punishment in the Nineteenth-Century American South* (New York: Oxford University Press, 1984); Alex Lichtenstein, *Twice the Work of Free Labor: The Political Economy of Convict Labor in the New South* (New York: Verso, 1996); Vivien M.L. Miller, *Crime, Sexual Violence, and Clemency: Florida's Pardon Board and Penal System in the Progressive Era* (Gainesville: University Press of Florida, 2000); Douglas A. Blackmon, *Slavery By Another Name: The Re-Enslavement of Black Americans from the Civil War to World War II* (New York: Doubleday, 2008); James Campbell, *Crime and Punishment in African American History* (Basingstoke: Palgrave Macmillan, 2013). Northern convicts also laboured for the private sector but usually within centralised prisons. See for example, Glen A. Gildermeister, *Prison Labor and Convict Competition With Free Workers in Industrializing America, 1840–1890* (New York: Garland Publishing, 1987); Rebecca L. McLennan, *The Crisis of Imprisonment: Protest, Politics, and the Making of the American Penal State, 1776–1941* (Cambridge: Cambridge University Press, 2008).

[21] See Miller, *Crime, Sexual Violence, and Clemency*, Introduction and Chapter 1.

Siberia in Florida

From the late nineteenth century, American readers were informed of corrupt institutions, politicians and financiers, of numerous social, economic and political abuses in northern urban-industrial centres, and of the morally indefensible southern practices of convict leasing, debt peonage and lynching by a proliferation of investigative journalists, social reformers and "muckrakers." New Orleans' native, writer, essayist and national prison reformer George Washington Cable decried the exploitation of prisoners for private gain, the disproportionate numbers of African American convicts and the lengthy sentences at hard labour being handed down in southern courts, particularly for larceny and burglary convictions, to ensure the availability of black chained labourers for planters and industrialists. Drawing on official reports and statistics as well as first-hand accounts, Cable's exposé of convict leasing was published as *The Silent South* in 1885, but did not include Florida.[22] It is possible, although not confirmed, that Powell's book was envisaged as an addendum to Cable's study, even though it was more memoir than empirical study.

Extant sources allow for a fragmentary biographical sketch of J.C. Powell to be pieced together. According to the 1880 US Census, Florida "Captain of the Guard" John C. Powell was twenty-nine years old, originally from Georgia, married, and living in Suwannee County in northern Florida. In 1885 he and his wife Elizabeth, also a native of south Georgia, were residents of Clayton District No.3 of Suwannee County as were their two sons and two daughters.[23] A portrait of Powell in the 1891 publication shows a gaunt-looking man with a "full, slightly drooping mustache," and a receding hairline, that historian William Warren Rogers thought looked more like a clerk or farmer than a convict captain.[24] Powell was an unpopular figure,

---

[22] Cable's address on the defects of convict leasing to the National Conference on Charities and Correction in September 1883 was published in *Century Magazine* in February 1884. See Arlin Turner, "George W. Cable on Prison Reform," *Huntington Library Quarterly* 36.1 (1972), 75. African American critics of leasing included Timothy Thomas Fortune of Florida. See Herbert J. Doherty, Jr., "Voices of Protest from the New South, 1875–1910," *Mississippi Valley Historical Review* 42.1 (1955), 49–50. For examples of (often paternalistic) white southern female criticism, see Rebecca L. Felton, "The Convict System of Georgia," *Forum* 11 (1887), 484–90, and Julia S. Tutweiler, "Our Brother in Stripes, in the School-Room," National Education Association, *Journal of the Proceedings and Addresses: 1890* (Topeka: National Education Association, 1890), 601–8.

[23] "United States Census, 1880," index and images, *FamilySearch* (https://familysearch.org/pal:/MM9.1.1/MNZC, accessed 23 December 2013), John C. Powell in household of William Howren, Precinct 1, Suwannee, Florida, United States, Sheet 297A, NARA microfilm publication T9-0132; 1885 FLORIDA CENSUS "Florida, State Census, 1885," index and images, *FamilySearch*, accessed 23 December 2013, http://familysearch.org/pal:/MM9.1.1/MNJD-LJC 2013, JC Powel, 1885. Another infant was killed during an accident with an open hearth in 1879. See Powell, *American Siberia*, 116–17.

[24] William Warren Rogers, "Introduction," to Florida Bicentennial facsimile edition of *The American Siberia* (Gainesville: University Press of Florida, 1976), ix.

and his employment had been interrupted in 1879 when he was one of several guards indicted for cruelty to prisoners, although the case was subsequently dismissed, and he later resigned following a dispute with his lessee-employers.[25] He was literate (his reading of newspapers is remarked on in the memoir) and this fact distinguished him from the majority of nineteenth-century southern convict camp personnel who were typically people of minimal education.

Through his descriptions of frequent convict escapes and necessary pursuit of fugitives, and his later duties as "a forwarding agent" transporting convicts from county jails to convict camps, Powell provided many details of frontier Florida, of dense forests and of rivers and lagoons infested with alligators and "fat, bloated water-moccasins."[26] The sparseness of the settlements, particularly in the southern section of the state, is evident in Map 9.1. The memoir also contains ethnographic snapshots of late nineteenth-century Cracker life, for example of a "frolic" with self-taught fiddlers, copious amounts of moonshine and raucous dancing, backwoods distillers at war with revenue agents, and the exotic "others" including Seminole Indians and "negro priests of voodooism."[27] Yet, Powell was a largely unsympathetic chronicler, and his prejudices against Crackers, African Americans, Native Americans, Jews and lower-class women were all very clear. Rogers believed that much of *The American Siberia*, particularly the Cracker and African American dialects and the detailed descriptions of the Florida interior, was authored by Powell, but quite how it or he came to the attention of northern publishers remains unclear.[28] Further, although Florida convict camp personnel might have travelled to other US regions for military or naval service or as migrants seeking economic opportunity in the post-Civil War years, surviving guard applications suggest that very few would have had any direct knowledge of Russia or Siberia. Yet, it is also not clear whether Powell had actually read any of Kennan's recent essays in *Century Magazine* or if the decision to include the comparisons with Siberia was his or an editorial one, particularly as they are limited to only one small section of the narrative.[29]

Powell's account opens with an occasional sight for residents of leasing states and one which generally drew crowds of curious spectators:

[25] Ibid., xx; Powell, *American Siberia*, 117–19.
[26] Powell, *American Siberia*, 154, 188, 194. See also, James M. Denham and Canter Brown, Jr. (eds), *Cracker Times and Pioneer Lives: The Florida Reminiscences of George Gillet Keen and Sarah Pamela Williams* (Columbia: University of South Carolina Press, 2003); Eric Musgrove, *Suwannee County* (Charleston: Arcadia Publishing, 2011).
[27] Powell, *American Siberia*, 99, 152, 197–8, 327, 333.
[28] Rogers, "Introduction," xvi–xvii. Cash believed also in the veracity of Powell's account as "the present writer knows from first-hand authority that much of what Powell relates occurred substantially as he has told it." See William T. Cash, *The Story of Florida*, vol. II (New York: American Historical Society, 1938), 520.
[29] Powell, *American Siberia*, 121–2.

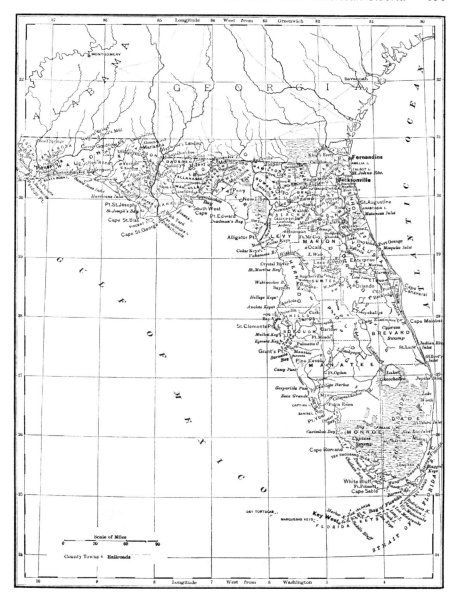

Map 9.1 Map of Florida in the 1880s

Source: Brown & Co., Encyclopædia Britannica (9th ed.), v. 9, 1879, facing p. 338. This image is accessible at: http://commons.wikimedia.org/wiki/File:EB9_Florida. jpg?uselang=en-gb.

In the fall of 1876 a singular spectacle might have been observed at the little town of Live Oak, in Northern Florida. A train had just arrived, and from one of the cars some thirty odd men disembarked and formed an irregular procession by the road-side. The sun never shone upon a more abject picture of misery and dilapidation. They were gaunt, haggard, famished, wasted with disease, smeared with grime, and clad in filthy tatters. Chains cluttered about their trembling limbs, and so inhuman was their aspect that the crowd of curiosity seekers who had assembled around the depot shrank back appalled.[30]

Powell informed the reader that this "ragged battalion" of filthy, diseased and emaciated convicts were survivors of a severely mistreated railroad gang building the line between St. John and Lake Eustace through "tropical marshes," "palmetto jungles" and "pestilential swamps."[31] The report of Surgeon for Convicts, J.S. Hankins, noted that twenty-seven prisoners, nineteen of whom were suffering from chronic dysentery and typhoid fever, were received from Lake Eustis in August 1877 (not 1876), and that in his opinion, "if the state had not sent the prisoners to Lake Eustis the mortality at the stockade [in Suwannee County] would not have exceeded 8 or 10 [13 deaths were recorded]."[32]

Half of the 110 state prisoners, including two women, had remained at the state prison at Chattahoochee, which was overseen by the Adjutant General, from 1868 to 1888, and surgeon's reports were generally positive, although a high prevalence of chronic disease among prisoners was remarked upon.[33] Nevertheless, in the 1930s, Florida historian William T. Cash drew on Powell's memoir to portray conditions there as "so disgusting and disgraceful as to be almost unbelievable" under corrupt and cruel warden Malachi Martin and callous guards who indiscriminately tortured and shot at inmates:

After he had extracted every ounce of toil from his unfortunate prisoners that flesh and blood could stand, [Martin] would then inflict punishments upon them for failing to perform their tasks – punishments worse than the agents of the Czar of Russia inflicted on the prisoners sent to Siberia.

However, Mildred Fryman's 1978 evaluation of Malachi Martin was significantly different from that of Powell and Cash, and indeed leasing

---

[30] Ibid., 7. George Washington Cable recalled a similar sight on a train in Alabama in September 1884. See Cable, *Silent South*, 28.

[31] Powell, *American Siberia*, 11–12.

[32] *Biennial Report of the Adjutant General, 1877–1878* (Tallahassee: C.E. Dyke, Sr, 1879), 16.

[33] See, for example, *Report of the Adjutant General, 1874* (Tallahassee: Floridian Office, 1875), 33.

historian Matthew Mancini.[34] She concluded that while conditions at Chattahoochee were "disgraceful" and Martin was an inept administrator, criticisms of the Republican-appointed "carpetbagger" were highly politicised in the wake of the re-establishment of Bourbon-Democratic political rule in Florida in 1876–1877, thus "[Martin's] regime was not, as Powell asserted, 'one of almost unrelieved barbarity'."[35]

Florida officials had first experimented with leasing in the late 1860s and early 1870s. Forty-four Florida prisoners were sent to the Great Southern Railroad in 1873 for example, and in 1876 – as described in Powell's account – about half of the state convicts were leased to Live Oak merchant Major H.A. Wise [Wyse] for turpentine harvesting, and to Leon County farmer "Green Cheers" [G.A. Chaires]. In 1879, during the administration of Governor George F. Drew, the state prison was abolished and the labour of all state convicts was sold to the highest bidders.[36] These arrangements prevailed in Florida at the state level until 1919. In return for an annual fee for each person convicted of a felony, lessees (usually local landowners or transplanted northern capitalists) were expected to feed, clothe, work and discipline prisoners.[37] Most Florida counties adopted similar practices until 1923. Thus, from the late 1870s state prisoners and guards slept in crude log houses in temporary camps and stockades scattered across northern and central Florida and laboured ostensibly in public, but usually in the remote backwoods, within a radius of a few miles from the main camp. Convicts and camps moved as turpentine sap was exhausted or railroads were completed, or when new lessees took over. Powell initially oversaw the prisoners leased to Wise.[38] Thus, imprisonment in Florida did not mean a permanent place of total confinement but rather forced labour in a remote and temporary place of detention. Decisions as to the location of camps and the assignment of state prisoners were made largely by lessees rather than state officers in Tallahassee.

Harvesting turpentine was exhausting, back-breaking, year-round labour, and convicts were particularly attractive to operators who struggled to recruit free workers. Powell observed, "The work is severe to a degree almost impossible to exaggerate, and it is very difficult to control a sufficient quantity of free labor to properly cultivate any great number of trees."[39] The waist chains of each convict were looped together while they worked and then attached to the building chains as they slept. Leg irons were riveted to each convict's ankles and then fixed to additional "stride chains" at night that enabled prisoners to

[34] Mancini, *One Dies, Get Another*, 33–4.
[35] Mildred L. Fryman, "'Career of a Carpetbagger': Malachi Martin in Florida," *Florida Historical Quarterly* 56.3 (1978), 338.
[36] *Report of the Adjutant General, 1874*, 13; Edward C. Williamson, "George F. Drew, Florida's Redemption Governor," *Florida Historical Quarterly* 38.3 (1960), 208–12; Miller, *Crime, Sexual Violence, and Clemency*, 23.
[37] *Biennial Report of the Adjutant General 1885–1886*, 26.
[38] Powell, *American Siberia*, 16, 39.
[39] Ibid., 27–9.

take only the few steps to the privy. The constant clanking of chains was thus as ubiquitous in Florida as it was in Siberia. Florida convicts ate supper under burning pine knots and while sitting in rows on bunks akin to ship's berths or the sleeping platforms in Siberian *kámeras*. Fat white bacon, corn bread and cowpeas were cooked "hunter fashion, on a bank of dirt under a lean-to shelter." After supper, convicts were ordered to lie down and sleep; they had to ask a guard's permission to change position or to get up.[40] Indeed, Powell suggested that the sleeping platforms (which he called "nares") in Siberian cellhouses, the use of stride and waist chains, the general uncleanliness of the prisoners, and the physical layout of the prisons were "absolutely identical" to conditions in Florida.[41]

Permanent infestations of fleas, lice and bedbugs on prisoners and rodent-infested cellhouses or stockades were also common to both Florida and Siberia. Kennan decried the "humiliating sense of physical defilement that was almost as bad as a consciousness of moral degradation" from being "forced to live for weeks at a time in clothing infested with vermin from the unclean bodies of common criminal convicts."[42] He described a dull-red band of crushed and bloodied bedbugs on the white-washed walls above the cell-house sleeping platforms in Ust Kara and Algachí. Powell wryly observed, "Mr. Kennan need not have gone so far away from home. In summer time these insect pests were almost impossible to exterminate, and it took only a few weeks for the convicts at the [Florida] camps to paint a dado on the walls exactly similar to that which Mr. Kennan observed."[43]

In Florida, unsanitary conditions, poor diet and general mistreatment led to frequent outbreaks of sickness and disease, often fevers, skin infections, bronchitis, pneumonia and even scurvy. Dysentery was rife throughout 1876–1877 and "a large proportion" of Camp Padlock inmates died. In 1880 there was a serious measles outbreak at Camp Hillyard followed by a terrifying outbreak of spinal meningitis that decimated the camp population as there was no treatment for this disease. Powell was among those who recovered, but only slowly over several months.[44] Whereas after 1890, local doctors were paid to treat inmates in nearby convict camps, medical care in the 1880s was provided by guards and captains. Powell sewed up at least two sliced throats following unsuccessful convict suicide attempts, another inmate who "drove his axe through his foot" died "in great agony" after gangrene set in, while untreated bullet wounds sustained during escape attempts could also result in fatal infections. Of the nine convict deaths recorded in 1881–1882 (which equated to a death rate of 3 per cent), one was from gunshot wounds and

[40] Kennan, *Siberia and the Exile System*, 1: 110, 114, 364; Powell, *American Siberia*, 17–19, 22.
[41] Powell, *American Siberia*, 121.
[42] Kennan, *Siberia and the Exile System*, 1: 364–6.
[43] Ibid., 1: 366; 2: 147, 293; Powell, *American Siberia*, 122.
[44] Powell, *American Siberia*, 22–3, 144–51.

eight from unspecified "diseases," but surgeon's reports also indicated the prevalence of non-fatal sickness in the camp.[45]

Florida convict guards and captains were generally young white men from local farming families or recent economic migrants from neighbouring Georgia or the Carolinas doing badly paid and routinely dangerous work. Powell described several of these men, including Bill Newland (alleged to have been manipulated by a "villainous negro" called Griffin), W.B. Phillips ("a tall, raw-boned, wild-looking native – rather harum-scarum, but a nervy fellow and a dead shot"), and Captain Charles P. Jolly [C.R. Joly] of "Passum Trot" turpentine camp.[46] Most convicts were young, African American lower- or working-class men in their late teens or early twenties from counties across the state. Inmate hierarchies quickly developed. "Trusties" or privileged inmates – trusted or rewarded by camp personnel – did not wear leg irons, were often employed as camp cooks or tradesmen, and thus had greater freedom of movement, but could incur the enmity of the gunmen or ordinary and fettered inmates. One-armed Jesse Simpkins was rumoured to be the guards' spy.[47] Violent interracial confrontations between prisoners, and prisoners and guards were common and some were fatal. In February 1886, black prisoner George Ball, serving fifteen years for burglary, was "killed while leading a mutiny and in the act of assault, with a knife and bludgeon, the Captain of the guard."[48] Guards shot at fleeing convicts and some were "lamed for life."

Powell's memoir may be described as an early muckraking exposé but his main concern was to restore his reputation and honour which had been tarnished by what he perceived to be unwarranted criticisms of his treatment of prisoners, rather than to elicit sympathy for an unjustly imprisoned or mistreated inmate class. Thus, he had few complimentary things to say about his charges, who he characterised as "Cracker outlaws" and "cut-throat negroes" who had been sentenced "for crimes of the most atrocious character," and who were always plotting to escape. "Noted desperado" Jim Ota was part Native American and part African American, had been convicted of burglary and the attempted rape of "the wife of one of the leading citizens of Pensacola,"

---

[45] Ibid., 60–3; *Biennial Report of the Adjutant General 1881–1882*, 30.

[46] Powell, *American Siberia*, 30, 71, 257, 258, 304–5, 320. These are probably references to W.R. Newlan and W.D. Phillips. See "Florida, State Census, 1885," index and images, *FamilySearch*, accessed 23 December 2013, https://familysearch.org/pal:/MM9.1.1/MNJD-CNS and https://familysearch.org.pal:/MM9.1.1/MNJD-H9L, W.R. Newlan in entry for J.B. Newlan, 1885; W.D. Phillips in entry for E.N.W. Phillips, 1885. Jolly was a former foreman of convicts under Major Charles K. Dutton's lease. See *Biennial Report of the Commissioner of Agriculture for the State of Florida, 1893–1894*, 64.

[47] Powell, *American Siberia*, 106. Frost and Kennan had encountered privileged inmates or the *maidánshchik* at several Siberian prisons who were permitted "to keep a small stock of such luxuries as tea, sugar, and white bread for sale to his fellow-prisoners; and at the same time with the aid of the soldiers of the convoy whom it is not difficult to bribe, he deals surreptitiously in tobacco, playing-cards, and *vodka*." See Kennan, *Siberia and the Exile System*, 2: 358–9.

[48] *Biennial Report of the Adjutant General 1886–1887*, 29.

and had avoided several threats of lynching. He fled on several occasions.[49] Thomas Nix, a "big, gaunt, Cracker" serving fifteen years for incest, attempted to escape with another white convict by leaping from a moving train, as did black prisoner Smith Oliver on a different occasion.[50] Powell was particularly irritated by Richard "Dick" Evans, former saloon keeper and marshal of Pensacola, serving five years for murder, who attempted several escapes, and with the help of other camp employees supposedly instigated a plot against Powell. Evans' Radical Republican political allegiances and his public interracial sexual conduct rendered him especially disreputable in Powell's assessment.[51] By contrast, Kennan had found the "faces of the [Siberian common] prisoners generally were not as hard, vicious, and depraved as the faces of criminals in America. Many of them were pleasant and good-humored, some were fairly intelligent, and even the worst seemed to me stupid and brutish rather than savage or malignant."[52]

American Siberia provided a compelling portrait of the brutal and bloody world of convict leasing. Several convicts were young first-offenders, including fifteen-year-old "Archie" who disappeared in mysterious circumstances.[53] In fact, Powell indicated that several prisoners were lynched while supposedly under the protection of lessees. Eighteen-year-old "mulatto" trusty John Evans was nearing the end of a three-year sentence for assault to rape when he was accused of raping an elderly white woman during an absence from the camp, and was lynched within earshot of the camp by "an armed mob of over 200 men."[54] Jewish inmate Gus Pottsdamer, a former Lake City town marshal, sentenced to life for killing Columbia County sheriff John C. Henry in January 1880, arrived under threat of lynching but secured a pardon shortly after.[55]

There were few female state prisoners in late nineteenth-century Florida. For example, in December 1878, there were three "colored" and one white female prisoner "on hand," along with twenty-four white and 135 "colored" male convicts, and a total of eight black female convicts in 1886.[56] In this period, female prisoners were generally not separated from males and

---

[49] Escapes are recorded for James Ota – described as "yellow" (i.e. mulatto), sentenced to life imprisonment for burglary offences in Escambia County in December 1881 – in July 1890 and August 1891. See *Biennial Report of the Commissioner of Agriculture for the State of Florida, 1889–1890* (Jacksonville: DaCosta Printing, 1891), 149; ibid., *1891–1892*, 124.

[50] Powell, *American Siberia*, 186.

[51] Ibid., 84–8, 219, 246–7, 276–7.

[52] Kennan, *Siberia and the Exile System*, 1: 114, 116.

[53] Powell, *American Siberia*, 310.

[54] Ibid., 316–18; *Biennial Report of the Adjutant General 1886–1887*, 29.

[55] Powell, *American Siberia*, 125. Gottschalf "Gus" Pottsdamer was pardoned by Governor Edward A. Perry. He subsequently relocated to Suwannee County where he was elected as sheriff for three terms in 1889–1893 and 1913–1914. See William Warren Rogers and James M. Denham, *Florida Sheriffs: A History, 1821–1945* (Tallahassee: Sentry Press, 2001), 129–30, 201, 306.

[56] *Biennial Reports of the Adjutant General 1877–1878*, 27; ibid., *1886–1887*, 34.

were usually employed in domestic or agricultural labour, and endured both physical and sexual violence (as did male inmates also). Talitha LeFlouria's work on Georgia's black women prisoners assigned to railroad construction, coal mining and domestic work, and Mary Ellen Curtain's study of African American prisoners in Alabama, highlight the different regimes in other southern states but commonalities of neglect and mistreatment of convict women.[57]

In both Powell's and Kennan's accounts, convict leasing and imprisonment in exile had particularly deleterious effects on women, thus providing further evidence of cruelty and degradation. The descent into insanity of several female political exiles was described by Kennan, as were many suicides.[58] Powell related the stories of a handful (mainly white women) under his care, including Maud Foster whom he collected from Key West in March 1881. Originally from a "well-to-do, eminently respectable" New York City family, she had run off to Cuba with "another silly girl" in search of romantic adventure but became ensnared in Havana's "demi-monde." Foster's adventure ended with a conviction for larceny in Key West. Powell described her arrival at Camp Hillyard:

> It was altogether a sorrowful sight. I regret that I ever saw it. I felt sorry for the girl, and as time passed it hurt me to see how shame and desperation did their work. She donned the stripes in a paroxysm of wild grief, but before long she hardened herself to her degradation and abandoned herself to it. It made a bad woman out of her, and her beauty was practically all that remained of her former self.

However, she was discharged one year later, swapped convict stripes for fine clothing and resumed her former life of luxury.[59] Another "voluptuous young negress" turned out to be a man, a young "double-sex thief" operating in female disguise as part of a gang of thieves in north Florida.[60] Georgiana Abbott, called "Mamma" by the black women, was the only white female convict in 1890, serving a life sentence for infanticide, by which time most women were kept at the central headquarters camp in Jefferson County and

[57] Talitha LeFlouria, "'The Hand that Rocks the Cradle Cuts Cordwood': Exploring Black Women's Lives and Labor in Georgia's Convict Camps, 1865–1917," *Labor: Studies in Working-Class History of the Americas* 8.3 (2011), 47–63; Talitha LeFlouria, *Chained in Silence: Black Women and Convict Labor in the New South* (Chapel Hill: University of North Carolina Press, forthcoming); Mary Ellen Curtain, *Black Prisoners and Their World, Alabama, 1865–1900* (Charlottesville: University Press of Virginia, 2000). Similarly, Kennan witnessed female convicts breaking up ore in the mine of Algachí and elsewhere. See Kennan, *Siberia and the Exile System*, 2: 298, 304.

[58] Kennan, *Siberia and the Exile System*, 2: 213–16.

[59] Powell, *American Siberia*, 41, 176–8, 288.

[60] Ibid., 289–90.

worked either in the fields, as domestic servants, or sewing striped convict suits.[61]

Powell had charged that stringing prisoners up by the thumbs and other tortuous punishments had been practised at Chattahoochee, but in his camps, the strap, which he implied was more benign, was used. While Powell was a strict disciplinarian, Rogers considered him to be "a conscientious but not a cruel man" who did not engage in malicious torture. However, Powell's own description of the flogging of black trusty William Hadley who he caught stealing camp rations for his free black "inamorata" suggested otherwise. Powell ordered each to punish the other: "I told Hadley to get down for punishment, and handing my strap to the negress, requested her pretty shortly to lay it on to the best of her ability," which she did but Powell urged her to exert more and harder strokes. He then ordered Hadley to whip the woman, a sight that Powell seems to have taken great, almost pornographic, satisfaction from:

> An instantaneous change came over the darky. His sullen look disappeared like magic, and he snatched the leather as drowning men snatch straws. Revenge is sweet. He whirled the strap and brought it down with a resounding whack. "Oh, Lord! Oh, Mr. Hadley!" yelled the negress. "Give it to her, Number 54," I said; "remember how she tanned your hide."[62]

Convict leasing was supposed to deliver a compliant and dependable labour force but the punishment beatings, frequent work stoppages and other forms of inmate resistance, and the numerous escapes described by Powell, generated a portrait of ill-discipline and inefficiency.[63] Powell frequently portrayed himself as the relentless pursuer of escapees, surmounting physical pain, danger and numerous obstacles, thus displaying a heroic fearless masculinity that triumphed over spineless and conniving fugitives. Some convict escapes were planned, including one mass breakout from a railroad gang just before knocking off time, where work tools were used to cut each man's leg irons. Others like Daniel Bass ran to the Suwannee River to shake off the trailing hounds, and hid out for months in the "coast jungles" of the Florida interior that were said to be inhabited by "typical forest robbers and outlaws." Others headed for the cities: Walter Shavers, serving a ten-year sentence for robbery, was pursued to a "robber's roost of the ugliest type" in Jacksonville's "negro section" but Powell searched for him for two weeks without success even though he was hidden in plain sight in feminine disguise as "the young mulatto girl who sat against the wall in the gambling den."[64]

---

[61] Abbot had been sentenced to life imprisonment on 26 October 1881 in Madison County and secured a pardon on 19 November 1894. See *Biennial Report of the Commissioner of Agriculture for the State of Florida, 1893–1894* (Tallahassee: John G. Collins, 1895), 78.

[62] Powell, *American Siberia*, 8, 21, 130–1; Rogers, "Introduction," xix.

[63] Powell, *American Siberia*, 77, 101, 231, 239, 245, 299.

[64] Ibid., 165–6, 168. During a previous sentence, Shavers had led a strike of ninety inmates for which he was severely whipped by Powell. Ibid., 133, 137.

Florida and Siberia

Use of familiar images to explain foreign concepts or vistas is found in all types of writing, and Kennan and Powell both used transnational comparisons to convey particular images or features to their respective audiences. Kennan associated parts of Western Siberia with the southern sections of New England, while a recently discovered gold placer in Mongolia was known throughout Siberia as the "Chinese California."[65] The area around Tiumen was compared to "Florida or Culexia, since flowers and mosquitoes are its distinctive characteristics and its most abundant products."[66] Tomsk forwarding prison, particularly the stockade and log buildings with grated windows, armed sentries and "throngs of convicts" milling around in "gray, semi-military overcoats," reminded Kennan of the Union prison at Andersonville during the American Civil War.[67] Powell compared Florida's Marion County jail to the "Black Hole of Calcutta" as prisoners were kept in a dark underground dungeon.[68] Many comparisons were infused with paternalistic, racial and nativist inflections and stereotypes. The unpainted shanties and dilapidated huts and cabins occupied by ticket-of-leave convicts at Kara were compared to the notorious Irish and German "shanties on the rocks" in New York City, populated by immigrant communities that were not quite "white" in the antebellum US imagination, and later cleared to make way for Central Park.[69] While comparisons with penal conditions in Siberia were designed to reinforce the barbarity of Florida's early leasing system in Powell's memoir, they could also be read as evidence that conditions in Florida were neither anomalous nor unusual.

Just as Kennan viewed the condition of Siberian prisons as the worst feature of penal servitude, Powell found the condition of Florida's camps to be the worst aspect of convict leasing. At the same time, Powell was not as vexed by punishment at hard labour for the hardened murderers, robbers and thieves that were sent to labour in naval stores operations, railroad construction or farming, and he was clearly willing to discipline non-compliant convicts, and

---

[65] Kennan, *Siberia and the Exile System*, 1: 283; 2: 71.

[66] Ibid., 1: 71.

[67] Ibid., 1: 308–22. See also William Marvel, *Andersonville: The Last Depot* (Chapel Hill: University of North Carolina Press, 1994).

[68] Powell, *American Siberia*, 261–2; Noel Ignatiev, *How the Irish Became White* (Milton Park: Routledge, 1995, 2009). There was of course also a "Chinese California" in the United States. Chinese immigrants to the West Coast were recruited to work gold placers in California after the 1849 Gold Rush and to construct the transcontinental railroads in the 1860s, but three years before Kennan's exile journey and investigation, severe restrictions on Chinese immigration had been implemented. See for example, Andrew Gyory, *Closing the Gate: Race, Politics, and the Chinese Exclusion Act* (Chapel Hill and London: University of North Carolina Press, 1998), and Sue Fawn Chung, *In Pursuit of Gold: Chinese American Miners and Merchants in the American West* (Chicago: University of Illinois Press, 2011).

[69] Kennan, *Siberia and the Exile System*, 2: 151–2; Robert Ernst, *Immigrant Life in New York City, 1825–1863* (Syracuse: Syracuse University Press, 1994), 40–1.

shoot at those who attempted to escape or engaged in mutiny. But the focus of Powell's ire was the lack of administrative oversight of the leasing system and woeful state supervision of lessees and prisoners. Kennan was also a severe critic of the "corrupt, shiftless, and inefficient" management of prison affairs throughout Eastern Siberia and denounced the imperial bureaucracy as "a huge administrative maelstrom of ignorance and indifference."[70] Thus, *American Siberia* offered an angry and bitter assessment of the failings of conservative white Democratic rule in post-Reconstruction Florida, from one of its own supporters who had abhorred Radical Republican rule and had blamed the poor conditions at the earlier state prison on its corrupt and cruel agents, only to see these perpetuated under the new leasing arrangements.

Criticism of convict leasing, exposés of horrible conditions and convict mistreatment, as well as the greater profitability of government-financed road building projects (with gangs of chained prisoners working outdoors and sleeping in often dilapidated and unsanitary camps), led to its decline in the 1890s, thus by 1900, only four southern states, Florida, Alabama, Georgia and Virginia, still leased their convicts to private contractors. Virginia legislators would vote to end the system in 1901 and Georgia followed suit in 1908. While reviews of *American Siberia* appeared in newspapers and journals in different US regions, and also in London, and Powell achieved short-lived acclamation, the memoir had very limited impact on the conduct of leasing or the treatment of prisoners in Florida. State legislators approved the establishment of a Department of Agriculture in 1889 and the newly appointed commissioner was given responsibility for the management and supervision of state convicts, the same year that racial segregation in all aspects of the state and county penal systems was codified. By this time, there were 588 convicts under contract to Major Charles K. Dutton and still harvesting turpentine sap. Of the 563 incoming convicts, 473 or 85 per cent were African American or "colored."[71] More effective state oversight of leasing was attempted in Florida in the early twentieth century, and there were some improvements to the prisoners' lot. However, W.J. Hillman who had worked for Powell, and motivated by "a deep interest in the welfare of the convicts both on their account and that of the good name of the state of Florida," became one of the state inspectors of lessee camps and prisoner treatment in the later 1890s. His resignation letter of 1899 recorded his disappointment that "many of the evils complained of" in the lease had yet to be eradicated.[72] As convict leasing remained remarkably profitable for both the state treasury and private

[70] Kennan, *Siberia and the Exile System*, 2: 313, 374.

[71] *Report of the Commissioner of Agriculture, 1889–1890*, 139. In 1889, 473 "colored males," ten "colored females," seventy-nine white males, and one white woman are recorded as newly-convicted convicts to be assigned to the lessees.

[72] W.J. Hillman to W.J. Wombwell, 9 October 1899, in Board of Commissioners of State Institutions, *Convict Lease Program, Subject Files 1889–1916*, Record Group 890, Series 42, Box 7, File 6. Hillman was a lessee of state convicts in the 1890s and 1900s.

contractors, and a state prison building was not constructed until 1913, many features of the "American Siberia" period endured long after publication of Powell's account. In a sparsely-populated frontier state such as Florida, located on the periphery of the continental United States, and without a central penitentiary, the journey from punishment as public spectacle to something that was hidden from public view was a long and uneven one. While criminal justice systems and penal operations provided centralising and unifying roles, particularly after 1889, the profitability of leasing together with the need to discipline a predominately black male convict population ensured its durability.

Part III

Desistance

10 'What is a man that is a bolter to do? I would steal the Governor's axe rather than starve'

Old lags and recidivism in the Tasmanian penal colony

Hamish Maxwell-Stewart and Rebecca Kippen

Between 1787 and 1868 the British government dispatched over 160,000 convicts to its penal colonies in New South Wales, Van Diemen's Land (renamed Tasmania in 1856) and Western Australia. A question that has interested historians of crime about this mass transportation of convicts has been its impact on colonial offending rates. Several studies have explored the rate of reconviction amongst offenders shipped to Australia's penal colonies. While these authors have drawn very different conclusions about the effects of transportation on recidivism rates, they have been largely silent about the factors that helped some convicts to 'go straight' while others found themselves back before the courts long after their original sentence had expired. In this chapter we use a detailed analysis of life cycle offending amongst a cohort of male convicts shipped to Van Diemen's Land to address these issues.

Transportation to Van Diemen's Land can be split into two phases: assignment, which for men lasted until 1839, and the probation system which replaced it. If transportation really did help to make Tasmania a relatively crime-free colony as has been argued by some then it is probation, rather than assignment, that should take the credit. Using data for a cohort of 1,124 male prisoners arriving in the probation era (1840–1853) we calculate that the actual reconviction rate was about 21 per cent. We also find evidence that high levels of punishment experienced under sentence significantly increased the chances of reconviction. In order to contextualise our findings on the impact of pre-transportation offending histories, colonial punishment, education levels and colonial on post-emancipation reconviction rates, we use a detailed exploration of the life of one transported convict, James Ashcroft.

While transportation to Tasmania was widely condemned in the nineteenth century, recent reassessments have been more positive[1] Criminologist John Braithwaite in particular has argued that convict transportation was notable for its success in reducing crime rates in colonial Australia, whereas in

---

[1] For contrasting views, see Robert Hughes, *The Fatal Shore* (London: Collins Harvill, 1988), 103 and Babette Smith, *Australia's Birthstain: The Startling Legacy of the Convict Era* (Sydney: Allen & Unwin, 2008), esp. 1–7.

the post-revolutionary United States a reliance on the penitentiary had the opposite effect. He attributes the difference in outcomes to the way in which former convicts and their descendants were integrated into colonial society, a process that encouraged desistance, while the penitentiary effectively stigmatised offenders – particularly those who were black.[2] In Braithwaite's view, a marked difference between the two penal regimes was the emphasis that the former placed on the effective utilisation of the skills of convicts. In order to achieve this, the state and private sector combined to supply adequate levels of clothing, accommodation, nutrition and medical care. These interventions had a direct impact in that they lowered mortality.[3] Braithwaite argues, however, that they also had a long-term effect in that they helped to resocialise former offenders. The practice of rewarding good behaviour was particularly prevalent in the private sector, but government-bestowed indulgences such as small monetary payments, better rations and quarters, were far from insignificant. Combined, these amounted to a system of 'restorative justice'.[4] Braithwaite's analysis supports Henry Reynolds' view that these processes were further aided by Tasmania's comparatively high investment in social welfare, particularly through the supply of institutional care for its aging former convict population.[5] As Braithwaite points out, Tasmania not only received 42 per cent of all convicts transported to Australia, but also a disproportionately small share of nineteenth-century free migrants.[6] It was thus the Australian colony most shaped by the transportation experiment. Despite this, it became, in Braithwaite's words, 'one of the most serene places on earth by the 1880s'.[7]

Such positive views are shared by others. Echoing Russell Ward, Babette Smith has recently argued that transportation resulted in the creation of a remarkably egalitarian and inclusive society, but not all agree.[8] Both James Boyce and Shane Breen point to the stratified nature of post-transportation Tasmania.[9] They argue that, as in other colonies, the transition from unfree to free labour was not as straightforward as is sometimes imagined. For example,

---

[2] John Braithwaite, 'Crime in the Convict Republic', *The Modern Law Review*, 64.1 (2001), 16–17 and 19–21.

[3] Stephen Nicholas, 'The Care and Feeding of Convicts', in Stephen Nicholas (ed.), *Convict Workers: Reinterpreting Australia's Past* (Cambridge: Cambridge University Press, 1988), 180–98, and Mark Staniforth, 'Diet, Disease and Death at Sea on the Voyage to Australia, 1837–9', *International Journal of Maritime History*, 8.2 (1996), 119–56.

[4] Braithwaite, 'Crime in the Convict Republic', 27.

[5] Henry Reynolds, '"That Hated Stain": The Aftermath of Transportation in Tasmania', *Historical Studies*, 14.53 (1969), 30.

[6] Ibid., 21.

[7] Braithwaite, 'Crime in the Convict Republic', 18.

[8] Smith, *Australia's Birthstain* and Russell Ward, *The Australian Legend* (Melbourne: Oxford University Press, 1958).

[9] James Boyce, *Van Diemen's Land* (Melbourne: Black Inc, 2008), 213–43, and Shayne Breen, *Contested Place: Tasmania's Northern Districts from Ancient Times to 1900* (Hobart: Sugar Hill, 2012), 136–201.

aggressive Master and Servants Acts were introduced in Van Diemen's Land in 1837 and 1854; these included lengthy custodial sentences (twice as long as provided for by similar legislation in England and Wales) for those who broke employment agreements.[10]

Although there is evidence that comparatively few former convicts were reconvicted in higher courts, many were prosecuted by magistrates' benches. Employing data from Western Australia, David Cox and Barry Godfrey found that former convicts accounted for a disproportionate number of offenders and that there were significant recommittal rates 25 years or more after prisoners had first arrived in the colony. Cox and Godfrey conclude that transportation, like long prison sentences, hit some offenders hard. Many former convicts found it difficult to remake their lives after gaining freedom and often reappear in court and other records as vagrants and petty offenders. As such, they disproportionately contributed to the level of minor crime in Western Australia.[11] In Perth, in 1870, two years after transportation had ended, for example, former convicts were responsible for about one-third of all convictions. Despite declining numbers due to death and migration, former convicts still accounted for one in three defendants that appeared in Western Australian courts a decade later.[12]

Examination of Tasmanian convictions reveals a similar picture. An analysis of information about convicted offenders circulated by the colonial police reveals that long after transportation had ceased former convicts accounted for a significant number of Tasmanian convictions. In the period 1865 to 1875 a total of 4,721 former 'lags' were responsible for 63 per cent of all convictions recorded in the *Tasmanian Police Gazettes*. In the 1857 census – the last to capture civil status – convicts or former convicts accounted for just 37 per cent of the male population. The majority of these former convict reoffenders, 81 per cent, only had one recorded reconviction; the remaining 19 per cent were responsible for 40 per cent of all recorded former-convict offending and 27 per cent of total Tasmanian incarcerations.[13] Thus, long after the last transport vessel had docked in Hobart, a small number of former convicts comprised a disproportionate number of defendants.

[10] Michael Quinlan, 'Australia, 1788–1902: A Workingman's Paradise?', in Douglas Hay and P. Craven (eds), *Masters, Servants and Magistrates in Britain and the Empire, 1562–1955* (Chapel Hill: University of North Carolina Press, 2004), 219–50.

[11] Barry Godfrey and David Cox, '"The Last Fleet", Crime, Reformation, and Punishment in Western Australia After 1868', *The Australian and New Zealand Journal of Criminology*, 41.2 (2008), 245–6.

[12] Barry Godfrey, '"Convict Stain": Desistence in the Penal Colony', in Judith Rowbotham, Marianna Muravyeva and David Nash (eds), *Shame, Blame and Culpability: Crime and Violence in the Modern State* (London: Routledge, 2012), 96–108.

[13] Tasmanian Government, *Census of the island of Tasmania, March 31, 1857: abstract of the returns of the population, houses, &c. in the several districts of the island of Tasmania* (Hobart, 1857) and *Tasmanian Police Gazette* 1865–1875.

The shift between the pre-1839 assignment and the probation system which replaced it marked important structural differences in the way that convict labour was organised. Under assignment, disembarked convicts were routinely handed over to the private sector as cheap labour. Settlers supplied with convict workers had to feed, clothe and house their charges but could not administer corporal punishment. Any master wishing to disciple a convict assigned to him or her had to bring charges before a magistrates' bench. Although magistrates could not hear cases that involved their own assigned servants, the majority were themselves the masters of convict labour and were therefore far from disinterested parties.[14] It is thus not surprising that assignment attracted considerable criticism from metropolitan penal reformers, who argued that convicts in the Australian colonies were not punished according to the severity of the crime that they had committed in Britain and Ireland, but according to how useful they were as cheap colonial labour. Like slavery, this system of forced labour extraction was characterised as morally corrupting because it provided masters of convict labour with arbitrary powers (flogging was singled out for particular criticism) and convicts with little moral direction.[15] Following publication of the 1837–1838 report by the British Parliamentary Select Committee on Transportation, newly arrived male convicts had to serve a period in a probationary gang. The length of time to be spent in this gang was fixed according to the length of the convict's sentence. The new system was designed to placate the opponents of transportation by aligning the colonial treatment of transported convicts with the precepts of the British penitentiary system. It included, for example, much greater use of incarceration within cells, and it was only after successfully negotiating probation that convicts became eligible for service in the private sector.[16] The new regulations also stipulated that employers had to enter into contracts with their transported workforce, who were to be financially remunerated for their services, albeit at lower rates than those received by free workers.

The introduction of probation was associated with a shift in punishment away from flogging in favour of solitary confinement (see Figure 10.1). This change came at considerable cost to the colonial administration (the cost to convicts has yet to be evaluated). Unlike flogging, solitary confinement was expensive to administer in that it necessitated the construction of cells. The number of days spent in solitary confinement per male convict declined after 1841 as the colonial administration found it difficult to maintain the ratio of cells to prisoners in the presence of increasing arrivals from Britain and

---

[14] Hamish Maxwell-Stewart, *Closing Hell's Gates: The Death of a Convict Station* (Sydney: Allen & Unwin, 2008), 157–63.

[15] Kirsten McKenzie, *Scandal in the Colonies: Sydney and Cape Town 1820–1850* (Melbourne: Melbourne University Press, 2004), 121–6.

[16] Ian Brand, *The Convict Probation System: Van Diemen's Land 1839–1854* (Hobart: Blubber Head Press, 1990), 3–106, and Cassandra Pybus and Hamish Maxwell-Stewart, *American Citizens British Slaves: Yankee Political Prisoners in an Australian Penal Colony 1839–1850* (Melbourne: Melbourne University Press, 2002), 83–94.

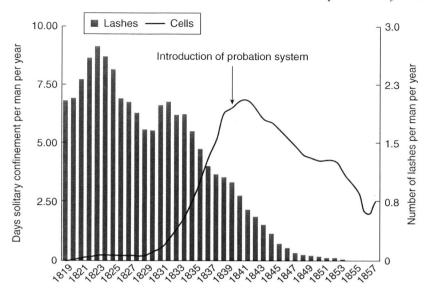

Figure 10.1 Number of lashes and days spent in cells per male convict, Van Diemen's Land 1819–1857 (moving five-year average).

Source: Systematic 4 per cent sample of entries in TAHO, Conduct Registers for Male Convicts Arriving in the Assignment Period, Con 31/ vols 1–48; Supplementary Conduct Registers, Con 32/ vols 1–5; Conduct Registers for Male Convicts Arriving in the Probation Period, Con 33/ vols. 1–115.

Ireland. As a result they fell back on the use of sentences to road gangs and chain gangs, the former consisting of convicts working out of irons and the latter with fetters on their legs although prisoners were not chained to one another. Thus, while it is true that flogging diminished in the 1830s and 1840s, it is a misnomer to equate this with a shift from physical to psychological punishment. While the use of solitary confinement became increasingly important, so did the shackling of convicts and the extraction of labour through the use of ganging.

If transportation to Tasmania really did help to make the colony one of the 'most serene places on earth' then probation rather than assignment was the influential factor. In the two decades after 1840, some 28,000 male convicts passed through probationary gangs before signing 'passholder' contracts with colonial employers or being issued with tickets-of-leave which further eased employment restrictions.[17] In the remainder of this chapter we will examine

---

[17] Passholders could sign a contract to work for a colonial employer for small monetary payments. A convict in receipt of a ticket-of-leave could negotiate for a higher rate but had to reside within a particular district. See David Meredith and Deborah Oxley, 'Contracting Convicts: The Convict Labour Market in Van Diemen's Land 1840–1857', *Australian Economic History Review*, 45.1 (2005), 45–72.

the extent to which the life course histories of a longitudinal sample of male probationers can shed light on this question.

The reasons why some transported offenders continued to offend after their arrival, probation and release in Tasmania and why others built futures away from offending are obviously complex. In an attempt to explore these issues in greater depth we collected information about pre-transportation court appearances, sentencing, occupation, religion, literacy, place of birth, age and height as recorded on arrival in Australia. In the case of a systematic sample of 1,124 convicts we expanded this information by transcribing the summary data entered in each individual's conduct record. This included the date of each magistrates' bench encounter, a description of each offence and information about punishments as well as indulgences and other notations. This amounted to a total of 9,672 events (8.6 per sampled convict). The sample itself was selected by taking every record for a convict with a police number ending in the digits 06, 33, 56, 83 who had an entry in the 115-volume probation conduct registers.[18] This technique was designed to draw a representative 4 per cent longitudinal sample that would reflect changes in convictions and punishments over time.

We linked each sampled conduct record to information contained in death registers, absconding notices and lists of issued certificates of freedom, conditional pardons and absolute pardons.[19] This enabled us to determine the number of convicts who died under sentence or escaped without recapture, and to calculate the amount of time served by those who negotiated a legitimate exit. Further, any serving convict who wished to marry had to apply to the colonial government for permission to do so and we also linked the sample to the register of these applications and, in turn, to civil marriages, to determine if proposed unions were actually solemnised. Information about post-sentence emigration was extracted from departure records. While these are incomplete, they survive for an estimated 30 per cent of all former convict departures. Coverage is particularly good for northern Tasmania ports in the period 1846–1854 and, importantly, these years span the Victorian gold rush of 1851.

Information about reconviction was taken from the *Tasmanian Police Gazette* for the period 14 June 1861 to 2 November 1900. The principle purpose of the *Gazette* was to circulate information about offenders, or likely offenders, between police offices in Tasmania and other police forces in Australia and New Zealand. To this end, the paper carried descriptions of all of those who were wanted for questioning, had been arrested or had been discharged from prison or a pauper establishment.

---

[18] Conduct Records for Male Convicts arriving in the Probation Era, Con 33. Tasmanian Archives and Heritage Office (henceforth TAHO).

[19] A certificate of freedom was issued when a sentence expired. A conditional pardon freed a convict prior to the expiration of their sentence to transportation on the condition that they did not return to Europe. An absolute pardon removed this condition. The only way convicts sentenced to transportation to life could obtain their freedom was through a conditional or absolute pardon.

Table 10.1 Life events identified for a 1-in-25 sample of 1,124 male convicts transported to Van Diemen's Land, 1840–1854

Event	N	%
Died while still under sentence[a]	88	8
Escaped[b]	67	6
Applied for permission to marry while still under sentence[c]	141	13
Issued with a certificate of freedom or conditional or absolute pardon[d]	927	82
Known to have departed the colony[e]	166	15
Re-arrested 1861–1900[f]	100	9
Admitted into a pauper institution[g]	81	7

Sources:
[a] Tasmanian Archives and Heritage Office (TAHO): Conduct Registers for Male Convicts arriving in the Probation Period, Con 33/ vols. 1 – 115; Con 63/1–2, Register of Convict Deaths; GO 33, Quarterly Returns 1834–48 returns of casualties included in the despatches sent to the Secretary of State for the Colonies by the Governor of Van Diemen's Land. National Archive, UK: HO 10/51 Reel No 80, Muster 1841; HO10/39 Reel No 74, Muster 1849.
[b] TAHO, Con 33/1–115, *Tasmanian Government Gazette*, 3 January 1840 – 25 December 1860.
[c] TAHO, Permission to Marry Registers, Con 52/1–7.
[d] TAHO, Con 33/1–115, *Tasmanian Government Gazette*, 3 January 1840 – 25 December 1860.
[e] TAHO, Lists of Departing Passengers, CSO 20/23; CSO 95/1; Cus 33 1-3; Cus 36 1-560; Pol 220 1-2; Pol 459 1-2.
[f] *Tasmanian Police Gazette*, 14 June 1861 – 2 November 1900.
[g] TAHO, *Tasmanian Police Gazette*, 14 June 1861 – 2 November 1900, HSD 274/1; SWD 10/38.

As all these records provided the name of the convict vessel that had first brought the offender to the colony, it was possible to link information with some degree of certainty.[20] The results of this process are summarised in Table 10.1.

The linked data enabled a detailed reconstruction of convict life courses. To provide an example: James Ashcroft was born in Manchester in 1809. A bricklayer and slater by trade, he was raised by his uncle although he spent frequent short stretches in prison. He confessed that prior to being transported he had served one sentence of seven days and another of four months for stealing coal as well as being convicted four times for vagrancy. He was tried on 31 August 1840 for housebreaking and sentenced to seven years' transportation.[21] Embarked on the *Duncan*, he arrived in Van Diemen's Land in the following year and was described as aged 32, 5 feet 5 inches tall, and with light brown hair and grey eyes. His other distinguishing features were a hairy chest and three blue dots on his right arm.[22] He also had a ring tattooed

[20] We searched a total of 2,154 editions of the *Tasmanian Police Gazette* issued between 1861 and 1900. These had been converted to machine-readable text using optical character recognition software (OCR). The method we adopted was to match by convict vessel and then name.
[21] TAHO, Con 14/1/5.
[22] TAHO, Con 18/27, 101.

on the middle finger of his right hand but declared that he was single. He could read and write, possibly as a result of schooling he had received while in prison and on the voyage to Australia. The ship's surgeon also noted that he had been punished three times while onboard the *Duncan*.[23]

Following his arrival and processing in Hobart, Ashcroft was sent to the Brown's River probation station, where he was punished four times in a period of two and a half months for being absent without leave.[24] On the fifth occasion he was sent to Port Arthur penal station where he spent nine months clocking up another three offences. He was then returned to Brown's River where he was charged in quick succession with being absent without leave and refusing to work, and for which he was sentenced to 15 months hard labour in chains at Salt Water Creek on the Tasman Peninsula. While labouring there he was convicted for being absent without leave four times, as well as for misconduct, namely having his irons off at night, having potatoes in his possession, and giving bread and meat to a prisoner undergoing solitary confinement. After his seventh offence he was relocated to the nearby Coal Mines, where he was punished once more for being absent, and twice for trafficking government jackets. Returned to Salt Water Creek, he was subsequently charged with mislaying a spoon and his shirt, as well as for having potatoes and turnips in his possession. He was then transferred to the Prison Barracks in Hobart from where he absconded and was thus sentenced to 12 months' hard labour in chains, and then sent back to the Coal Mines where he was once more charged with refusing to work. After serving out his sentence in irons, he was transferred to Impression Bay where he was stationed when he finally emerged from probation. When he received his certificate of freedom just over a year later, on 1 September 1847, he had already served 116 days in solitary confinement, 1,200 days in chains and had ground out 42 days on the treadwheel as well as receiving 133 strokes of the lash.

Upon gaining his freedom, Ashcroft walked from Hobart to Launceston, a distance of just over 100 miles, in search of work. Alexander Milligan, later a witness against Ashcroft, recounted that the 40-year-old approached him complaining that 'he was better off when under government'. Milligan took pity on him and gave him an axe to cut some wood in return for the promise of food, but the former convict disappeared along with the axe. Ashcroft was subsequently sentenced to a further seven years' transportation at the Launceston Quarter Sessions in August 1859 even though the axe was only valued in court at one shilling.[25] He had been free for less than two years.

During the second transportation sentence, Ashcroft was hired out as a convict labourer to a property holder in Bothwell in central Tasmania, but was charged with neglect of duty and placed in a road party at Ross. Although his initial sentence to hard labour was only for three months, it was extended

[23] TAHO, Con 33/8.
[24] TAHO, Con 33/8 and Con 27/8.
[25] *Cornwall Chronicle*, 11 August 1859.

after Ashcroft was also charged with being idle, neglecting work, absconding, and falling asleep while employed as a watchman. In July 1851, while in the Prison Barracks in Launceston, he was sentenced to an additional 12 months' imprisonment and hard labour for insubordination. Following this offence, he was transferred to Norfolk Island, and arrived at this notorious and remote South Pacific penal station on 14 September 1851. While there he was sentenced a further 31 times for petty breaches of prison regulations. This earned him 61 lashes and he was kept at constant hard labour for nearly four years (a result of multiple extensions to the sentence that had resulted in his transfer from Van Diemen's Land). On 25 August 1854 he was shipped to Port Arthur and just over a year later to the Hobart Prison Barracks. From there he was sent to work as a convict passholder on a property at Swanport on the east coast, only to be convicted again and sentenced to a further nine months' hard labour in irons for exposing his person. He finally regained his freedom on 10 February 1857 when he was 48 years old after a stint with the Douglas River Coal Company.[26]

On 17 July 1858 Ashcroft was once more charged with stealing an axe from a property in Warwick Street, Hobart. In his defence he pleaded that he was 'in liquor at the time and was now extremely sorry for what he had done'. This time he only received six months' imprisonment with hard labour.[27] Following his discharge from gaol he temporarily swapped his obsession with axes for weightier items. He was charged twice in August and September 1860 with stripping lead from the top of a pump and the roofing of a government gun battery.[28] Sentenced to 12 months' imprisonment he served yet another stint at Port Arthur. Following his release on 24 October 1861, he was convicted of gross indecency with Charles Littleton on 10 February 1862. Both men were sent to the house of correction in Hobart; Ashcroft for three months and Littleton for two.[29] In May of the same year Ashcroft borrowed a wheelbarrow from Elizabeth Winter of Hampden Road, Hobart, under the pretext that he needed it to collect some bones. After she acquiesced he promptly decamped, and was arrested after he had sold the barrow for nine shillings.[30] In February 1863, he was convicted of stealing a brass tap valued at five shillings and was sentenced to 12 months' hard labour.[31] While serving this sentence he absconded from the gang on the Government Domain, returned to Elizabeth Winter's house, and stole another wheelbarrow from her. He received sentences of 12 months' hard labour in chains for absconding and six years for the larceny.[32]

[26] TAHO, Con 37/1, 1553.
[27] *Hobart Town Daily Mercury*, 20 July 1858.
[28] *Mercury*, 25 August and 8 September 1860.
[29] *Tasmanian Police Gazette*, 25 October 1861, vol. 1, issue 37 and *Mercury*, 11 February 1862.
[30] *Mercury*, 22 May and 31 May 1862.
[31] *Mercury*, 24 February 1863.
[32] *Mercury*, 18 December 1863, 23 December 1863 and 29 January 1864.

Ashcroft was released on 26 September 1868 after serving four years at Port Arthur. His description circulated in the *Police Gazette* reveals that his hair had now turned partially grey and he had acquired the image of a sailor on his left arm to add to the ring tattooed on the middle finger of his right hand.[33] A month later he was charged with being an idle and disorderly person with no means of support. The offence was exacerbated by his bad police character and his possession of a tin can for which he could not satisfactorily account, and he was sentenced to a further six months in gaol.[34] He absconded seven days later from the gang employed at Government House, but was almost immediately rearrested for stealing yet another axe.[35] When charged, he told the arresting constable: 'What is a man that is a bolter to do? I would steal the Governor's axe rather than starve.' He was equally assertive in court when addressing some 'very defiant observations to the Bench' and as a result was sentenced to two years' imprisonment with hard labour.[36] By the time he was discharged on 8 February 1871 he was now blind in one eye.[37] However, on the very same day he was released he was charged once more with stealing a wheelbarrow. Now described as 'a repulsive looking old man', he was sentenced to a further two-year stretch.[38]

When Ashcroft was discharged from prison on Christmas Day 1872, his hair was now fully grey and his height measured one and half inches less than when he arrived in Tasmania 21 years earlier. With no means of support he gained admission to the Brickfields Invalid Depot (an institution which housed paupers) on 4 January and remained there until he was discharged on 3 March 1873.[39] The following month he was charged with being idle and disorderly and sentenced to another three months' imprisonment. Discharged on 9 July, he again gained admission to the Brickfields depot 13 days later by claiming he was unable to work. He remained there until 25 August when he discharged himself and walked to the Midlands town of Oatlands, where he was promptly arrested for begging, sentenced to one month's imprisonment, and sent back to Hobart.[40] Released from gaol on 15 October he once more walked to Oatlands where he was charged 16 days later with being idle and disorderly and sentenced to two months' imprisonment.[41] Following his

---

[33] *Tasmanian Police Gazette*, 25 September 1868, vol. 7, issue 390.

[34] *Mercury*, 23 October 1868.

[35] *Tasmanian Police Gazette*, 30 October 1868, vol. 7, issue 395 and *Mercury*, 31 October 1868.

[36] *Tasmanian Police Gazette*, 13 November 1868, vol. 7, issue 397 and *Mercury*, 4 November 1868.

[37] *Tasmanian Police Gazette*, 10 February 1871, vol. 10, issue 604.

[38] *Tasmanian Police Gazette*, 17 February 1871, vol. 10, issue 605 and *Mercury*, 9 February 1871.

[39] *Tasmanian Police Gazette*, 27 December 1872, vol. 11, issue 702 and 14 March 1873, vol 12, issue 713.

[40] *Tasmanian Police Gazette*, 11 July 1873, vol. 12, issue 729 and 29 August 1873, vol. 12, issue 736.

[41] *Tasmanian Police Gazette*, 17 October 1873, vol. 12, issue 743 and 2 January 1874, vol. 13, issue 754.

discharge on New Year's Eve 1873, he was arrested 12 days later for begging on the streets of Hobart on a Sunday. Now described as 'an infirm old man', he was sent to gaol for six months.[42] He was admitted to the Colonial Hospital in Hobart on 26 February 1875, and died there the following month. The cause of death was recorded as 'senilis'.[43] Although Ashcroft's age was estimated as 75 he was probably only 66 years old, but by the time of his death he had been brought before a court of some description on at least 96 occasions.

Ashcroft's long history of encounters with the colonial state was far from atypical. In all, at least 100, or 9 per cent, of the 1,124 convicts in our sample were reconvicted in the period 1861–1900. The actual rate of reoffending was much higher, however, than these figures suggest as many convicts had either died or left the colony. Using death registers and conduct records and musters, we determined that 88 convicts in the sample died while under sentence (death rates were particularly high in the first year in the colony due to the knock-on effects of a long voyage at sea).[44] A further 18 deaths that occurred after the convicts in the sample became free were recorded in these sources. We know, however, that this is an underestimate of the number of former convicts who died in the period prior to 1861. Employing Tasmanian age-specific mortality rates and the age structure of our sample, we estimate that a further 102 convicts are likely to have died prior to the issue of the first edition of the *Tasmanian Police Gazette*.[45]

At least 166 other former convicts migrated to Victoria and elsewhere in Australia and New Zealand, although this too is an underestimate. The rate of emigration from Van Diemen's Land increased dramatically as a result of the news of the discovery of alluvial gold in Victoria, officially announced in September 1851. A register of departures was kept by the Tasmanian government which often listed the ship of arrival in the colony and the status of the departing individual (conditional pardon, free by servitude, etc.) but these details were often not filled out. Some registers are also missing. The colonial government, however, sent aggregated totals of the number of former convicts known to have departed the colony between 1846 and 1852 to the Colonial Office in London, and these were subsequently published in British Parliamentary Papers.[46] Taking both sets of figures, it is possible to estimate that the true rate of departure was closer to a third (as opposed to the 15 per cent of our cohort linked to a departure record). Our estimates of the number

---

[42] *Tasmanian Police Gazette*, 2 January 1874, vol. 13, issue 754, 17 July 1874, vol. 13, issue 782 and *Mercury*, 13 January 1874.

[43] Colonial Hospital death register, 26 February 1875, TAHO, HSD, 145/1.

[44] Hamish Maxwell-Stewart and Ralph Shlomowitz, 'Mortality and Migration: A Survey', in David Boyd Haycock and Sally Archer (eds), *Health and Medicine at Sea 1700–1900* (Suffolk: Boydell Press, 2009), 137.

[45] R. Kippen, 'Death in Tasmania: Using Civil Death Registers to Measure Nineteenth-Century Cause-Specific Mortality', PhD thesis (The Australian National University, Canberra, 2002).

[46] British Parliamentary Papers, *Crime & Transportation Series* (Shannon: Irish University Press, 1970) 11 (1851–1854), 93; 12 (1852–1853), 299.

Table 10.2 Observed and estimated death and migration rates for 1-in-25 sample

	Observed	Estimated actual
Recorded in Conduct Record as escaped	67	67
Deaths 1840–1860	106	210
Migrants 1847–1860	166	380
Remaining members of sample on strength in Tasmania 1861	785	467

in our cohort who were alive and located in Tasmania in 1861 are provided in Table 10.2.[47] We calculate that the actual reconviction rate was about 21 per cent.

In terms of their rate of reoffending, 46 of the 100 recidivists were only charged once and 85 were charged on fewer than five occasions. In all, 46 per cent of all charges laid were brought against just 15 individuals, who were each charged five times or more. Conversely, those with longer records tended to receive shorter custodial sentences. The five worst offenders in terms of number of recorded convictions were sentenced to just seven months per offence compared to 19.4 months for those who were charged only once over the period (see Table 10.3). Like Ashcroft, the other multiple offenders in the cohort had significant numbers of convictions for vagrancy and for being idle and disorderly.

A breakdown of all 270 charges brought against the cohort is provided in Table 10.4. While comparatively few of these were serious, defendants convicted of burglary, housebreaking, robbery, sexual assault and murder were more likely to be one-off rather than repeat offenders. As Godfrey and Cox found for Western Australia, the majority of convictions were for relatively small-scale offences, many of which were tried in lower courts.[48]

While recidivism rates were significant amongst former probation-era male convicts who remained in Tasmania, there was little to physically distinguish those with a record of reconviction from their more law-abiding shipmates. They were the same age on arrival and their adult heights were almost identical. There was nothing to suggest that a nutritionally deprived childhood contributed to subsequent offending. Lack of schooling does not appear to have influenced reoffending rates either. Both cohorts had near identical literacy scores upon disembarkation in Van Diemen's Land.[49] Reoffenders were not more likely to speak with an Irish brogue, or for that matter any other

---

[47] This is almost certainly an overestimate as considerable numbers of migrants returned to Tasmania.

[48] Godfrey and Cox, "'The Last Fleet'", 245–6.

[49] We gave each convict a literacy rating as follows: 0 = neither read nor write; 0.5 = read a little; 1 read; 1.5 read and write a little; 2 read and write. Gaelic and Welsh monoglots were scored as though they had the equivalent level of proficiency in English.

Table 10.3 Number of re-offenders, percentage of all charges and mean length of sentence per offence, 1-in-25 sample

	No. of offenders	Percentage of all charges	Mean length of sentence per offence (months)
1 offence	46	17.0	19.4
2 to 4	39	37.4	13.0
5 to 9	10	21.5	16.1
More than 10	5	24.1	7.0
	100	100	Mean for cohort as a whole = 13.3

Table 10.4 Re-offenders by type of offence, 1-in-25 sample

Offence	Number of prosecutions
Murder	1
Robbery, burglary and housebreaking	11
Animal theft	5
Indecent assault	6
Larceny	85
Absconding	5
Unlawfully on premises	3
Arson, destruction of property	10
Hawking without a license	1
Non-maintenance of a dependent	2
Harbouring prostitutes	1
Uttering, obtaining goods under false pretences	10
Assault, resisting arrest	25
Breach of Masters and Servants Act	17
Non-payment of fine or bill	2
Possessing an illicit still	2
Indecency	8
Idle and disorderly, disturbing the peace, begging, vagrancy	68
Breach of prison discipline, non-compliance with an order, using threatening language	8
Total	270

kind of accent, nor were they of a particular religious persuasion. They were also not more likely to be either urban born or unskilled. Indeed, it would be impossible in terms of the data collected on arrival in Australia to identify a future recidivist. In this respect our powers of prediction turn out to be no better than the nineteenth-century criminal and military courts that sentenced convicts to transportation in the first place. The number of years that the future recidivists were ordered to serve was nearly identical to those with no record of subsequent offending. There is nothing to indicate that those convicts who reoffended were in some way disadvantaged upon arrival

Table 10.5 Bivariate analysis of reconviction status

Bivariate analysis		Reconvicted after sentence	No record of reconviction	P
Age on arrival (years)		27.4	27.3	0.923
Height (inches)		65.3	65.4	0.731
Literacy		1.26	1.27	0.864
Country of birth	Ireland (%)	9.5	90.5	
	Other (%)	10.2	89.8	0.784
Place of birth	Urban (%)	9.5	90.5	
	Rural (%)	10.3	89.7	0.736
Religion	Protestant (%)	10.6	89.4	
	Catholic (%)	9.0	91.0	0.472
Industry	Agriculture (%)	9.7	90.3	
	Labourer (%)	12.4	87.6	0.309
	Urban semi-skilled, skilled (%)	8.3	91.7	0.518
Length of sentence (years)		10.3	10.5	0.685

in Australia or were considered by the metropolitan authorities to be particularly problematic, although we intend to expand the sample size to re-examine this issue in the future.

Prior to disembarkation in Australia each convict was questioned about their record of former employment, next of kin, and previous convictions. Before this interview with the principal colonial officials charged with running the penal colony each prisoner was also told that their inquisitors were already familiar with the broad outline of their record having perused the hulk and gaol reports forwarded with each transport vessel. Falsehoods, prisoners were warned, would result in punishment. We have no means of knowing the extent to which, anxious to get off to a good start in the penal colony, convicts revealed the truth about their past. It is revealing, however, that they routinely confessed to having committed more offences than those recorded in their gaol reports.

We compared the number of confessed prior convictions for recidivists and those convicts for whom we had no record of conviction after emancipation. As an added test we also calculated the number of months that both groups admitted to having been sentenced to. The future recidivists confessed to slightly more convictions, but to having served less time in correctional institutions. There was a danger that the length of time served was unduly influenced by a small number of convicts in the sample who revealed that they had been previously transported. Sentences to imprisonment tended to be short, usually under two years and frequently less than six months. Indeed many were for petty matters, such as vagrancy, theft of firewood and apples, and breach of employment contract. Since the minimum sentence to transportation was seven years we excluded these longer sentences to make sure

Table 10.6 Confessed conviction record prior to transportation by reconviction status.

	Reconvicted after sentence	*No record of reconviction*
No. of prior convictions	1.5	1.3
No. of months served	8.0	10.1
Months served omitting sentences > 7 years	6.4	6.7

that a few atypical cases did not unduly influence our results. With these cases omitted, the amount of time the two groups confessed to have spent in gaol was nearly identical. We could find no statistical evidence that the colonial recidivists had a worse record of offending prior to transportation. In short, there is no indication that they constituted a lumpen or criminal residuum. To turn a memorable phrase on its head – they were not, as Humphrey McQueen once quipped, a 'deformed stratification ... vomited up by the maelstrom which was delineating class in Britain'.[50]

If the factors that impacted upon the life of convicts prior to their arrival in Van Diemen's Land do not appear to have influenced the extent to which they were able to desist from offending post-sentence, then much the same can be said for colonial marriage. While slightly fewer future recidivists were named in the permission to marry registers, the difference – at the 5 per cent level – was not significant. As a check on these results, we linked the applications to the civil marriage registers in to order to see whether a greater number of recidivists were jilted or otherwise disappointed grooms. We could find no evidence to support this hypothesis. These results are particularly surprising since other studies indicate that marriage can positively impact upon desistence rates. Indeed, this is one of the points argued by Braithwaite.[51]

It is possible that the permission to marry indexes are a poor guide to the actual rate of marriage amongst our two cohorts. The persistent offenders were less likely to be released early than those for whom we have no evidence of reoffending. There was a tendency for prisoners who spent longer under sentence to apply for permission to marry, while others waited until they were free, thus circumventing the need to obtain state as well as clerical sanction. Thus, it is possible that a statistically significant difference may emerge when actual marriage rates are compared. It is also possible that unions that involved future recidivists were less likely to result in issue. Children might have a greater bearing on recidivism rates than marriage alone. Former convicts who failed to form a colonial family had no relatives to turn to for support as

[50] Humphrey McQueen, 'Convicts and Rebels', *Labour History*, 15 (1968), 24–5.
[51] Braithwaite, 'Crime in a Convict Republic', 26. See also Barry Godfrey, David Cox and Steve Farrell, *Criminal Lives: Family, Employment and Offending* (Oxford: Oxford University Press, 2007).

Table 10.7 Rate named in permission to marry register by reconviction status.

Bivariate analysis		Reconvicted after sentence	No record of reconviction	P
Permission to marry	PTM (%)	11.3	88.7	
	No PTM (%)	13.5	86.5	0.731

they aged and it is possible that this was an important determinant of offending in that vagrancy charges often triggered a pattern of post-transportation sentence reconvictions.

It is also true that in some circumstances marriage can increase offending rates.[52] This was indeed the case for some of the more serious charges brought against our cohort of persistent offenders. Thomas Reynard, for example was accused of sexually assaulting his step-daughter, although he was acquitted.[53] Michael Bakey, the only recidivist charged with murder, was convicted at the Supreme Court in Hobart, on 20 February 1877, of poisoning Thomas Lynch. The unfortunate victim had drunk rum doctored with Steiner's vermin-destroying paste from an old case bottle found amongst raspberry canes owned by Denis O'Reilly. Bakey had planted the case bottle in the hope that O'Reilly, who was having an affair with his wife, would find it and consume the contents. However, the plan went badly wrong when O'Reilly gave the bottle to Lynch.[54] We might also add that marriage is unlikely to be a powerful shaper of post-emancipation behaviour since colonial sex imbalances ensured that few former male convicts had the opportunity to find a partner of the opposite sex. Indeed this may have been one of the factors that drove emigration rates.[55]

When the record under sentence of recidivists and their more law-abiding shipmates was compared significant differences emerged. Those who subsequently reoffended spent more days per year in solitary confinement or undergoing hard labour on the roads (both significant at the 1 per cent level). They were also more likely to be fined (significant at the 5 per cent level). Perhaps not surprisingly given this record of treatment, disproportionate numbers of them tried to abscond (significant at the 1 per cent level). In short, James Ashcroft's shocking experience of transportation was shared by other future recidivists. It is perhaps worth reminding ourselves here that his numerous magistrates' bench appearances were overwhelmingly for petty breaches of

[52] See, for example, Jeffrey S. Alder, *First in Violence Deepest in Dirt: Homicide in Chicago 1875–1920* (Cambridge, MA: Harvard University Press, 2006), 45–84.
[53] *Mercury*, 23 July 1879.
[54] *Mercury*, 21 February 1877.
[55] For the impact of marriage on offending see Robert J. Sampson, John H. Laub and Christopher Wimer, 'Does Marriage Reduce Crime? A Counterfactual Approach to Within-Individual Casual Effects', *Criminology* 44.3 (2006), 465–508.

Table 10.8 Convict experience under sentence of transportation by reconviction status.

Bivariate analysis	Reconvicted after sentence	No record of reconviction	p
Length of sentence (years)	10.3	10.5	0.685
Years served	9.4	8.7	0.021*
Days in cells per year	1.8	1.1	0.001**
Days in chains per year	11.4	7.5	0.129
Days hard labour per year	47.7	13.9	0.000**
Days on treadwheel per year	0.2	0.2	0.833
Number of lashes per year	0.5	0.5	0.698
Shillings fined per year	0.8	0.4	0.034*
Average number of absconding attempts	0.73	0.38	0.000**

Notes: * = significant at the 5 per cent level; ** = significant at the 1 per cent level.

prison discipline. It was repeated charges of being absent while at Brown's River, for instance, that precipitated his slide down the rungs of the convict system. Whatever the wrongs and rights of this we can be sure of one thing: if the punishment meted out to Ashcroft was meant to deter him from breaking the criminal law, it failed. To mangle Jeremy Bentham's famous phrase – probation was a machine that ground some rogues dishonest.

There is powerful evidence that the probation system made it more difficult for some offenders to adjust to life post-emancipation. Braithwaite does acknowledge that transportation created a 'brutalised minority who responded to injustice with escalated defiance'.[56] Our study suggests, however, that this minority may have been considerable and that it left its mark on the colonial court system long after the last transport vessel had arrived. It is of course possible that this was a trait that was peculiar to the probation system and that assignment was more effective at resocialising offenders. Probation was intended after all to reposition transportation in order to make it more acceptable to its critics. Part of this repositioning included an increase in the surveillance and segregation of newly arrived convicts, features which were designed to mimic the penitentiary experience. Even under the assignment system, however, large numbers of convicts spent many months labouring in road gangs, chain gangs and penal stations under the watchful eye of overseers and other minions of the state. These were experiences that were far from benign. In fact, our data suggests that the amount of prosecutions brought against serving convicts varied considerably, reaching a peak in 1838 before declining substantially in the 1840s (see

[56] Braithwaite, 'Crime in a Convict Republic', 25.

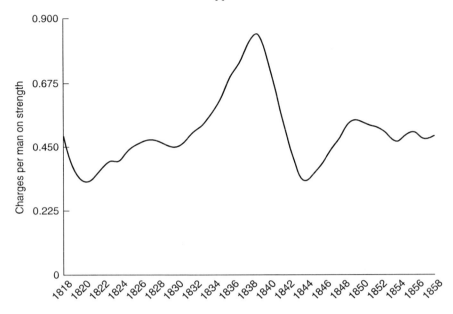

Figure 10.2 Mean number of charges brought per male convict per year, Van Diemen's Land 1818–1858 (moving five-year average).

Source: Systematic 4 per cent sample of entries in TAHO, Conduct Registers for Male Convicts Arriving in the Assignment Period, Con 31/ vols 1 – 48; Supplementary Conduct Registers, Con 32/ vols 1 – 5; Conduct Registers for Male Convicts Arriving in the Probation Period, Con 33/ vols. 1 – 115.

Figure 10.2). In other words, there is no evidence to suggest that assignment was less coercive than probation.

As Godfrey and Cox found for Western Australia, Braithwaite's assessment of the impact of transportation on colonial society significantly underestimates the proportion of former transported convicts who appeared before the lower courts. Nevertheless, our data suggests that the underlying premise, that the Australian convict experiment resulted in much lower rates of reoffending than later systems of incarceration, is sound. While the full range of factors that helped former transported convicts to desist require further study, some issues are clear. There was an association between the levels of punishment incurred under sentence and a failure to desist from reoffending post-release, for example, and solitary confinement and hard labour were not successful agents of reform. It is thus possible that the introduction of the probation system, which aimed to make transportation politically acceptable by aligning it more closely with the precepts of the penal reform movement merely succeeded in retarding reform for a minority of prisoners.

It is harder to assess the impact that assignment had on reoffending because of the lack of an accessible pre-1861 source documenting encounters with lower courts for the entire transportation period – although this deficiency could be overcome through future archival work. While prosecution rates under assignment rose to a peak in 1839, ganging and cellular punishments were less prevalent and there was much more resort to flogging. Greater use was also made of convict labour in the private sector – under the assignment system the majority of convicts were sent to work on farms and other privately owned businesses. It remains to be seen whether these different circumstances aided successful long-term escapes from the judicial establishment, as the Braithwaite thesis would predict, or whether the lash and private sector exploitation blunted post-emancipation desistance rates.

11 On licence

Understanding punishment, recidivism and desistance in penal policy, 1853–1945

David Cox, Barry Godfrey, Helen Johnston and Joanne Turner

During the nineteenth and early twentieth centuries, British legislators reacted to the perceived growth in a hard core of violent repeat offenders and struggled to find solutions to the problem of recidivism. The concept of dangerousness, and the potential threat posed by those people who appeared to be less affected by civilising processes that appeared to be effective in making Britain a safer place to live, have since been a recurring topic of study for researchers of nineteenth-century society.[1] Others, such as Leon Radzinowicz and Roger Hood, have focused more on legislation such as the Penal Servitude Acts (1853–64), Habitual Offender Acts (1869–91) and the Preventive Detention Act (1908), which were designed to incapacitate offenders through the imposition of long prison sentences and extended police supervision.[2] In an attempt to make the system work effectively, a vast bureaucracy was created which was responsible for the identification and tracking of many thousands of former prisoners and convicts. This served to create a huge range and number of archived written documentary records – many of which can now be utilised by historians to examine the impact of particular forms of legislation on offenders and the length of their criminal careers. In this chapter we present some case studies in order to outline both the possibilities, and also some of the possible pitfalls, of using these bureaucratic records in modern research. We contribute to the debates initiated by Radzinowicz and Hood by examining the impact of penal practices and policies on repeat offenders in order to understand the relative effects of punishment and surveillance, and also other significant events in individual offenders' lives, on their offending over the whole course of their lives.

---

[1] Mark Brown and John Pratt (eds), *Dangerous Offenders: Punishment and Social Order* (London: Routledge, 2000); John Pratt, "Dangerousness and Modern Society," in Mark Brown and John Pratt (eds), *Dangerous Offenders: Punishment and Social Order* (London: Routledge, 2000), 35–48; John Pratt, *Punishment and Civilization: Penal Tolerance and Intolerance in Modern Society* (London: SAGE, 2002), 213.

[2] Leon Radzinowicz and Roger Hood, "Judicial and Sentencing Standards: Victorian Attempts to Solve a Perennial Problem," *University of Pennsylvania Law Review* 127 (1979), 1288–349; Leon Radzinowicz and Roger Hood, "Incapacitating the Habitual Criminal: The English Experience," *Michigan Law Review* 78.3 (1980), 1305–89.

The period under study, broadly the middle of the nineteenth century to the early twentieth century, was rife with changing conceptions of criminality, degeneracy and moral imbecility. The 1870s witnessed the beginnings of anthropomorphic criminology and Lombrosian theory. Biology was thought to be a central driver for criminality, and sentencing which was designed to deter the rational offender was beginning to be seen as ineffectual: more than that, in fact, inappropriate. Given that visceral criminality could not be deterred by normal sentencing tariffs, only very long sentences and surveillance post-release were thought to be capable of protecting society. By contrast to the whirl of ideas about why some people offended persistently, contemporary conceptions of desistance (an individual offender's movement away from a life of crime) were rudimentary (indeed almost non-existent). Desistance was considered improbable, and only possible through moral improvement supported by religiosity. However, by the 1890s, many offenders, even habitual ones, were thought capable of changing their ways with the support of rehabilitative policies enacted by the prison authorities. It would be many more decades before surveillance became associated with probation programmes designed to support individuals moving away from crime, but the social control measures increasingly introduced between the 1869 Habitual Offenders Act (which attempted widespread surveillance of repeat offenders) and the Probation of Offenders Act 1908 were important steps on the route to twentieth-century theories of desistance. Modern studies of desistance point to wider support networks as being important to convicts sustaining pro-social lifestyles rather than criminal identities, and also gaining education and employment and forming meaningful relationships.

Fortunately for our understanding of nineteenth-century offenders, the systems erected to watch over habitual offenders and ex-convicts created a huge range and number of bureaucratic records – many of which can be utilised by historians to examine the effectiveness of legislation and of other events outside of the criminal justice system, such as marriage, child-rearing and employment, on criminal careers. Recent studies by Godfrey, Cox and Farrall and Johnston and Godfrey have now supplemented existing research on desistance, and have provided valuable historical evidence of how and in what circumstances habitual or serious offenders continued, or alternatively, abandoned criminal careers.[3] In this chapter we describe the methodology we used to unlock the penal bureaucracy and present some examples in order to show the possibilities (and some possible pitfalls) of using these bureaucratic records in reconstructing the experiences of those subject to, and confined

---

[3] Barry S. Godfrey, David J. Cox and Stephen Farrall, *Criminal Lives: Family Life, Employment and Offending* (Oxford: Oxford University Press, 2007); Barry S. Godfrey, David J. Cox and Stephen Farrall, *Serious Offenders: A Historical Study of Habitual Offenders* (Oxford: Oxford University Press, 2010); Helen Johnston and Barry S. Godfrey "The Costs of Imprisonment: A Longitudinal Study," ESRC End of Award Report, RES-062-23-3102 (Swindon: ESRC, 2013).

under, such laws. To do this, we focus on the life and criminal stories of three offenders: locally 'notorious' offender Richard Edwards (1835–96) who left a life of crime behind him when he was in his fifties; the mercurial Walter Mitty-like Charles Dunning (1886–1967); and Catherine Bowden (1849–1913), a woman multiply convicted of theft and robbery who served long periods of time in prison.

Our data sources

The material presented here draws from two research projects: Godfrey *et al.* focused on the impact of individual parliamentary acts as well as the body of legislation as a whole to understand serious offending; Johnston and Godfrey applied the same methodological approach to examine those convict prisoners released on licence from Penal Servitude, after transportation to Australia had come to an end. For both projects we relied upon a mass of different historical records, as detailed below.[4]

To make sense of the records of offending in Godfrey *et al.* (2010), we first populated a database with information taken from the *Birkenhead Register of Offenders 1875–1909* (Chester Archives CJP 20/3/1). This register was created and maintained by Birkenhead Police from 1875 until the late 1930s; the last offence recorded was for burglary committed in June 1937, with the last updated records being entered in 1938. The register, which contains details of offenders born between 1818 and 1907, followed a similar pattern to the Metropolitan Police Habitual Criminals Register, with a physical description of the individual (including an exhaustive list of distinguishing features such as tattoos, scars or deformities), known aliases and previous offences, police remarks (which gave additional details such as the individual's reporting history) and general remarks (which could include the individual's trade and administrative details of correspondence between police forces concerning the individual). From this register we collected details of 99 offenders.

We then turned to the *Birkenhead Town Thieves Book 1879–1928*, a register which contains details and photographs of offenders born between 1838 and 1888, and covers offences carried out from 1869 until 1907 (Cheshire Archives CJP/20/10/1). It follows a similar pattern to the *Birkenhead Register of Offenders*, and includes individuals who carried out at least one larceny (any kind of theft) within the Birkenhead Police jurisdiction. Several of the offenders who appeared in the *Town Thieves Book* therefore also appeared in the *Birkenhead Register of Offenders*. This document provided us with details of 52 offenders. To this we added extracted details of 160 offenders identified as the more 'serious offenders' who appeared at Quarter Sessions or Assizes. These data sources, in total, provided us with 311 individuals for analysis.

---

[4] Godfrey *et al.*, *Serious Offenders*; Johnston and Godfrey, "Costs."

From these main sources, we were then able to trace these individuals using a wide variety of other extant sources. The most important sources of further information were the census returns from 1841 to 1911 inclusive (which detailed residence, family status and occupation at an individual level); online birth, marriage and death indices (which detailed if and when our offender was married, had children, and when they died); military records (mainly referring to the First World War); Cheshire Quarter Sessions Calendars of Prisoners (data on all offenders tried for indictable crimes, outcome of trial, details of the offence, and, crucially, previous criminal history and aliases); Cheshire Assizes Calendars of Prisoners (as above, but for those charged with very serious crimes); British Library Nineteenth Century Newspapers Online, *The Times* Digital Archive, and the *Guardian* Digital Archive (which provided trial reports); the Old Bailey Proceedings Online (several of our offenders were peripatetic and gravitated towards London at some time during their offending career, subsequently appearing at the Central Criminal Court); Home Office Criminal Registers (HO26 and HO27) that give details of offenders from 1805 to 1892; Metropolitan Police Habitual Criminal Registers (MEPO 6) covering 1881–1940 and Prison Commission records such as Prison Registers (PCOM 6), which contain details of all prisoners held at various English prisons from 1856 onwards. The now considerable data we had collected on individuals was then organised into life grids. Using this approach enabled us to analyse life events such as marriage, having children, gaining employment and so on, with patterns of offending and incarceration. Whenever possible we also constructed a narrative which helped us to understand the twists and turns of an individual's life story, as the examples below illustrate.

A similar approach was employed by Johnston and Godfrey with prisoners released on licence from convict prisons.[5] When penal transportation started to slow as a process from the mid-1850s, and more convicts were thereafter imprisoned in British prisons, the British government preserved the 'ticket-of-leave' system that released convicts in Australia before their sentence had ended, so that they could be employed to support the colonial enterprise. Whilst early forms of probation in the Australian penal context, to some extent, seemed to provide an opportunity for experimentation in rehabilitation; and the British appeared to have continued attempts to provide reformative opportunities for prisoners who behaved well on their sentence, there are three important caveats to be factored into this rosy picture. The first is that, although the ticket-of-leave system may or may not have played a strong part in helping offenders to rehabilitate, the system was primarily designed to provide labour to fuel the burgeoning Australian economy.[6] Any rehabilitative impact was a by-product of a system of un-free labour that punished criminals by squeezing work out of them.

[5] Johnston and Godfrey, "Costs."
[6] A new AHRC project will investigate the role of the ticket-of-leave system in rehabilitation. See www.digitalpanopticon.org.

Second, the British government seemed to give little conscious thought to why the Australian ticket-of-leave system should be repatriated in the 1850s. The ending of transportation was accompanied by the Tasmanian and New South Wales governments' belief that labour needs could be met by colonial-born workers and that a new influx of convicts was unnecessary (indeed unsettling) for the growth of most Australian colonies – although the Swan River colony at Perth, Western Australia, would still require convicts until 1868 to ensure growth. The British government was consequently faced with a penal crisis similar to the one it had faced after the American War of Independence ended convict transportation across the Atlantic and there is little evidence that administrators and bureaucrats either side of the Pacific paid attention to the advantages or disadvantages of the ticket-of-leave system. It was simply planted in Britain because it came as part and parcel of orthodox ideas about how a convict system was supposed to run.

Lastly, there is a natural inclination to link good behaviour whilst in prison to the reward of early release. However, although there is some correlation – those that committed offences inside prison, or who breached prison rules, did lose remission, and therefore became eligible for early release later in their sentence – even those that had a quite poor record in prison also gained release.[7] As Johnston and Godfrey have shown, the early release scheme was very useful to government in reducing the costs of the UK prison system. Saving money therefore went hand-in-hand with any attempt to reduce re-offending. Nevertheless, the licence system established in 1853 continues in a revised form today and remains a remarkable, if complex, example of transnational penal policy and practice.

In England and Wales, convicts were released on licence in order to prepare for their re-introduction to civil life, and so were allowed (indeed encouraged) to gain employment, reside where they wished, and otherwise resume (an honest) life. Convicts on licence were to all intents and purposes "free," so long as they did not commit further offences, or fail to report to the local police station, first within three days of release and to police each month during the 12 months following the granting of the "ticket." If a licence holder neglected to report to the police as required above, or was suspected of leading an irregular life, or had committed an offence, the licence was revoked and they were returned to serve the residue of their custodial sentence (colloquially, returned to "finish your ticket") in addition to any new period of incarceration.[8]

This is, of course, all contrary to the very prevalent modern view that the Victorians forced prisoners to serve their full sentence without remission – that it was a time when "life meant life." In fact, not even murderers (serving their penal servitude at home or transported for life to the colonies)

---

[7] Helen Johnston and Barry Godfrey, "Punishment Inside: Prison Offending 1853–1914," paper presented at the Social Science History Association Conference, Chicago, 21 November 2013.
[8] Johnston and Godfrey, "Costs."

could expect to serve their full terms, and all but a handful were given early release. In 1856, for example, nearly 3,000 ticket-of-leave men were released, and only 20 prisoners were refused applications for tickets and so went on to serve their full term in prison. The majority of serious offenders sentenced to long prison terms were released, albeit with certain conditions, long before their sentence had expired. In England and Wales, approximately 1,300 prisoners a year were issued with licences between 1854 and 1919. This meant that, as the annually published judicial statistics show, approximately a quarter of the sentenced convict prison population was released on licence each year.

Coding and interpreting life histories

Once we had constructed life grids and narratives for each of the offenders and prisoners, we turned to coding the information so it was suitable for aggregation. For example, the offenders in our sample committed many offences, some minor and some serious. Obviously the progression of their criminal careers was integral to our study, and we therefore used the following system of coding in order to determine whether each of their offences, and their offending pattern on the whole, was minor or serious:

- low-level (property crimes which did not involve a large sum of money or valuable property, common assault, all regulatory offences which did not endanger life, public order offences such as drunkenness and breach of the peace);
- medium-level (property offences which involved large sums of money, but which did not endanger life, violence which was not life-threatening and public order offences such as rioting or affray but which did not endanger life);
- high-level (life-threatening offences and offences of a serious violence and/or sexual nature, such as murder, manslaughter, rape, burglary, robbery and attempts to commit such offences, together with public order or regulatory offences which resulted in a loss of life).

To modern eyes, and indeed in line with our coding, many of the offences committed by offenders would today not be seen as serious. Concerns about property crime, the type of offending which actually comprised most of our sample, reflected prevalent Victorian and Edwardian attitudes about class and the protection of property. Although serious violence including murder and rape was treated seriously in the nineteenth and twentieth centuries, many other offences, such as indecent assault, affray, offences against minors, and even manslaughter, received comparatively light sentences. A quick survey of contemporary newspapers or court records will reveal manslaughters that resulted in less than a year's imprisonment; sexual assaults on children that resulted merely in fines, and so on. We have however coded these kinds of violent offences as "serious", and/or "dangerous," in line with modern values. Sexual violence or offences committed against children (or spouses) are now treated much more seriously, attracting a larger measure of public approbation, and longer prison sentences for perpetrators. We therefore faced a coding conundrum, since we could have followed contemporary historical mores and labelled these kinds of offences as "minor," or fallen in line with modern conceptions. In the end, that is what we did, since we wanted to avoid trying to guess what historic opinions of particular crimes actually were as we were not convinced we could always do this with accuracy. Second, we were interested in an individual's behaviour – taking things that did not belong to them, or killing another human being; and how punishment and other events in a person's life affected their offending/family lives – rather than how criminal acts were viewed in the media or in the public imagination.

Each person in our sample had committed at least two recorded offences, and, in fact, most had committed many more: the average number of offences committed by people in our dataset was just under nine. The focus of our research was an assessment of the impact of legislation passed between 1853 and 1908 on the offending careers and the daily lives of serious habitual offenders. By looking at the impact of lengthy periods of imprisonment and police supervision on criminal careers, employment and family life, we explored not just whether the Habitual Offender, and Preventative Detention Acts "worked," but at what cost to offenders. We therefore focused on the lives of offenders before and after they became subject to particular Acts. We divided the 1853 to 1940 period into three parts, grouping the legislation by what we consider to be its dominant characteristics; either to introduce heavy punishments designed to incapacitate the dangerous, or to establish supervision regulations designed to survey the movements of those too threatening to be left to their own devices.

In order to assess prisoners released on licence, we examined the record series *PCOM 3 & 4 (1853–87, 1902–08, 1912–42)* held in the National Archives which contains details of 45,000 convicts who had been released on licence. These penal records list details of the prisoner's name, sentence, where and when convicted, date and conditions of the current licence; previous convictions, age, previous occupation, when and from where the prisoner was released; and some also have photographs of the prisoner. They also tell us a great deal about the internal workings of prison in relation to these individuals; letters sent and received, visitors, medical attention, special requests as well as offences and breaches of the prison rules and regulations. These penal records were used in conjunction with the other records listed above to compile life-grids of 650 male and female convicts who were released during the mid to late nineteenth century, and utilised to evaluate the effectiveness of Victorian-era legislation and punishment on desistance.

Using our methodology to evaluate the effectiveness of legislation and punishment

Just as we configured the events in our offenders' lives, and the nature of their offending, we also divided the legislation passed in this time into three distinct periods – 1853–71; 1871–9; 1879–1908 – which helped to frame the development of thinking around incapacitating recidivists and the impact that different legislative regimes had on our offenders:

- *1853–71*: This is the period which largely marked the end of transportation as a viable penal policy, and the passing of the Penal Servitude Acts. Prison licence schemes were introduced which gave conditional release to the majority of prisoners well before their sentence had expired. In 1864, active police supervision following release from prison became a feature of prison licence conditions, and further punishment remained as the deterrent against recidivism with a minimum of seven years' gaol for repeat offenders. In 1869 reporting elements were strengthened; the frequency of reporting increased from monthly (1864) to fortnightly (1869). Registers with photographs of all offenders were kept by local police forces and a centralised bureaucracy was developed; and a mandatory period of police supervision for up to seven years was introduced. Punishments could now be imposed for breaching reporting and other regulations, and a maximum of 12 months' custody could be imposed for such breaches.
- *1871–9*: Although the reporting and other restrictions were still in place, with attendant penalties, supervision became a discretionary matter. From 1871, judges were able to impose differing periods of supervision, and chief constables were able to dictate the frequency of reporting. In 1876 photographing of offenders became limited only to particular types of offenders.
- *1879–1908*: The tariff of seven years' minimum sentence was removed in 1879. Penal servitude was reduced to between three and five years, and, in 1891, an alternative sentence of two years' imprisonment (with or without hard labour) could be substituted instead of penal servitude. In 1908 preventive detention largely replaced police supervision and, again, this was targeted against particular types of offenders, and indeed against particular individuals. Preventive detention became a reality in 1909 in order to deter dangerous offenders. Offenders with three previous convictions could be sentenced to a period of penal servitude followed by another five to ten years served under a more reformative regime.[9]

Through the use of the biographical life-grids constructed from a variety of criminal justice and civil records we have found examples of offenders – as in

---

[9] Godfrey *et al,*, *Serious Offenders*, esp. 60–84.

the cases discussed below – whose desistance was caused or at least severely impacted upon by legislation designed to incapacitate prolific offenders.[10] In some cases, for example that of Richard Edwards, the impact was only felt after the acts had been applied iteratively. Edwards, born in Cheshire in 1835, had accumulated over ten summary convictions for vagrancy and drunkenness by his thirtieth birthday. In 1865, he was found guilty of assault at Knutsford Sessions and sentenced to two months' hard labour. The following year he was found guilty of two more offences (an offence under the Criminal Justice Act, and an act of felonious intent) which saw him imprisoned for four months. Another conviction for larceny after a previous summary conviction for a similar offence again saw him in prison, this time for six months. He was then convicted of the larceny of a cotton dress at Tranmere in April 1870 and was sentenced to five years at Knutsford Quarter Sessions court. The *Liverpool Mercury* for 13 April 1870 reported that this labourer from Tranmere had "a long list of previous convictions" on his record. The 1871 Census listed Edwards as "labourer, convict at Gillingham prison," but he was at liberty in 1875, because he had been released on licence. His licence was not recalled however when he was convicted of another breach of the Criminal Justice Act and sentenced to six weeks' hard labour just a few months after his release from HMP Gillingham. A further theft followed shortly afterwards, and because he was now considered a persistent offender under the Habitual Offender Acts (this was in fact the third offence which qualified him as such under the acts), he was sentenced to seven years' penal servitude at Chester Sessions in 1877. The *Liverpool Mercury* (5 August 1877) was quick to identify him as "a notorious character" who would serve his sentence at HMP Portland this time.

Four years later, the 1881 census described Edwards as a "dock labourer." Released from HMP Portland the following year, Edwards stayed out of trouble for two years until he was convicted of larceny and sentenced at Chester Assizes to five years' imprisonment together with five years' police supervision. As was the usual practice, even with persistent offenders, he was released early from prison. By 1888 he had successfully completed his police supervision without any problems or incidents. Indeed, he did not commit any other offences until he died in Birkenhead in 1896. Our view is that the last long stretch in prison (mandated by the Habitual Offender Acts), coming on top of other long periods in custody, just wore him down, so that, when he was still in his early fifties, he was unable or unwilling to continue a life of crime. Other people, however, appeared to be completely unaffected by the strictures of the acts, and instead appeared to either desist through their own efforts and the support of friends and relatives, or they continued offending until they died.[11]

---

[10] See ibid., 35–49.

[11] See a summary of debates about the reasons for desistance together with some interesting thoughts about pace of desistance within individual offending trajectories in Ray Paternoster and Shawn Bushway, "Desistance and the Feared Self: Toward an Identity Theory of Criminal Desistance," *Journal of Criminal Law and Criminology* 99.4 (2009), 1103–56.

As part of our study we researched the desistance story of Yorkshire-born Charles William Dunning, a rather intriguing character. Born in 1886, Dunning clearly had a troubled adolescence as he was prosecuted for vagrancy and petty theft in his teens. Whilst living at home with his parents, he was convicted of an indecent assault and sentenced to two months' imprisonment in 1903. Two years later he was further convicted of larcenies in Yorkshire and in Northumbria. In 1906 he seems to have been in a somewhat frail mental state. He twice attempted to kill himself (the last attempt followed a conviction for being found on enclosed premises in Cheshire). Moving around the country frequently, his unsettled life continued in this manner for some time. He was convicted of housebreaking in Northampton in 1907, of being an incorrigible rogue in Northallerton in 1908, and for burglary in Nottingham in 1909 (for which he received five years' imprisonment). Released from prison at the start of the First World War, Dunning joined the 1st battalion Bantams (so-called due to their recruitment of smaller men under the regulation height of five feet three inches; Dunning was recorded as being just over five feet tall). He was then transferred to the 3rd Battalion Cheshire Regiment, a training regiment based in Cheshire that never saw service overseas, in December.[12] Dunning was discharged in 1917 after the army decided that he was unfit to serve.

After the war ended he was convicted of two accounts of shop-breaking in Peterborough and, in line with the Habitual Offenders Acts, he was given five years' imprisonment followed by three years' police supervision. Dunning was released in 1924 and found a job as a tram driver in Liverpool, but was again convicted of counting-house breaking and possessing housebreaking implements by night in Liverpool. Released early from his five-year sentence in 1929 he was quickly convicted of receiving stolen goods in Liverpool and of being a habitual criminal, and was therefore sentenced to three years' imprisonment and five years' preventive detention under the 1908 Act. Despite this, he was, however, released in 1930, after which there is no trace of him in criminal or other kinds of records for 15 years.

After the Second World War, Dunning found employment with Metropolitan Vickers (the wartime manufacturers of the Avro Lancaster) and also a faith, the Baha'i religion. He later told members of his church that his experiences during the First World War, where he had witnessed mass open graves in France (although we can find no evidence of him being overseas during 1914–18), had greatly disturbed him and caused him to seek solace in the Baha'i Centre in Manchester. He was a quick convert to the Baha'i faith, and he was keen enough to offer himself as a pioneer missionary to Belfast, which must have been a difficult place to establish the Baha'i faith since established faiths had strong adherence. His conversion/embracing of Baha'ism appeared to happen after his last offence had been dealt with, and his devotion and the support offered by the Baha'i religious community must have supported his efforts to lead a good and useful life.

12 Ancestry Medal Rolls Reg no 20854, http://www.ancestry.co.uk.

Dunning was certainly revered by members of the community and sub-sequent publications and memoirs talk glowingly about him.[13] However, we do not know whether other members of the Baha'i community who knew Dunning were aware of his previous life or his offences, arrests and terms in prison. Marion Hofman, a Baha'i member in the Orkneys (where members of the faith could find a welcome retreat), recalled her memories of Charles the "Knight of Baha'u'llah":

> Charlie was small, slightly strange-looking. The children in Kirkwall used to run after him and throw stones and sticks and call him names. He was simple and uneducated. Charlie went on pilgrimage during the time of the Guardian [during the visit of Shoghi Effendi, leader of the Baha'i faith]. At dinner the other guests were shocked because Charles spoke very forcefully to the Guardian telling his views – and wagging his finger at the Guardian to emphasize his points ... He was a rough diamond, done-up but still scruffy, a bit clown-like. This taught me powerfully that nobility comes in modest packages AND that the Guardian really knew the wheat from the chaff ... Charles was very little but 100% the real thing.[14]

Dunning eventually left Orkney in 1958 due to ill health and subsequently resided in a nursing home in Cardiff. In 1967 he died peacefully in his sleep on Christmas Day after having never fully recovered from a bad fall earlier that year.[15] It is possible to characterise Dunning as an ex-offender who almost literally changed from sinner to saint.

The advantages and disadvantages of our methodology

Although Charles William Dunning found faith and community with fellow Baha'i members that appeared to bolster if not initiate his move away from offending, the majority of offenders had more earthly reasons for desistance, such as a commitment to a loving life-partner, gaining and maintaining employment, and so on, which we were able to discern in the majority of cases. The advantage of our methodology is fairly self-evident. We were able to map changes in individual offenders' personal lives onto their criminal careers over the whole course of their lives, and by doing that, we could attempt to see the impact that particular events, such as marriage, finding a good job and

---

[13] The Bahá'í World – An International Record Vol XIV; Bahá'í Magazine for Children, accessed 27 December 2013, http://bahai-library.com/uhj_bahai_world_14.

[14] This information can be viewed in the Baha'i in Process, e-newspaper article, accessed 27 December 2013, http://processbahai.wordpress.com/2009/07/21/nobility-comes-in-rough-packages-shoghi-effendi-charles-dunning-and-the-cigarettes/.

[15] Charles Dunning, accessed 27 December 2013, http://bahaikipedia.org/Charles_Dunning.

having children, had on their routes out of crime. We can do this very easily by visually scanning, or 'eyeballing' the data, of course, but because we have been able to go beyond that through the consistent application of our coding system we have, in fact, been able to quantitatively analyse our life-grids in order to produce some statistical information about the impact of legislation, and that is discussed in *Serious Offenders*.[16]

There are some problems with our methodology, of course, as there are with all methodologies.[17] First, we may have made mistakes: tracing the events in people's lives through extant historical sources is, as we all know, an extremely difficult task, and we are prepared to admit that we may have missed some information that could have offered light on our subject, or we may have incorrectly identified our person of interest with someone else in a historical record – although we do think that we have avoided that particular error, and no one has come forward to say that we have made a mistaken identity (yet). Second, we are not in a position to know what people were thinking whilst they were undergoing these life-affecting events. For example, some of our individuals were married, but were they "happily married"? Again, this is not only a common problem for historians – it is also a problem for modern social scientists – none of us are mind-readers.

Third, in some cases, the information flow continues, and new data can challenge the conclusions we have reached. For example the 1911 census was released just before our project ended, and we scrambled to incorporate the new data which we had received (thankfully) just in time. In other cases, it is us, ourselves, who have sought to add further archival data in order to more fully understand the desistance routes we are describing. For example, many offenders described earlier in this chapter were released from prison on licence. Johnston and Godfrey initiated a project funded by the ESRC to investigate the propensity of licence-holders to desist from crime and to examine the impact of imprisonment upon their lives.[18] In their respective studies of Australian penal colonies, John Braithwaite, John Pratt and Barry Godfrey *et al.* have all suggested that the licensing scheme may have been important in providing a conditional form of release which could possibly have been used to support individual offenders' desistance from crime.[19] As such, our latest ESRC project has constructed a large sample of male and female licence-holders for the Victorian and Edwardian period.

As can be seen below, the life-grid methodology can easily be used to hold data gleaned from prison licences, and populated with data from other criminal and civil records (see Table 11.1).

[16] Godfrey *et al.*, *Serious Offenders*.
[17] Barry Godfrey, "Historical and Archival Research Methods," in David Gadd, Suzanne Karstedt and Stephen F. Messner (eds), *The Handbook on Criminology Research Methods* (New York: Sage, 2012), 159–75
[18] Johnston and Godfrey, "Costs."
[19] John Braithwaite, "Crime in a Convict Republic," *Modern Law Review* 64.1 (2001), 11–50; John Pratt, *Governing the Dangerous: Dangerousness, Law and Social Change* (Sydney: Federation Press, 1997); Godfrey *et al.*, *Serious Offenders*.

Table 11.1 The life-grid of Catherine Bowden née McGarry (General Convict Reg. J 72 Local Prison no. 129)

Year	Life events	Offending/punishment
1854	*Prison records say born in Runcorn but she is more likely born Ireland in 1849.*	
1855–60		
1861	Living at Wicksten's Hill with parents John (b.1820, Ireland) mother Bridget (1823, Ireland), she is unmarried aged 12 (b.1849, Ireland) and sister Margaret. Also living at property is a group of male boarders).	
1862–6		
1867	Married Thomas Bowden in Warrington.	
1868–9	Daughter Mary A. born in Runcorn (probably Mary Alice).	
1870		
1871	Living at 5 Wicksten Hill, Runcorn, with step-father Patrick McGarry, and mother Bridget. She is recorded as being 22 (b.1849), married, living with her child Mary A. Bowden aged one.	
1872	Daughter Catherine Bowden born in Runcorn.	
1873–7		
1878		Convicted of theft of boots and sent to Knutsford Gaol, for one month.
1879		Convicted at Cheshire Assizes of robbery with violence on 25th April, sentenced to 12 months. She is convicted with Henry Brindrick – and she is convicted in the name of Catherine Brindrick (and reported as his wife in the *Liverpool Mercury* account of the case). The robbery is carried out at knifepoint. Harry or Henry Brindrick gets five years' penal servitude.

1880	Convicted of theft (after previous conviction) from the person (a purse) at Knutsford QS and sent to prison for 12 months.
1881	In Knutsford prison as Catherine Bowden, aged 27 (b.1854) housekeeper. Says married. Her children (Mary recorded as Margaret, aged seven; and Catherine aged six) residing with father at 12 Mersey St. Her father has remarried.
1882	Convicted at Liverpool County Sessions in July for larceny from the person, sentenced to six months.
1883	Convicted on 26 February of criminal damage, imprisoned one month. Convicted at Cheshire Assizes of robbery with violence at Runcorn on 28 April; committed to higher court 17 May, convicted 21 July. Sentenced to five years' penal servitude. Newspaper report – attached to prison record – Bowden (29) of no occupation, and Henry Brindrick (28). In a pre-planned attack under an archway the two defendants, and a third man, punched victim and took his watch guard. Bowden was apprehended when she tried to pawn it in Runcorn. Whilst in custody the male prisoner was overheard to say that Bowden had caused him to be there, and that he may tell "the whole truth" about the affair. Brindrick was a ticket-of-leave man "and wished to say that he would lose his ticket with this offence". The learned judge in passing sentence, said "he knew what the previous conviction was for [*Brindrick and 'Catherine Brindrick' were convicted of robbery from person in 1879, he got 5 years and she got 12 months*]. Prisoners were dangerous people, having suffered together for another offence, but they had no sooner got out of prison again but they were repeating their evil practices." Brindrick got ten years.

Table 11.1 (cont.)

Year	Life events	Offending/punishment
		Received at Chester Prison 17 May 1883.
		Received at Millbank Prison, London 3 August 1883. She has five previous sentences by now.
		4 August 1883 – letter from Governor of Millbank asking Chester Prison Governor why they have not given date of her entry into HMP Chester. He replies stating this was 17 May 1883, and says that prisoner was anxious about welfare of her children when leaving Chester, and could the Governor of Millbank allow prisoner to have the letter from her father (below).
		4 August 1883 – letter from her father John McGarry telling her that her children are fine and all is well at home. Asks her to write to him.
1884		Weight on entry Millbank, 150 lbs, and 154 lbs on entry Woking, weight on leaving Woking was 168 lbs.
		Received at Woking Prison 10 July 1884.
		17 February 1884 – Millbank Prison get letter from Cheshire Constabulary at Runcorn stating "with regard to father of Catherine Bowden, John McGarry, he is well known here as a steady, respectable, hardworking man. He lives at 12 Mersey St." Prison chaplain notes on letter father's different name and address.
		13 April 1884 – letter from St Edward's RC Church to Governor of Millbank, in response to his enquiry. Priest says she was brought up as RC of Irish RC parents. Her whole family are RC "but very bad ones." Confirms that Catherine's children are attending his school.
		8 April 1884 – applies to change religion from C of E to RC. The Chaplain opposes the change, stating that she has not been in an RC church since her childhood, does not know RC religion, she was married in C of E church, and has been persuaded to this action by other women. Another letter from Rev William Kay (?) says there is no doubt she is RC and knows the priest at Runcorn, where she was born.
		10 April 1884 – Liverpool Prison reply in response to enquiry from Millbank stating that she is Protestant. Chester and Knutsford also reply to say "Church of England."
		17 May 1884 – Directors authorise change of religion.
		8 November 1884 – prison offence – fighting in the exercise yard with prisoner J104, Mrs Cormack. Received three days' close confinement and lost 12 marks.

1885
1886

Licence Number A42448/7392 – married woman, two children, Roman Catholic (C of E crossed out and dated 1884 "v. Director's order").

Good conduct, good health, no education (can't read or write).

Father given as John McGarry, 12 Mersey St Runcorn.

Features on first sentence in convict prison are:

Dark complexion, dark brown hair, 5' 4" tall, stout figure with oval face. Ears pierced. Has varicose veins, some scars, a mole. All these remain the same subsequently, except that her eyes appear to change colour, to hazel.

Trade is recorded as knitter and cleaner.

Has no property on entering prison.

Licence granted 18 February for two years and five months.

Discharged to East End Refuge, Finchley [*In 1864 the Sisters of the Good Shepherd bought East End House on the north side of East End Road, where until 1948 they maintained a refuge for distressed Roman Catholic women, including former prisoners. In 1900 they aided 180 "poor penitents" and 130 younger girls. New buildings on the site included a church in 1875 and a wing for the novitiate in 1886, when East End House became the provincial house for the order. After a fire in 1972 land was sold for housing and most of the buildings were demolished, although the original house remained, "Finchley: Roman Catholicism", A History of the County of Middlesex: Volume 6: Friern Barnet, Finchley, Hornsey with Highgate (1980), pp. 86–7. www.british-history. ac.uk/report.aspx?compid=22509. Date accessed: 9 January 2011.*]

Handwritten – "The Directors of the Convict Prison allow this person to leave the Refuge."

Letters from – "husband" [prison authorities' quotation marks] Thomas, c/o Samuel Ashby [can't trace this man in 1881 or 1891 in Cheshire], Prescott Terrace, Runcorn.

Letters to father 12 Mersey St, Runcorn.

Table 11.1 (cont.)

Year	Life events	Offending/punishment
1887–9		
1890		Convicted at Warrington of fighting. Chief Constable reports that she "can fight like a man, often does so, and is proud of her accomplishments." She received one month's custody reported the *Wrexham Advertiser* on 14 June.
1891		Criminal registers – 12 January convicted at Warrington QS as Bowden. Sentenced to 12 months.
		Newspaper report – Catherine Bowden and two other women "of doubtful character" took man to the pub in Dial St, and robbed him of £15 in gold at Helsby.
1892		Convicted at Chester Assizes of larceny from the person. Sentenced to nine months' hard labour.
		Newspaper report – Bowden, 34, laundress, convicted of theft of clothes at Halton. Two women got the man drunk and robbed him when he fell asleep by the side of the road. Her co-defendant was a woman of no fixed abode.
1893–4		
1895		Catherine Bowden convicted of theft of 9d at Warrington. Sentenced at Liverpool County QS to 1 day's imprisonment. She is reported as aged 39, laundress (newspaper report).
1913	Dies in Cheshire, aged approximately 64.	

Things all appeared to go wrong for Catherine Bowden between 1873 and 1877 when her husband either died or the couple became estranged. Her new beau Henry Brindrick became her accomplice and co-defendant; in the 1881 census he was recorded as being married, but by 1891 he was recorded as a widower, which suggests that he and Catherine either were never married, or that they had separated following Henry's long period in prison (he was in Borstal Prison in 1881 and in Portsmouth in 1891). To date, online newspaper databases (which end in 1900) have revealed that Bowden appeared to be quite capable of using violence, as the Chief Constable of Warrington noted, and her various prison sentences did not deter her from a fairly sustained criminal career. As she entered her thirties she appeared to have led a dissolute life, mixing with prostitutes and vagrants, and occasionally taking the opportunity to relieve drunks of their property. She appeared to commit her last offence when she was nearly 40 years old. Further study of early twentieth-century Cheshire newspapers may reveal whether she continued offending until she died.

The research on prison licensing has created a large dataset on those released from prison and has allowed us to examine the impact of periods of imprisonment and licence on individual people's life course. The licensing system did operate as a pressure valve for the prison population as a whole (reducing the numbers in prison and the cost) but at the individual level, although periods of custody were shorter due to its use, there was no intrinsic value. That said, looking across the life course of the offender, we can say that the period of licence did allow more time for the supportive processes relating to desistance, we have discussed in these individual examples, to take hold and also reduced the impact of institutionalisation. On that note, let us return again to Charles William Dunning.

Additional information provided by a Baha'i member after our study had concluded, revealed that Dunning had informed members of the church that he had a more "interesting" military career than the one we had recorded for him. Dunning claimed that he had re-enlisted in the forces at the outbreak of the Second World War (despite being 60 years of age by then), and served variously in the RAF (where he witnessed the bombing of Dresden in 1945) and the Welsh Commandoes (during which time he visited some Russian prisons – thereby providing him with his knowledge of prison life). We cannot find any evidence to support these claims. They appear to be little more than fanciful stories, and from our evidence, he clearly deceived his Baha'i biographers (and maybe himself) about his past. We have been able to ascertain, however, that Dunning did not commit any new offences after joining the Baha'i faith. It is possible to characterise him as self-deluded, maybe muddled, or some might even allege mental illness or criminal artifice, but he was also, as our original research concluded, a desister from crime.

12 'Whose prisoners are these anyway?'

Church, state and society partnerships and co-production of offender 'resocialisation' in Brazil

Fiona Macaulay

Brazil's prisons frequently hit the headlines of the international press for all the wrong reasons. In a typical episode of systemic violence, in December 2013, an attempt by state police to regain control of the lawless Pedrinhas penitentiary in the northeastern state of Maranhão resulted in inmates unleashing violence outside and inside the prison.[1] In four buses burned out in the state capital by their criminal associates, a six-year-old girl died, and inside the jail three inmates from a rival gang were decapitated. Filmed on an inmate's phone, leaked footage of the latter went around the world. But not all of Brazil's prisons have fallen prey to gang control, or generate such violence, whether between prisoners, prisoners and staff, or prisoners and the local community. Indeed, some are almost the mirror images of such hellholes, are innovative in terms of their approach to administration and rehabilitation, and have even prompted international imitation.

This chapter complements Sacha Darke's (Chapter 13) in exploring the particularities and lessons that can be learned from a small group of prisons – the so-called Resocialisation Centres (*Centros de Ressocialização* – CRs) in São Paulo state, a variant of the APAC prisons in Minas Gerais state that he analyses.[2] Both CRs and APACs are unusual, not just in the Brazilian or Latin American context, but also in terms of modern penal institutions overall. They are compliant with domestic and international human rights norms for the treatment of detainees, and have experienced no riots, little violence and very few escapes, despite operating with low security. They apparently

---

[1] In 2013 over 60 prisoners were murdered by their fellow inmates in this high security prison. Designed for 1,700 prisoners, it currently holds 2,200, but this represents an average level of overcrowding in Brazilian prisons.

[2] I first encountered prisons (in Pernambuco and Minas Gerais) run broadly according to the APAC ethos, or by the APAC organisation, in 1997 while researching prison conditions in Brazil for Amnesty International. A grant from the Socio-Legal Studies Association allowed me to spend several days in each of four CRs in October 2004, using semi-structured interviews and focus groups with the inmates, families, prison service and NGO staff, criminal justice system operators and opinion-formers in the local community. Access became difficult after 2006, so I began researching the APACs in Minas Gerais in 2007, and in July 2013 accompanied the prison authority team in Paraná state setting up new APACs.

achieve high levels of desistance, successfully reintegrate offenders back into their families and communities, and operate at around one-third to one-half the per capita cost of state-run prisons and commercially contracted-out facilities.

But there are two key differences between the CRs and APACs. The first is that the Catholic-run APACs make religious faith a central plank in their very explicit and prescriptive 'method'. The second is that the APACs are run entirely by volunteers and the prisoners themselves, without police or guards inside or outside the facility. The CRs, however, are run in a formal *partnership* between the state and local civil society, and the former provides both guards and key administrative posts in the units. These differences, apparently minor on the surface, reveal an underlying tussle over who can lay claim to the body and soul of the offender. The state, against whose laws they formally transgress? The community, which suffers fear of crime and disorder, and the family, which has to bear broken relationships? Or the Church, whose task is to save a sinner for God? In this regard the APAC franchise's insistence on a religiously saturated environment and the absence of the state is a challenge on two fronts, not just to the predominant prison culture of simultaneous state absence and violence (what Agamben refers to as 'bare life' and inmates call *o sistema* – 'the system'),[3] but also to the inherent capacity of the state prison authorities to enact and embody a more humane set of values, and to cede some control over the offender to civil society. This chapter examines the rise and fall from favour of the state-run CRs, whose operation both challenged the dominant prison system but also aimed at its perfectability, in order to explore these issues of contested 'ownership' and the potential of the state to improve the 'moral performance' of its penal institutions.[4]

The Brazilian prison system

A diversity of prison cultures is only to be expected in a country of such continental dimensions as Brazil. As of December 2012, Brazil's prison population – now the fourth largest in the world – stood at 548,003, distributed between its 26 states and Federal District, and held in 470 penitentiaries, 74 farm/factory prisons attached to 64 open prisons, 16 half-way houses, 821 public jails (intended for remand prisoners but frequently holding convicted prisoners for their full term) and 33 secure psychiatric units. Some 34,290 detainees were held in custody in police stations and police-run lock-ups and remand facilities. Brazil's prison population doubled in a decade, and, like many other developing countries, authorities have been desperately looking for transnational models to cope with a constant influx of inmates generated

---

[3] Giorgio Agamben, *Homo Sacer: Sovereign Power and Bare Life* (Stanford: Stanford University Press, 1998).

[4] Alison Liebling, *Prisons and their Moral Performance: A Study of Values, Quality and Prison Life* (Oxford: Oxford University Press, 2004).

by a combination of rising common and drug-related crime, and harsh laws and sentencing practices.[5] To this end, Brazilian prison authorities built more prisons overall, and constructed a new generation of 'super-max' facilities (both state-run and federal) to handle violent organised crime. It also turned to the private sector to partially run and, more recently, finance and build prisons, through public–private partnership agreements. The government also attempted to divert and decarcerate more minor offenders, through the use of non-custodial sentences and diversionary measures such as community service and attendance at drug courts. Whilst the penal code is federal law, however, the organisation and running of the prison system falls largely within the remit of the 27 sub-national administrations, with the federal government providing only matched funding for prison construction and guidelines for management, rehabilitation, staff training and so forth. The emergence of multiple and distinctive penal regimes and models, including the APACs and CRs which swim against the punitive tide, is a function both of the specificities of Brazil's administrative structure (decentralisation) and historical political context (authoritarian rule and transition to democracy), and of the way in which these produced a certain configuration of civil society, and state–civil society relations.

From APACs to CRs

In 1972 Brazil was in the eighth year of a military dictatorship. The repressive forces of the state were far more interested in arresting 'subversives' than in the control of common crime. Civil society was cowed by draconian legislation, and the Catholic Church as an institution, along with its international human rights allies, focused on the regime's political torture and abuse. Nobody cared about prison conditions for ordinary detainees.[6] So, as Darke notes, when Catholic laymen, led by Dr Ottoboni, attempted to improve conditions in their town's decrepit and overcrowded police lockup, the state justice authorities were indifferent, and the local police ambivalent. The NGO they set up with the acronym APAC (which initially stood for *Amando ao Próximo, Amarás a Cristo* – By Loving Your Neighbour You Will Love Christ)[7] first took over

---

5 Fiona Macaulay, 'Modes of Prison Administration, Control and Governmentality in Latin America: Adoption, Adaptation and Hybridity', *Conflict, Security and Development* 13.4 (2013), 361–92.

6 Honourable exceptions are two pioneering ethnographic studies of individual prisons: José Ricardo Ramalho, *Mundo do crime: a ordem pelo avesso* [The World of Crime: Order Turned Upside Down] (Rio de Janeiro: Graal, 1979) is a study of the São Paulo House of Detention, Brazil's – and Latin America's – largest prison; and Julita Lemgruber, *Cemitério dos vivos: análise sociológica de uma prisão de mulheres* [Cemetery of the Living: A Sociological Analysis of a Women's Prison] (Rio de Janeiro: Achiamé, 1983), a study of the Talavera Bruce women's prison in Rio de Janeiro.

7 Over the years the acronym has stood for a number of very slightly different names. Some confusion is caused by some of the NGOs working in the CRs in São Paulo state having adopted the APAC acronym, whereas the Minas Gerais group see themselves as the 'true',

from the police the provision of services to the prisoners, and then built and ran a new wing for 75 prisoners on day-release schemes. Closed down for five years due to police brutality and hostility, the prison reopened in 1984, this time under the APAC group's sole control. Another APAC group also established itself in Itaúna in Minas Gerais state in the mid-1980s, formalised its running of the local jail in 1991, and began to attract attention in the mid-1990s. As the prison population soared and riots and breakouts became weekly occurrences in the police lock-ups and jails, the National Congress conducted a parliamentary inquiry and the Brazilian Catholic Church launched a campaign on prison conditions.

The APAC model was also replicated, but in significantly modified form, in another jail (Bragança Paulista) in São Paulo state when Dr Nagashi Furukawa, then the local judge, helped a group of local volunteers to sign a partnership agreement with the state in 1996.[8] Once appointed head of the state's prison system in 1999, in large part on the basis of his advocacy of this model, he established a total of 22 such prisons, mostly purpose-built, which he called CRs, each holding around 210 prisoners and jointly run by the state and a local NGO. Meanwhile the original, religiously-based APAC group moved its headquarters to Minas Gerais state.[9] Thus, by the early 2000s, the CRs constituted numerically the largest group of prisons run in formal partnership between the state and civil society.

In 2006, however, Furukawa was forced to resign from his post following an extraordinary show of force by the *Primeiro Comando da Capital* ('First Capital Command', PCC), an organisation that functions both as an inmates' union and organised crime network. The PCC has managed to penetrate most of the state's prisons following its foundation in the early 1990s.[10] In response

faith-based APAC. Many of the facilities run by the 'true' APAC group are also referred to as Resocialisation Centres, adding to further muddling of the two strands.

[8] An NGO with the name *Associação de Proteção e Assistência ao Condenado* (Association for the Protection and Assistance of the Convicted Prisoner), set up in 1978 by concerned citizens in Bragança Paulista, was blocked by the local judge but revived in 1993 by individuals linked to the justice system, including the prosecution service, Bar Association, Civil Police and the Community Council (a civil society oversight body linked to the court).

[9] This move occurred in part because the original APAC, in São José dos Campos, was closed down in 1999, and later reopened as a CR, that is, in partnership with the state rather than being under the full control of the APAC group.

[10] Within the PCC there are various foundational myths about when (between 1989 and 1993) and in which prison it was founded. (Karina Biondi, *Junto e misturado: Uma etnografia do PCC* [Mixed Together: An ethnography of the PCC] (São Paulo: Editora Terceiro Nome, 2010), 69–70). What seems clear, however, is that it quickly garnered support among the prison population due to the brutality of the prison system, such as the extrajudicial execution by military police of 111 prisoners who had surrendered after a riot in the House of Detention in 1992, the harsh super-maximum security conditions in Taubaté prison (a unit for disruptive inmates), and the violent anarchy permitted to reign in the prisons. The PCC set out a statute governing prisoners' relations with one another, and with the authorities. Inmates opt to join the PCC and to take on leadership and bargaining/conflict resolution roles, but all those in 'PCC prisons' are expected to adhere to their rules. Camila Caldeira Nunes Dias, *PCC: Hegemonia nas*

to the authorities' intention to isolate gang leaders, it unleashed a wave of violence in the city, killing dozens of police and prison guards, attacking criminal justice and economic targets, and paralysing the city, and coordinated riots across 82 prisons in São Paulo state alone. His successor in the post, Antônio Ferreira Pinto, was a former military police officer and criminal prosecutor. A hardliner, he expressed a visceral dislike of the CR experiment, both for its perceived 'soft' approach to prisoners and the involvement of non-state actors,[11] and leaked to the press 'evidence' of 'irregularities' committed by the NGOs, aimed at discrediting them and their champion.[12]

It was not politically possible to close the CRs down, however, given that they had received the strong backing of the previous state governor, whose successor was from the same party. As a result, the new director of the prison service opted simply not to renew the contracts of the partner NGOs, with the result that as of early 2014, nine CRs had reverted to state control with no local community involvement. In the meantime, as Darke indicates, the 'original' faith-based APAC model has expanded in Minas Gerais, backed by senior justices, and in states further afield. The CR experience is now largely forgotten and unknown in a state in which most prisons are controlled on a day-to-day basis by the PCC.[13]

Religious civil society and the state

The core disagreement between Ottoboni and Furukawa, the originators of the APAC and CR approaches, concerns the role of religion and of the state in the rehabilitation of the offender, an old debate in historical, comparative terms. The monopolisation of the punishment function by the state, wrested from the sovereign and from private individuals, is a feature of modern penal systems. However, as the modern carceral institutions emerged in the United States, Europe and Latin America from the late eighteenth century, in certain locations religious organisations were involved in shaping and running some penal institutions, both complementing and substituting for the state, and then, eventually, competing with the secular authorities both to control the ethos and running of these facilities and to determine the fate of inmates. Quakers designed and ran the first penitentiaries in the United States – Newgate in New York and the Walnut Street jail in Philadelphia – whilst in Latin America separate women's penitentiaries were often run by orders of

---

prisões e monopólio da violência [PCC: Hegemony in the Prisons and Monopoly of Violence] (São Paulo: Editora Saraiva, 2013).

[11] Interview with Antônio Ferreira Pinto, July 2007.

[12] Dr Furukawa claimed these allegations were either untrue, or the facts had been twisted to smear him and his administration. Interview July 2007 and 'Furukawa diz que apurou irregularidades em presidios de SP', 7 December 2006, http://g1.globo.com/Noticias/Brasil/0,,AA1378554-5598,00.html.

[13] The CRs are specifically intended for those who want to avoid gang involvement. A few other prisons, for example those for sex offenders, host rivals to the PCC.

nuns in the nineteenth century.[14] But in all cases tensions around disciplinary power over offenders were resolved in favour of the consolidation of state penal authority.

Civil society was slower to develop in Brazil than in North America and Europe, although intellectuals from the legal field were concerned with the proper modernisation of the prison system. São Paulo's state penitentiary, built in the 1920s, was hailed as a model institution, attracting visitors from far afield.[15] However, after decades of political upheaval and gradual decline of this ideal of modernity, it was not until the democratic transition of the 1980s that prisoners again attracted attention, first from religious civil society. Throughout the dictatorship, a liberal Catholic Church had provided a space for the defence of diverse vulnerable groups, and in 1986 the Brazilian Conference of Bishops set up the prison pastoral service (*Pastoral Carcerário*), which was legally constituted in 1988. The Pastoral, however, saw its main role, alongside other civil society groups, as one of advocacy and defence of prisoners' *human rights*, for which the guarantor had to be a perfectible, democratic state. As such, the Pastoral refrained from proselytising and has been very ambivalent about taking over the running of prisons, seeing this as the function of the state within the rule-of-law. Indeed, at times it has regarded Ottoboni's APAC group with some suspicion.[16] That said, Brazil's size and the decentralised operation of the Pastoral have allowed for variation. In 1996 the coordinator of the Pastoral in Pernambuco state, a doctor, stepped in as director of the then relatively small Juiz Plácido de Souza prison in Caruaru, taking over from a string of military police directors. Notably, the Pastoral group there was composed of individuals with a background of liberal/left *political* militancy and mixed, or no, religious belief or affiliation. The way that this director, and his successor, a former prison guard, ran the prison was much more akin to the secular, partnership-based ethos of the CRs than that of Ottoboni's APACs.

The very presence of the grassroots Catholic APAC model in prisons, however, seems to have suggested to the established Church that this was a sphere in which it *should* intervene. In Minas Gerais the first ever purpose-built APAC prison opened in Santa Luzia in 2006, sponsored by the Pontifical Catholic University, the Archdiocese and the Pastoral in Belo Horizonte.[17]

[14] Carlos Aguirre, 'Prisons and Prisoners in Modernising Latin America (1800–1940)', in Frank Dikötter and Ian Brown (eds), *Cultures of Confinement: A History of the Prison in Africa, Asia and Latin America* (Ithaca: Cornell University Press, 2007), 27.

[15] Fernando Salla, *As prisões em São Paulo 1822–1940* [Prisons in São Paulo 1822–1940] (São Paulo: Anna Blume/FAPESP, 1999), 196.

[16] This was certainly the view expressed to me in the late 1990s by Padre Francisco 'Chico' Reardon, late coordinator of the Pastoral, and by his successors.

[17] Possibly the APAC venture has attracted both Church and government support in Minas Gerais because of the higher level of expressed Catholicism there (73 per cent, compared to 66 per cent in São Paulo, according to the 2010 Brazilian Institute of Geography and Statistics survey). The most Catholic states are in the under-developed northeast, with the exception of Pernambuco whose level of Catholic adherence is similar to São Paulo's. Minas Gerais was the

This involvement should be read within a dynamic context in which Christian groups, both orthodox Catholic and evangelical Protestant, have become more influential in political life and social welfare administration, both cooperating and competing with each other.[18] Pentecostalism has also been displacing Catholicism in Brazil in recent decades, with data suggesting that a quarter of the Brazilian population now identify themselves as 'born again' Christians, rising to over 50 per cent in some urban areas. Pentecostal churches recruit successfully in prisons, not least because they offer adherents exemption from the rules, rites and violence of the wider prison system.[19] However, Pentecostal groups have restricted themselves thus far to providing welfare and material support to inmates, and have not attempted to collaborate formally with, or substitute for, the state.

This tension between the officially secular character of the Brazilian state and the reality of variable and diverse forms of religiosity in society at large, and among decision-makers, will probably, as Darke notes, affect the spread of APACs, with some local actors embracing or rejecting it precisely on these grounds. Ottoboni's criticism of Furukawa's CRs for lacking 'methodology' (the 12 components listed by Darke) is actually an attack on its secularism.[20] Indeed, despite the CRs' consistency of practice, achieved through the training of new staff and NGO personnel, there was no manual, written methodology or explicit analytical framework. All the CRs had some autonomy to interpret and implement the core elements, for example by adopting slightly differing internal routines and disciplinary rules, allowing the staff, NGO personnel and, importantly, the prisoners themselves some creativity and latitude in responding to the socio-economic characteristics of the locality and the offenders they took in.[21] The failure of the CRs to articulate explicitly their

---

only state where, in colonial times, Portugal prohibited convents and monasteries, leaving the running of everyday religious practice in the hands of brotherhoods of lay people. See Caio César Boschi, *Os leigos e o poder: irmandades leigas e política colonizadora em Minas Gerais* [Laypeople and Power: Lay Brotherhoods and Colonising Policy in Minas Gerais] (São Paulo: Editora Ática, 1986). It is, of course, hard to prove whether this has left a cultural trace that made key actors in that state more receptive to the APAC model of lay engagement.

[18] The parliamentary cross-bench evangelical group has grown considerably in the last decade, now standing at 70 out of 513 federal deputies and three out of 81 senators.

[19] Camila Caldeira Nunes Dias, *A igreja como refúgio e a bíblia como esconderijo: Religião e violência na prisão* [The Church as Refuge and the Bible as Bolt-hole] (São Paulo: Editora Humanitas, 2008). Some prisons may see the presence of a single Pentecostal, or fundamentalist church, whilst others may have several. Pastors may visit frequently to conduct religious services, whilst followers inside often self-segregate in their own cells or wings.

[20] This methodology is contained in the writings of its ideologue Dr Mário Ottoboni, *Vamos matar o criminoso? Método APAC* [Are We Going to Kill the Criminal? The APAC Method] (São Paulo: Paulinas, 2001); *Ninguém e irrecuperável* [No One is Irredeemable] (São Paulo: Cidade Nova, 2001); *Seja solução, não vítima! Justiça restaurativa, uma abordagem inovadora* [Be the Solution, not a Victim! Restorative Justice, an Innovative Approach] (São Paulo: Cidade Nova, 2004).

[21] For example, the internal standing orders in the Sumaré CR were drafted by prisoners and staff together, and could be modified after consultation with both.

own, non-religious modus operandi, however, has meant that this alternative path for state–society collaboration has undermined the wider resonance of this model.

State and society: invited participation, co-production, substitution

The CR partnership approach is in fact consistent with, and extends, the forms of collaboration between state and civil society on social policy issues that were made possible, even mandated, by the 1988 Constitution. The latter created spaces of 'invited participation' in the form of Management Councils jointly composed of civil society and state representatives.[22] Some, often those dealing with specific social groups (disabled, elderly, women, blacks), have a largely watchdog role that involves monitoring the state and its protection of rights, whilst others in the areas of health, welfare, housing and youth police have a more deliberative role aimed at modifying bills in the relevant legislature, shaping state policy, and ensuring it is implemented. They do not actually 'co-produce' the public good they monitor, however, as the CR partnerships do, in the sense of signing a formal partnership with the state and actually delivering the service (in this case, offender rehabilitation) inside the state institutions. Criminal justice has also traditionally been the social policy area most closed to civil society input due to its association with the 'security' concerns of the state. The only civil society groups akin to these Management Councils with a legal remit for involvement in prison matters are the so-called Community Councils (*Conselhos da Comunidade*), which emerged from the Brazilian state's attempts to bring the country's penal systems into line with international human rights norms. The 1984 national Sentence Serving Law (*Lei de Execução Penal*) provides for such bodies in any jurisdiction with a prison. However, many areas still have no such prison community councils as they can be set up only by the local judge, and receive little institutional support. There is also an increasing tendency to downgrade their rather unclear watchdog role (some had been very active in inspecting, then publicly decrying human rights abuses in, local prisons), a role now played in civil society by the Pastoral and the Brazilian Bar Association. Increasingly criminal justice actors seem to be emphasising their 'gap-filling' role, that is, providing material and human welfare assistance to prisons where the state cannot meet needs, which is only one of their four legal functions.[23]

---

[22] Andrea Cornwall, 'New Democratic Spaces: The Politics and Dynamics of Institutionalised Participation', *IDS Bulletin* 35.2 (2004), 1–10.

[23] They are required to visit prisons monthly, interview inmates and report to the state-level Prison Council (also of mixed state–civil society composition, which handles issues such as parole applications) and the local judge. However, it is not specified to what end they should do this. Maria Palma Wolff, 'Participação social e sistema penitenciário: uma parceria viável?' [Social Participation and the Prison System: A Viable Partnership?] Unpublished paper available on Ministry of Justice website: http://tinyurl.com/qyq5kuw.

The CR partnership with the state in offender rehabilitation highlights the philosophical difference between the Ottoboni and Furukawa models regarding the nature and 'redeemability' of the state, and whether such collaboration constitutes a radical challenge to the state monopoly on force and disciplinary power, or simply co-opts civil society into a hegemonic, essentially neoliberal, project of mass incarceration. The literature on co-production of public services suggests such a divergence of views, with one strand stressing 'equal and reciprocal' relations between professionals, service users, family and community,[24] whilst another sees it as a means for the public sector and citizens to make best use of one another's resources in the pursuit of efficiency (lowered costs) and effectiveness (better outcomes).

In this instance, co-production has certainly reduced the cost of incarceration to the state. The APACs and CRs are much cheaper than prisons run entirely by the state because the NGOs are free from certain constraints such as the tendering arrangements that tie the state authorities to 'preferred suppliers' and in turn inflate costs and encourage backhanders. They buy cheaper and better goods and services from local businesses, thus contributing to the local economy, and can switch suppliers when necessary. Their staff members are also not state employees, whose protections under Brazilian labour law makes them very hard to dismiss, even when they fail to fulfil their contracts, as is the case with many hourly-contracted professionals in prisons, such as doctors. These same advantages are, of course, also held by commercial companies that have entered into partnerships with the prison authorities. However, greater flexibility in purchasing and contracting is offset in the private sector by the need to generate profit, so there is very mixed evidence in Brazil as to whether operating costs in semi-privatised prisons are actually lower than in the state sector.[25] By contrast the NGOs are driven by non-economic, moral factors. They take pride in their careful guardianship of resources, reinvesting any surplus in improved services to prisoners. Cost reductions are also possible because as community-based organisations they are more persuasive in seeking free donations of food or material. The relationship between the two partners of *gestão compartilhada* or *co-gestão* [shared administration or co-administration] thus provides not just a division of labour but also a value-added element through the synergy that can be achieved through the distinctive contributions of both.

The CRs, at least, were also subject to strict systems of accountability on the part of the state authorities. In their heyday Dr Furukawa considered having the NGOs take on the administration – not the rehabilitative services – of nearby large penitentiaries simply to reduce costs. This proposal, however, prompted the APAC group to criticise the CR partnerships as constituting privatisation by another name. Indeed, the division of labour in the

[24] New Economic Foundation, *Co-Production: A Manifesto for Growing the Core Economy* (London: New Economics Foundation, 2008).
[25] Macaulay, 'Modes of Prison Administration', 374–5.

partnership arrangement does resemble the European form of semi-privatisation in which the state provides the prison guards and authorities, but not the rehabilitative and 'hotel' services. Yet, it does not go as far as the 'hybrid' form of contracted-out prisons in Brazil whereby guards are also supplied by the private company but the state maintains a supervisory presence inside the prison, appointing state employees to the post of warden, deputy warden and head of discipline, as a minimum.[26]

Further, the Ottoboni-ite APACs also make an especial virtue of voluntarism, whereby the key rehabilitative services – education, healthcare, psychological support, social work, legal aid – should be provided by volunteers from the community, with the directors of the facility as the only paid staff. In addition, they prefer to receive donations from local businesses to meet their running costs. On two occasions, however, this arrangement jeopardised the sustainability of their flagship facilities and so they were forced, reluctantly, to accept financial support from the state prison authorities. This dependency on the state goes against their autonomist inclinations, but in a country such as Brazil, where there are still considerable gaps in welfare coverage and which has a limited history of philanthropy, demands on local civil society are multiple and draining and often make collaboration with the state and its resources inevitable.[27]

Competition with the criminal justice system

The lower running costs and greater effectiveness and efficiency of the CRs were insufficient in themselves, however, to sell the model to sceptical state criminal justice operators whose cooperation with this project of rehumanising and resocialising the offender is also required. Conventional criminal justice systems are state-centric. The state determines the nature of 'crime' through legislation, and offenders are deemed to have wronged the state. Whilst the CR model allows the local community to assert its interest in the fate of its 'own' offenders, it also brings the NGOs into conflict with the state, which retains legal responsibility for the custody of the offender. Moreover, the different branches of the state also compete for disciplinary power over the prisoner. Although the executive branch is responsible for the arrest of offenders, it is the judiciary that prosecutes, in most cases passes sentences, and then oversees the serving of that sentence in Brazil. Indeed the 1984 Sentence Serving

[26] Sandro Cabral, Sergio G. Lazzarini and Paulo Furquim de Azevedo, 'Private Entrepreneurs in Public Services: A Longitudinal Examination of Outsourcing and Statization of Prisons', *Strategic Entrepreneurship Journal* 7.1 (2013), 6–25. Brazil's is the sixth largest economy in the world but is ranked eighty-fifth on the Human Giving Index and eighty-third on the World Giving Index.

[27] Alex Segura Ubiergo, in *The Political Economy of the Welfare State in Latin America* (Cambridge: Cambridge University Press, 2007) characterises Brazil's welfare as ambitious and egalitarian in intent, but with 'limited efficiency and high regressivity' in practice (29n17).

Law (LEP) specifically 'judicialised' prison sentences, with the intention that judicial oversight would guarantee fair treatment of detainees. But Dr Furukawa's term in office saw a 'dejudicialisation' process, as he argued that certain rights to which prisoners were entitled, such as progression from a closed to a semi-open prison regime, parole or final release were not being granted on the basis of objective criteria, such as time served, but rather at the discretion of the local judges responsible for the correct serving of the sentence. In particular, Furukawa abolished the legal requirement for these local judges to base their decisions in these matters on a formal assessment conducted by a psychologist or social worker who had never met the offender before. This was replaced by a similar assessment carried out by prison and NGO staff in the CR, who then sent their recommendation to the judge.[28] But this created a problem.

The principle in the LEP of 'individualised sentences' requires subjective assessments of the prisoner's progress. However, the judge, NGO technical staff and CR prison administration (Director and the Head of Discipline) all believed that *their* judgement was the one that should prevail, and this led to frequent differences of opinion. Divisions arose because the judge continued to hold *legal* responsibility for the prisoner, the state prison authorities had *security* concerns with regard to offenders, whilst the NGOs believed they had been handed the *moral* responsibility for offenders under the terms of the contract with the authorities. Thus the presence of state agents and civil society actors on an apparently equal footing within the CR prisons generated contests that are absent within the APACs run without state agents. As Darke notes, the APACs have managed to establish a penal space within which the volunteers and the prisoners themselves determine the progress made by an offender, and have pushed state criminal justice system operators to the margins.

Criminal justice system operators seemed to divide into two groups in relation to the CRs. Some local judges were very enthusiastic and were instrumental in bringing the community into the local jails, first through the APAC groups and then through the establishment of a CR. Others, however, were indifferent or even hostile, especially in São Paulo state. Each new CR had a purpose-built room where judges could come and conduct pre-trial hearings or deal with business related to sentencing, such as approving sentence remission, exeats, parole or regime progression. This was intended to cut out the need for police escorts to take prisoners to court, freeing police for other duties, and allowing judges to be more efficient. In a number of cases the judges refused to set foot in the CR, however, preferring to stay in their own territory and maintaining their social distance from the inmates. Similarly, many local judges and prosecutors failed to carry out the monthly visits to penal facilities under their jurisdiction that are required by the LEP and were entirely ignorant of the work of the CRs. This is partly due to a technical-

---

[28] Interview with Dr Furukawa, October 2004.

bureaucratic understanding of their responsibilities in relation to prisoners, which ignores the substantive element of ensuring that offenders are rehabilitated, as the LEP demands.[29] It may also be a characteristic of the post of the judge responsible for overseeing sentence serving, which some appeared to view as an undemanding sinecure.[30] In the APAC prisons in Minas Gerais, however, the upper echelons of the state judiciary formally support the initiative, making it more difficult for local judges to boycott them.[31]

Police, on the other hand, seemed to maintain an almost uniformly hostile attitude to the CRs, which they regarded as 'soft' on offenders. My fieldwork in 2004, the heyday of the CRs, suggested that officers were the most anxious to maintain the stigmatisation of offenders on which, in large part, their own professional identities depended and allegedly wasted no opportunity to give inmates a reminder of their proper status. I heard accounts from prisoners and staff of prisoners being beaten in the police vans on the way to court for hearings. Police frequently tried to reproduce what Garfinkel calls the 'status degradation ceremonies' prevalent in the mainstream criminal justice system by handcuffing non-violent prisoners, and insisting that prisoners kept their eyes downcast, and refrained from interacting with the officials. Moreover, they also deliberately 'invaded' the CR space with police dogs, and attempted, through sexual innuendo and other means, to undermine the authority of the mainly female prison governors. This notable gender dimension was the result of Dr Furukawa appointing social workers or psychologists, professions with high proportions of women in Brazil, which reflected both his emphasis on rehabilitation and the creation of an explicitly domestic environment that rejected the hyper-masculinity and violence of the mainstream prison system.[32]

Judges, prosecutors and police are criminal justice agents largely external to the day-to-day running of the prison. However, the governors of the CRs also had the task of managing several relationships within the facilities, between guards and prisoners, and between the state employees and the NGO staff. Volunteers also claimed that they had to resocialise not only the prisoners but also the guards, who took about a year to adjust themselves to the CR culture. The guards were challenged especially by the much reduced social distance between themselves and prisoners, and by an understanding of security

---

[29] In one CR, I witnessed an inspection by two representatives of the state prosecution service's internal affairs department. They evinced little interest in the rehabilitative regime and effectiveness of the CR, being most exercised by the fact that on their monthly visits local prosecutors were failing to sign a separate log from the judge, as required by the LEP.

[30] In some jurisdictions criminal judges also fulfil this function, whereas in larger ones judges are specifically appointed to this role.

[31] Jane Ribeiro Silva, *A execução penal à luz do método APAC* [Sentence Serving in the Light of the APAC Method] (Belo Horizonte: Tribunal de Justiça do Estado de Minas Gerais, 2012).

[32] This feminisation is less evident in the APACs, whose core leadership group is still mainly men. However, as the model diffuses to other locations in Brazil it is often being advocated by women in the justice system.

that relies on human interaction rather than physical barriers and the threat of force. Some never adapted and went back to working in the mainstream prison system. The rest – some of whom chose to work in the CRs; others who were simply transferred – generally accommodated themselves to a trade-off. They earned less money than in a large penitentiary (salaries are linked to staff/prisoner ratio and degree of risk), but benefited from the far less stressful environment and access to good food, free health services and better working conditions. Again, this problem was circumvented in the APACs, which have regarded state prison guards and their mentality as an obstacle to their method. Rather than retrain the guards they have simply replaced them with volunteers and trustee prisoners. This is an understandable circumvention of the problem. When I asked the governor of Bragança Paulista CR in the early days whether he attributed success to good staff, he laughed, and explained he had six guards on a rotating shift, 'two are drunkards, two are incompetent, and the other two have to keep an eye on them'.[33]

The other issue evident in the CR model related to the NGOs and their relationship to the prison staff. Both the APAC and CR models are hostage to the variable density and character of civil society. Sometimes existing NGOs offered to take on the CR partnership, as was the case of a group active around HIV/AIDS, which was already working with prisoners as a high risk group. In other cases, NGOs formed out of professional and social networks, such as the Rotary or Lions Club and the Bar Association. In Bragança Paulista, many of the volunteers and staff had been work colleagues at the local branch of Itaú Bank. APAC groups have a similarly heterogeneous composition, but increasingly include members of the criminal justice service, such as local prosecutors and judges. NGO members are also not immune from more ignoble motivations, such as personal advantage and status enhancement. Therefore, in all but the longest established CRs, it took time to iron out the tensions between the key figures in the prison administration, and the NGO as they negotiated a number of boundaries concerning discipline, security, 'expertise' in regard to the prisoners, mutual accountability and oversight, and status. In my interviews with CR prison governors and the head of the NGOs, I heard frequent complaints about their counterparts.[34] The limited supply of interested and competent civil society groups skewed the balance in the early days, so that when conflicts arose between the NGO and the prison service staff, the head of the prison service found it easier to replace a prison governor, rather than look for a new NGO. This is not unconnected with the constraints of voluntarism in a country with uneven density of civil society highlighted earlier, though doubtless the APAC group would argue that the quality control exercised over the franchise by the central APAC greatly reduced their instability as a partner NGO.

---

[33] Field visit with Amnesty International, June 1998.
[34] Field notes, October 2004.

Community, family and the offender

As ideas about a 'modern' penal regime consolidated in the early and mid-nineteenth century in the United States and Europe, institutions quite deliberately turned their backs on the surrounding communities. The chaos of the jails of the eighteenth century would be replaced by order, discipline, isolation, penitence and work. The prison was to be a place of rehabilitation of the prisoner's soul, achieved precisely by *de*socialising him and dramatically restricting his contact with other prisoners, his family, the community from which he came, even from the guards, for fear of contamination in both directions. Post-colonial Latin American states, influenced by European penal debates, articulated a similar aspiration to such practices and values, even if their capacity to implement them was much weaker.[35] Localised practices created penal institutions that were far from being closed or total institutions, exposing local communities in recent years to violence (through riots, breakouts and crime, prisoners bribing guards to let them out at night), and infectious disease such as tuberculosis and HIV spread to families and community on visitors' day and on release.[36]

The CRs and APACs are thus an attempt to turn this porosity to good ends, and resocialise the offender; that is, reconnect them with his or her community, and participate within the community of fellow offenders, analysed by Darke. The CRs and APACs donate to local nurseries, schools and hospitals the surpluses of the fruit and vegetables produced in their kitchen gardens, and food cooked on site. Some inmates are visible outside the prison, working in local businesses and on community projects. All CRs work with the offenders' families (a key criterion for transfer to a CR or APAC is that a relative living nearby will engage positively with them), and some extend to the families the prison's health, education and occupational training services. The level of contact between the local community and CR population varies, of course, and often reflects the character of the NGO that has taken on the co-administration. Some are closely linked to narrow professional groups (such as lawyers linked to the Brazilian Bar Association), whilst others have a broader social base. The former tend to be more 'professionalised' whereas the latter tend to make more use of volunteer labour and donations from the community, forming a broader bridge.

'The community' is not always initially well disposed towards penal institutions of any type. In one town I visited, the local media had whipped up a mild moral panic when a CR was proposed, and the municipal authorities refused to offer any land. However, once the old jail was closed down and the new CR operating following compulsory purchase of land, the mayor who had so

---

[35] Aguirre, 'Prisons and Prisoners in Modernising Latin America', 18.

[36] Visitors' day in a Brazilian prison is a whole day affair, with families mingling freely inside the prison, often eating food their relative has prepared for them or they have brought in. Conjugal contact is routine.

strenuously opposed it boasted in his campaign literature for re-election that he had been responsible for bringing it to the town. Attitudes towards the CRs tend to change when the population sees that offenders from elsewhere will not be 'imported' into their community, bringing with them an influx of poor families visiting or moving to be close to their incarcerated relatives, as would be the case with a normal penitentiary. An attitudinal survey demonstrated a high level of 'ownership' of offenders by people in towns with a CR, who were far less likely to agree with propositions such as 'prisoners should be treated badly because they have done wrong' and more likely to agree that 'prisoners should be treated with humanity', and 'the rehabilitation of prisoners is the responsibility of everyone, not just of police, judges and the prison authorities'.[37]

Conclusion

This analysis of the CRs, in contradistinction to both the mainstream prison system and its close relative, the APACs, raised questions about how 'the community', via organised civil society, in *partnership* with the state, can reassert some ownership of the criminal justice system, from which it is largely excluded. Restorative justice, developed in other parts of the world, represents one way of rebalancing relationships between offender, state and community. Indeed the CRs (implicitly) and the APACs (explicitly) see restoration as a key aspect of resocialisation.[38] The reclamation of the offender for the community has been attempted in other ways, specifically through the complete, or partial, occupation of the penitentiary space. The CR experiment, in particular, is a liberal one that places its faith not in God's redemption, but in the potential for a democratic state to deliver on justice, fairness, safety, order, humanity, trust and opportunities for personal development (Liebling's measures of 'moral performance'), even as the Brazilian prison authorities maintain contradictory, but interpenetrating, penal universes where the state either enacts, or permits others to enact, multiple forms of violence and exclusion. For example, just four months before Pedrinhas prison exploded, a new APAC unit was set up in a wing of that prison to take prisoners eligible for a semi-open regime. The prison system, like the police, craves society's legitimation and requires its collaboration, but resists ceding power to it. However, whilst the dimensions of Brazil's prison crisis may overcome the resistance of state agents to working with civil society, issues of partnership, power, ownership and ethos will remain very much a contested and negotiated terrain.

[37] Secretaria de Administração Penitenciária, 'Centros de Ressocialização: A questão penitenciária e a opinião pública' [Resocialisation Centres: The Prison Issue and Public Opinion] (São Paulo: Governo do Estado de São Paulo, 2002).

[38] Restorative justice, as a concept, was barely known in Brazil until the late 1990s, when a number of conferences were held with international experts. It is still not much referenced with the criminal justice system as a whole, even when restorative practices are used – for example in the small claims courts when offenders have to pay fines, do community service or undertake therapy.

13 Recoverers helping recoverers

Discipline and peer-facilitated rehabilitation in Brazilian faith-based prisons

Sacha Darke

At 5 p.m. on 10 July 2012 a scuffle broke out in the semi-open unit of Franz de Castro prison,[1] when an inmate from the unit's prisoner council, the CSS (*Conselho de Sinceridade e Solidariedade* – Sincerity and Solidarity Council), approached another inmate in the workshop to escort him back to his cell. Both had to be physically restrained by other prisoners. The president of the CSS immediately called for a disciplinary hearing, where, following brief witness testimonies, it was decided that the second prisoner, who had picked up a metal instrument, was mostly to blame. When the president informed the CSS that the governor's immediate reaction to the incident had been to suggest both prisoners return to the closed unit, members were defensive of their colleague. They further complained that the governor was also partly to blame, having only that morning overridden a decision they had made not to allow the second prisoner to work for the day after he had refused to stand up during morning prayers. Later I discovered that while the CSS was solely responsible for dealing with breaches of low-level offences, the governor had been right to insist prison rules only required the offender lose a day's association. Nonetheless, some members insisted it was still a decision that was theirs to make, and the governor had not understood that the culprit, a known troublemaker, was bound to use the fact he had worked all day as an excuse for argument. In a clear show of defiance, each witness, including several CSS members, told the president they had not seen any weapons being raised. Still, at the end of the meeting the CSS explained to the governor they would be recommending the second prisoner return to the closed unit, but that the first receive no more than a few days' cellular confinement. When the prison's disciplinary committee received the CSS's formal report on the incident, it agreed to their decision.

Franz de Castro is one of over 30 voluntary sector administered APAC (*Associação de Proteção e Assistência ao Condenado* – Association for the Protection and Assistance of Convicts/the Condemned) prisons that have opened in Brazil over the past 40 years. The title APAC is associated with a Catholic Cursillo group that in the early 1970s opened Brazil's first voluntary

---

[1] Franz de Castro is a pseudonym. It is located in the state of Minas Gerais, Brazil.

sector prison wing at Humaitá, São José dos Campos, São Paulo, before taking full control of the prison in 1984. Of primary importance to its founders was that the prison was able to operate apart from the common prison system, with minimal interference from state authorities. In 1985 the group established a second non-profit legal entity to inaugurate a new prison in Itaúna, Minas Gerais.

Only a handful of APAC prisons opened over the next 20 years. The movement has advanced considerably since the mid-2000s, however, principally in Minas Gerais, where in 2001 judicial authorities instigated a project aimed at encouraging judges to support requests to open new APAC prisons, and from inmates in the common prison system for transfer to them. More important still, in 2006 state legislation came into effect that authorised prison authorities to enter into formal agreements to fund the building and maintenance of APAC prisons irrespective of the fact they operated without state employees, including police or prison officers.[2] In the past few years the APAC movement has spread to other parts of Brazil, for instance Maranhão and most recently Paraná (which opened their first APAC prisons in 2008 and 2013 respectively).

Since 1995 APAC prisons have been regulated by FBAC (the *Fraternidade Brasileira de Assistência aos Condenados* – Brazilian Fraternity for the Assistance of Convicts). Founded by the original APAC group in São José dos Campos, FBAC moved to Itaúna in 2004. By 2012, 147 voluntary sector organisations had been registered with FBAC across 17 states, including 94 in Minas Gerais.[3] Although the majority of these groups had only recently been constituted and had not yet secured permission or funding to start building, 41 APAC prisons were in operation by the end of 2013, 35 in Minas Gerais.[4] Significantly, FBAC no longer regulates Humaitá or other prisons in

---

[2] Two factors help explain the recent successes of the APAC movement in Minas Gerais. First, and more generally, the Brazilian justice system is largely fragmented. Institutions and practitioners enjoy levels of autonomy that generally work as a shield to outside criticism, but at the same time may open up spaces for penal reform when local actors are particularly demotivated and indifferent to prisons and prisoners, as they were in Minas Gerais in the early 2000s. See Fiona Macaulay, "Civil Society-State Partnerships for the Promotion of Citizen Security in Brazil," *SUR – International Journal on Human Rights* 2.2 (2005), 141–65. Here, it should also be noted that the Brazilian Ministry of Justice has limited influence on local authorities, allowing for quite different prison policies to operate in different states. See Fiona Macaulay, "Modes of Prison Administration, Control and Governmentality in Latin America: Adoption, Adaptation and Hybridity," *Conflict, Security and Development* 13.4 (2013), 361–92. Second, APAC prisons attracted the attention of state authorities for the fact they were being run at a third of the cost per prisoner as state prisons. See Carlos Eduardo Guerra Silva, *Gestão Social em Perspectiva: Entrevista com Valdeci Antônio Ferreira*, Universidade Federal de Minas Gerais, accessed 17 December 2013, www.ufmg.br/proex/cpinfo/ufmgtube/gestaosocial/valdeci-antonio-ferreira.

[3] Fundação AVSI, *Um Novo Olhar além dos Muros: O Potencial Gestão no Fortalecimento das APACs de Minas Gerais* (Belo Horizonte: Fundação AVSI, 2012).

[4] Tribunal de Justiça do Estado de Minas Gerais, "Programa Novos Rumos – Metodologia APAC," Tribunal de Justiça do Estado de Minas Gerais, accessed 18 December 2013, www.tjmg.jus.br/portal/acoes-e-programas/programa-novos-rumos/apac.

São Paulo. A further 21 voluntary sector prisons were opened in the state following the introduction of government funding in 1996, many by groups that were likewise constituted under the title APAC. In contrast to the situation in Minas Gerais, however, these CR (*Centro de Resocialização* – Resocialisation Centre – CR) prisons are administered in partnership with prison authorities (see Chapter 12, this volume). State prison guards retain responsibility for discipline and security. Moreover, since 2006 prison authorities have gradually replaced their contracts with the voluntary sector with private sector provision.[5]

Similar to the CR prison system, APAC prisons are renowned for being more humane and therapeutic than other penal institutions in the country, and for having lower levels of recidivism. From this starting point, accounts of CR/APAC prisons typically centre on one of four issues: inmates' access to rehabilitation-orientated activities such as education, therapy and work; the extent that the apparent success of the prisons is the result of them operating as a "system within a system" which means they can refuse entry to and expel prisoners they consider unsuitable; the role (more so in the case of APAC prisons) played by religion; and whether (again, mostly concerning APAC prisons) they are replicable across the country and in other parts of the world.[6] These are debates to which I directly contribute only in the conclusion. Less explored in the literature, and my focus here, is the self-governing nature of APAC prisons, in particular the role of prisoners and former prisoners, or in APAC terminology, the role of *o recuperando ajudando o recuperando* (recoverers helping recoverers). I pay most attention to the position held by the CSS, not only in the adjudication and administering of punishments, as highlighted in the event used to open this chapter, but also in maintaining prison routines. We will see that such prisoner participation is at the heart of the APAC vision, including its approach to rehabilitation. Most of my illustrations are likewise taken from Franz de Castro, a men's prison that I visited on a number of occasions in 2012. Between 2010 and 2012 I conducted extended visits to a further four men's and two women's APAC prisons in Minas Gerais, as well as one men's CR prison in São Paulo. Over four days I also participated in the fortieth anniversary/seventh national conference of the APAC movement in Itaúna, attended by prison staff and inmates from across the country, and

---

[5] Brazil opened its first private prison in 1999. In contrast to North American and European models of prison privatisation, in most states the private (or voluntary) sector provides services but not prison guards. See Macaulay, "Modes of Prison Administration," 373. The APAC prison system remains the only exception.

[6] For literature on APAC prisons in English, see for example Byron Johnson, "Assessing the Impact of Religious Programs and Prison Industry on Recidivism: An Exploratory Study," *Texas Journal of Corrections*, February (2002), 7–11; César Leal, "The Prison System in Brazil: The APAC Experience," *Caribbean Journal of Criminology and Social Psychology* 4.1/2 (1999), 254–67; Jonathan Burnside (with Loucks, N., Adler, J. and Rose, G), *My Brother's Keeper: Faith-Based Units in Prisons* (Cullompton: Willan, 2005); Lyla Bugara, "Unique Brazilian Prison Alternative Celebrates 40-Year Anniversary," *Prison Legal News* March (2012), 44.

in a one-day joint staff–prisoner event held in preparation for the conference. During these days I was accommodated by FBAC alongside Mário Ottoboni, founder of APAC and FBAC, and author of numerous books on the APAC methodology.

Self-governing prison communities

What drew my attention to APAC prisons was not so much the conditions in which they hold people, but the extent to which they are administered by their inmates, alongside, but mostly in place of, prison staff. This has been the central focus of my research on Brazilian prisons to date. In previous publications, I have focused on the common prison system, particularly the means by which, in circumstances of material deprivation and acute staff shortage, officers and inmates cobble together customary orders in which prisoners are required to take on the role of janitors and sometimes prison guards; I have also examined the reasons why prison wings are left in the hands of inmate hierarchies, sometimes managed by prison authorities, but more often left to develop organically or under the influence of criminal gangs.[7] Meanwhile, inmates and prison staff rely on prisoners' families and the voluntary sector to provide essential goods and service such as clothing, medicines, health care and legal representation. I have conceptualised these characteristics of Brazilian prisons in terms of situational adjustments to state abandonment, and addressed the challenges the self-governing nature of Brazilian prisons poses to our understanding of post-colonial prisons more widely. Within this framework of analysis, I have questioned the explanatory value of the classic sociology of prison life literature to prisons beyond the developed world, in particular theories on panopticism, the pains of imprisonment and total institutions associated with Michel Foucault,[8] Gresham Sykes[9] and Irvine Goffman.[10] I return to panopticism in the conclusion to this chapter. We will

---

[7] See, principally, "Managing without Guards in a Brazilian Police Lockup," *Focaal – Journal of Global and Historical Anthropology* 68 (2014), 55–67; "Entangled Staff-Inmate Relations," *Prison Service Journal* 207 (2013), 16–22; "Inmate Governance in Brazilian Prisons," *Howard Journal of Criminal Justice* 52.3 (2013), 272–84. Note that in this literature I warn against falling into the positivist trap of treating Brazilian prison gangs as necessarily predatory or hierarchical. Prisoners tend to be allocated to gang wings on the basis of living in an area under the gang's control rather than being active members of it, and inmate leaders are as likely to be selected as a result of the length of time they have been incarcerated as their affiliations on the outside. As such, I have emphasised the need to analyse prison gangs and organic prisoner organisation as a continuum: to regard the former as a rather chaotic attempt by prisoners and staff to formalise the latter.

[8] Michel Foucault, *Discipline and Punish: The Birth of the Prison* (London: Penguin, 1977).

[9] Gresham Sykes, *The Society of Captives: A Study of a Maximum Security Prison* (Princeton: Princeton University Press, 1958).

[10] Ervin Goffman, "On the Characteristics of Total Institutions," in Donald Cressey (ed.), *The Prison: Studies in Institutional Organization and Change* (New York: Holt, Rinehart and Winston, 1961).

see that Foucault's work on the "birth of the prison" provides limited tools for analysing the common prison system, but is of greater use in analysing APAC prisons.

As such, APAC prisons are fascinating for the extent to which they depart from certain aspects of the common Brazilian prison system, but also comply with others. In the words of Ottoboni, what the APAC movement rejects is the view that the majority of prisoners are "beyond recovery, social rubbish."[11] The prisoner, as the abbreviation APAC indicates, is condemned by society and becomes "the repository of distrust."[12] Even in the best prisons, the inmate is eventually forgotten: "they give the prisoner a profession, but forget him as a man. At the end of his sentence, he returns to the community as a delinquent with a profession, with no points of reference but the police."[13] What the APAC methodology embraces, though for very different reasons (rehabilitation rather than survival), Ottoboni stresses, is the need to maintain prisoners' connections to the community and for prisoners, as people who have lost sight of what it means to be part of the community, to learn to care for one another:

> We have discovered that social defence best resides in the treatment of the delinquent ... we know that the state is impotent to exercise this mission and only with the participation of the community, preparing the prisoner and supervising the work of those responsible for the security and administration of penal institutions, will it be possible to reduce reoffending rates ... We know, finally, that the convict, on gaining liberty, returns to their city of origin ... It is fundamental to teach the recoverer to live in community.[14]

This emphasis on community/peer-facilitated rehabilitation is reflected in the definition of an APAC prison used by FBAC. To qualify as an APAC prison, we have seen that a penal institution must operate without the presence of police or prison officers. From here, FBAC divides the prisons that it regulates into two categories: those that fulfil all aspects of the APAC methodology, allocated to just four prisons (three men's prisons and one women's prison), and the remainder that do not. The methodology itself contains 12 components, of which seven (*trabalho* – work; *assistência jurídica* – judicial assistance; *religião* – religion; *assistência a saúde* – health assistance; *valorização humana* – human valorisation; *mérito* – merit; *jornada de libertação com Cristo* – programme of liberation with Christ) concern methods of rehabilitation. Of greater interest for the moment, five (*participação da comunidade* – participation of the community; *o recuperando ajudando o*

---

[11] Mário Ottoboni, *Vamos Matar o Criminoso? Método APAC* (São Paulo: Paulinas, 2006), 30.
[12] Ibid., 66.
[13] Ibid., 45.
[14] Ibid., 37, 67.

recuperando – recoverers helping recoverers; *família* – family; *educador social e o curso para sua formação* – literally, social educator and their training course; *Centro de Reintegração Social* – Social Reintegration Centre) relate to the vehicles by which rehabilitation is delivered. I return to peer-facilitated rehabilitation and the concept of recoverers helping recoverers in a moment. First I turn briefly to the broader notion of community participation, of which the remaining three elements of the methodology (family, social education and social reintegration) form major parts.

Community-facilitated rehabilitation

To quote Ottoboni once more, APAC prisons are essentially designed to restore prisoners' bonds to their community: "[Punishment should take] the form of a dialogue between prisoners and society, and this is only possible if society is present in prisons."[15] To this end, APAC prisons should be small and only accept prisoners from the local area. This was the case at four of the men's APAC prisons I visited in 2012, which all had fewer than 70 inmates, and both of the women's prisons, which had around 35 inmates. All of these prisons are located in towns of less than 100,000 inhabitants.

From this point of departure, the APAC methodology adds three further official and one unofficial requirement. First, in order to fulfil their role as centres of social reintegration, and allow inmates to serve their full sentence close to home, APAC prisons are required to contain open and semi-open as well as closed units. In Franz de Castro, the semi-open units are sub-divided into two regimes, one for inmates given permission to work outside the prison, the other for inmates working in the prison bakery (which sells to local shops) or, more significant here, in full-time trusty positions (I return to this in the next section). The women's prisons both take remand as well as sentenced prisoners, in recognition that, due to the relatively small number of women offenders in the towns, there are no local women's prisons where they might otherwise be sent by the courts to await trial.

Second, it is stipulated that inmates should not only have the right to weekly visits from their families, as in the common prison system, but the prison should also support inmates' families. Each prison has a team that regularly visits families, and where necessary provides them with a *cesta básica* (basket of essential goods required by a family for one month). Families are also invited to participate alongside prisoners in the programme of liberation with Christ, a yearly three-day event based on the methodology of the Catholic movement from which the first APAC group emerged. Besides these common requirements, I observed a number of areas of specific practice aimed at maintaining contact between inmates and their families, and equally, wider contact between the prison and local community. At one of the men's

---

[15] Mário Ottoboni, *Testemunhos de minha Vida e a Vida de meus Testemunhos* (São José dos Campos: Netebooks, 2012), 52.

prisons, for instance, *reuniões da família* (family reunions) are held between families, prisoners and staff every Monday (family reunions are also held at many other APAC prisons, though not always with the same frequency). In addition, inmates held in semi-open conditions are involved in building and repairing families' homes. The family of the inmate nominated *recuperando do mês* (recoverer of the month) is provided with a *cesta básica* worth R$200 (£57).

Next, the methodology emphasises social proximity between inmates and prison staff. Three major points follow. First, not only prisoners but prison staff should live in the locality of the prison. During my research, inmates and staff often emphasised the advantage of having known each other prior to prison. Sometimes these relationships were personal. For instance, I met one *plantanista* (caretaker, the APAC equivalent of a prison guard) whose close relative was incarcerated in the prison where they worked. One prison director and one FBAC employee had wives or husbands that were currently imprisoned within the APAC system. Equally important, the emphasis on social proximity also means staff positions should be filled by volunteers, again including prisoners' relatives. In Minas Gerais the only salaried APAC prison positions are the director and *plantanistas*. Recruited as social educators, the APAC methodology emphasises that the work of APAC staff should be based on "gratuity, on service to others."[16] Finally, staff have to be trained not just to support, but also to set a good example to prisoners: "to be correct in your private life, to have exemplary conduct in your family, to avoid any type of privilege and to be a friend of everyone."[17] Married volunteers are also expected to become a *padrinho* (godparent) to a prisoner, to oversee their rehabilitation, and to provide a substitute family.

Finally, many former prisoners return to work within the APAC prison system. While ex-prisoner participation does not form a part of the official methodology, it is a central feature of APAC practice. In addition to those who return as volunteers, former prisoners make up a significant number of paid members of staff. In 2012 four of the 11 FBAC staff were former APAC prisoners. These included two prison inspectors and two senior managers, one of who was in charge of developing the methodology. Several APAC prison governors also had prison experience as inmates, including the governors of at least two of the prisons I visited. The current governor of Franz de Castro was the first not to have been a prisoner. One FBAC manager became governor at the prison while he was still on conditional release. One of the current former-prisoner APAC governors that I met was likewise still on licence. Similarly, many people that serve time in APAC prisons return to work as *plantanistas*. Many, perhaps the majority of *plantanistas*, were previously incarcerated at the prison where they work. One *plantanista* at Franz de Castro was among the first prisoners in Humaitá. One of the former-prisoner

---

16   Ottoboni, *Vamos Matar o Criminoso?*, 89.
17   Ibid., 90.

governors I met made the journey from prisoner representative to (within 18 months of release) *plantanista* and later governor. The seventh national APAC conference included a parallel session on the role of former prisoners. Participants spoke of the advantage of former prisoners "knowing the ropes," and of the added legitimacy that they held in the eyes of current prisoners. Most of all they spoke of the unique position they held as former offenders that had themselves been reformed by the APAC prison system. As one former-prisoner *plantanista* put it, their main role was to act as mentors to current prisoners.

Peer-facilitated rehabilitation

Former-prisoner participation bridges the gap between the ideals of community and peer-facilitated rehabilitation. As for the role assigned to current prisoners, the first point that needs to be noted is that all APAC inmates work full-time. At the beginning of their sentence, and as part of the first stage of rehabilitation (which focuses on learning to live communally), inmates are required to engage in *trabalho laborterápico* (work therapy), centred on the production of arts and crafts. Towards the end of their sentence, and as part of their final stage of rehabilitation (reintegration into the wider community), they are entitled to paid *trabalho especializado* (skilled work), though as in the common prison system this largely depends on companies setting up prison workshops (I did not come across any active workshops at the prisons I visited) or on prisoners securing jobs outside. Of particular significance for this chapter, as a major part of the middle stage of rehabilitation (learning to serve) APAC inmates are recruited to run their prisons. Again, similar to other Brazilian prisons, inmates are involved in almost every aspect of prison work, both on and off the wings. However, unlike other prisons, all inmate roles are officially recognised and compensated (though, as is typically the case in the common prison system as well, they gain their statutory right to one day's remission in sentence for each three days worked, but few gain their statutory right to be paid three-quarters of the minimum wage). In all cases, including the sale of arts and crafts, deductions are made by the prison for inmates' keep. Inmates are also required to contribute to a *caixa comum* (collection box) used by prisoners to purchase common goods, for instance, televisions, art materials or decorations for family days. The APAC methodology terms all prison work *trabalho social* (social work).

At Franz de Castro half of inmates work in some form of *trabalho social*, including a third of prisoners on the closed unit and two-thirds of prisoners on the semi-open unit (those that do not work externally). Every inmate is involved in *trabalho social* in the open unit of Franz de Castro and at least one of the women's prisons I visited, for the simple reason that they are required to take it in turns to cook. The majority of inmates at Franz de Castro work in domestic positions. Among these, the only paid positions are in the bakery, the kitchen, and at a small farm outside the building, which produces all of the meat and vegetables consumed at the prison.

More controversially, APAC prisons also recruit inmates to help take care of security. Formally known as *porteiros* (doormen) and *auxiliares de plantão* (assistant caretakers), these prisoners support the (one or two) *plantanistas* on duty at any time, assisting at the front gate, and taking charge of the entrances to the cell block, individual wings, cells and dormitories. Other security-related duties include patrolling the prison, searching prisoners returning to the closed unit from external visits, and checking food parcels delivered by families for prisoners on the closed unit. Although they are not authorised to open the front gate or step outside the prison, one *porteiro* at Franz de Castro was recently commended when he pursued and apprehended a cousin who had escaped.

Finally, inmates are engaged to support staff in teaching other prisoners how to live communally. Here the APAC methodology emphasises the role inmates should play in managing everyday prison life, in organising activities, and keeping order. Prisoners entrusted with these tasks are divided into two groups: *representantes da cela ou dormitório* (cell or dormitory representatives) and the CSS. Again, the parallels with the common prison system, where inmate leaders are left in charge of much that happens on the wings, are at first sight quite extraordinary.[18]

APAC prisoners are typically held four to a 12m^2 cell in closed units, and in six to 12-bed dormitories in semi-open units. Each cell or dormitory is represented by one prisoner. At the staff–prisoner event held prior to the seventh national APAC conference, the FBAC employee in charge of developing the APAC methodology explained that *representantes* are essentially tasked to manage five areas of anti-social behaviour among their cell-mates seen as forming the basis of crime or recidivism: indiscipline, lack of leadership, irresponsibility, disorganisation, and the inmate "code of honour" (principally, not to inform on one another) that they might previously have been exposed to in the common prison system. These underlying principles of the APAC approach to rehabilitation are reflected in the prison rules produced by FBAC.[19] *Representantes* have 18 specific obligations, including holding weekly *reuniões da cela* (cell meetings) to discuss prisoners' obligations, anxieties and needs, organising cleaning rotas, enforcing rules of conduct such as being silent between 10 p.m. and 6 a.m. and being clean, tidy and well presented (in addition to a general clause on in-cell discipline), and (as voluntary prison staff) encouraging and demonstrating (by example) exemplary conduct, as well as participating in all prison activities.

Cell and dormitory *representantes* are themselves selected and accountable to the CSS. The presidents of the three CSSs in an APAC prison (one for

---

[18] For analysis of the role played by inmate leaders in the common prison system, see Darke, "Inmate Governance in Brazilian Prisons."

[19] FBAC, *Regulamento Disciplinar APAC* (unpublished, 2012).

each unit) are accountable to the prison governor. Once appointed by the prison administration, the presidents select up to eight other CSS members. According to the APAC prison rules, the overriding task of a unit's CSS is to "guide inmates on the organisation [of the prison], distribution of tasks, discipline and safety."[20] Besides supervising the work of the *representantes*, major CSS tasks on a unit include: looking after the physical infrastructure of the prison (buildings, sewage, water and electrical supplies and so on); managing, as previously noted, the *caixa comum*, as well as keeping records on the purchase, storage and sale of, for instance, tools, canteen and art supplies, and the sale of artwork and confectionaries; arranging appointments with doctors and psychologists; maintaining medical records and dispensing medicines; advising the prison administration on the needs of individual inmates and the suitability of particular inmates to different forms of *trabalho social*; and, at one of the prisons I visited, writing reports on inmates' suitability for home visits. More generally, the CSS is responsible for monitoring everyday prison routines on its unit, for instance morning assemblies, work, meals, and use of communal televisions and DVD players in the evening. The CSS president acts as the link between the prison administration and all other inmates on their unit. Specific duties include ensuring prison orders are followed, informing the administration of potential risks to prison order, running weekly prisoner assemblies and weekly meetings between the CSS and *representantes*, explaining prison norms to new arrivals, and checking that *porteiros* and *auxiliaries de plantão* get to work. The president also plays a small, but critical role in security, supervising the work of *porteiros* in searching prisoners. (When *porteiros* search family parcels, on the other hand, they must do so in the presence of a *plantanista*.)

The most contentious duties of the CSS concern the role it plays alongside the cell and dormitory *representantes* in maintaining discipline. In part, this involves rewarding positive conduct. For instance, at the end of each month the CSS identify one prisoner and one cell/dormitory as the *recuperando modelo* (model recoverer) and *cela mais organizada* (most organized cell) *do mês* (of the month). At Franz de Castro a trophy is presented to the most organised cell/dormitories and a toy pig to the least organised. Of greater interest, in regards to the boundary between prison inmates and prison staff, is the task given to the CSS in enforcing the APAC prison rules. These contain 77 disciplinary offences (or house rules, as prisoners often refer to them). Low level offences include not following orders, using something belonging to another without permission, cleaning or drying clothes in a non-designated area, and wearing shorts in the presence of visitors or volunteers. Following verbal and written warnings, a third breach of discipline attracts an initial punishment of one day's loss of association; a fourth offence in a calendar month attracts a penalty of a week's loss of association; inmates lose the

---

[20] Ibid., 65.

right to both association and visits for a week in the case of a fifth offence. Medium level offences (punishable by up to seven days' segregation) include verbal abuse and hunger strike. Serious offences (which may result in 30 days in isolation, or in inmates being returned to the closed unit or the common prison system) include escape, subverting order and physical abuse. The CSS is solely responsible for adjudicating and administering punishments for low level offences. Medium level offences are dealt with by the prison governor, and serious offences by a disciplinary committee made up of the governor, and other senior prison administrators and *plantanistas*. However, prisoners investigate and write a report on all alleged breaches of discipline. They also make an initial suggestion of punishment for medium and serious offences. As we saw in the introduction to this chapter, combined with their role in adjudicating on the facts of alleged breaches, in practice this gives the CSS influence over the outcomes of all disciplinary hearings.

Recoverers helping recoverers

To summarise and conclude, the APAC methodology takes state abandonment of prisoners as its starting point. It aims to rescue inmates from the common prison system, where they are treated as being beyond reform. Its vision is of community self-governance, not state-governance, of community-led reintegration rather than state-led exclusion. This is reflected in three interrelating characteristics of APAC prisons. First, APAC prisons are self-governing in the sense that they are largely administered by their inmates. An extreme example of the acutely understaffed prisons found, across much of Brazil and other parts of the post-colonial world, that little if any significant distinction is made between trusty inmates and inmate leaders, prisoner collaboration and self-governance. In much the same way the term *faxina* came to signify all forms of prisoner participation in the infamous, now deactivated, Carandiru, Latin America's largest prison, in 1992 the scene of one of the world's most tragic prison incidents when inmate leaders in the "first-timers" block failed to prevent a minor dispute from escalating into a riot that resulted in a specialist police unit killing over 100 prisoners, most of whom had lain down their weapons and retired to their cells.[21] Just as important, in a radical interpretation of the therapeutic community model, the APAC methodology insists that all people working and incarcerated in the prisons come from the local community. Of particular note here, in the case of staff, a special case is made for people with past experience of prison, some of whom are fast-tracked to the top of their profession before they have even completed their sentence.

Finally, this time in a radical departure from the common prison system, APAC prisons can be described as self-governing in the sense that inmates

---

[21] Sacha Darke, "Estação Carandiru," *Prison Service Journal* 199 (2012), 26–28.

and local people participate in administering them in order to facilitate rehabilitation rather than survival, more specifically to facilitate prisoner self-help. Here the concept of recoverers helping recoverers comes to the fore. Similar to the methodologies utilised by peer-support groups such as Alcoholics Anonymous and Narcotics Anonymous, APAC prisons treat rehabilitation as a personal journey, moreover a journey that is best facilitated by fellow recoverers, on a reciprocal basis. As Burnside *et al.* explain in their analysis of the influence of the movement on therapeutic prisons in the United States and United Kingdom, the APAC vision of rehabilitation is premised on the view that prisoners' problems lie with themselves, but that the first step to recovery must be made by society. This requires the involvement of people who have been "healed enough to give an honest account of the failures in their [own] lives."[22] With its emphasis on empowerment, introspection and social connectedness, all of which are at the centre of theories on criminal desistance, there is plenty of scope for the APAC prison system to be replicated beyond Minas Gerais and Brazil. Importantly, the APAC prisons that have recently opened in other parts of the country, for example, in Paraná,[23] do not privilege religious service over other aspects of the methodology (though, it should also be noted that FBAC have resisted proposals to open secular APAC prison in Minas Gerais[24]). Yet all operate without prison guards. In the United States and United Kingdom, in contrast, the units analysed by Burnside *et al.* take religious service rather than prisoner participation as their starting points. As for the question whether APAC prisons are more effective than other prisons, Burnside *et al.* bemoan the methodological weaknesses of the only existing quantitative study,[25] which found a three-year recidivism rate of just 16 per cent for prisoners released from Humaitá in 1996. The informal records of recidivism maintained by individual APAC prisons consistently purport to demonstrate equally positive results. However, until a comprehensive study is completed, the validity of these statistics remains in dispute. As noted in the introduction, such a study will also need to take account of the fact that APAC prisons operate as a "system within a system," in particular that they only take prisoners who accept their guilt and express a willingness to participate in a full-time regime of activities.

This brings us onto the last characteristic of APAC prisons that falls within the recoverer-helping-recoverer paradigm, and to the usefulness of Foucault's theory of panopticism: the emphasis put on prisoners leading regimented lives. In general, there is a distinct lack of fit between Western European and North American analyses of the development of prison as a correctional

[22] Burnside *et al. My Brother's Keepers*, 11.

[23] Personal communication, Maria Tereza Uille Gomes, Secretary of Justice, Paraná, 13 July 2012.

[24] Personal communication, Andreza de Lima Menezes, President of APAC Feminina, Belo Horizonte, 30 June 2012.

[25] Johnson, "Assessing the Impact."

institution and the reality of everyday prison life in Brazil. According to Foucault, prisons are meant to be "complete institutions" that aim to transform inmates' characters through continuous observation and the imposition of rigid routines, work and education. A key characteristic of Brazilian and other post-colonial prisons literature are efforts to explain, on the contrary, the continuation of imperial and pre-modern prison practices of corporal punishments and social defence. Where radical critiques of Foucault in Western Europe and North America question the extent to which prisons have ever lived up to their purported aims to change as well as punish offenders, there is clearer consensus among post-colonial scholars that – irrespective of the expectations of the prison reformers who imported them – penal institutions in African and Asian colonies and post-colonial Latin America countries, including Brazil, were never institutions of reform.[26] It can be said that Brazilian prisons achieve certain levels of situational control, often with the implicit or explicit support of prisoners, but it is difficult to conclude that one of the objectives of the common Brazilian prison system is to rehabilitate offenders.

Yet, throughout this chapter I have endeavoured to emphasise the centrality of rehabilitation to the APAC mission. We have seen that prisoners' lives are micro-managed to the finest detail. APAC prisons depart from Foucault's analysis of the panoptic institution only in the sense that the "judges of normality" are not professionals, but ordinary members of the prison community. Finally, we have seen further that APAC prison regimes are based less on the ideals of mutual support as on mutual control, this time in contrast to wider developments in the peer-support/therapeutic community movement. In this regard, APAC prisons remain conservative institutions that are stuck in the past. Recoverers are held solely responsible for breaking their ties to the community, and the only thing required of the community is to provide the conditions for them to rehabilitate themselves.

---

[26] Frank Dikötter and Ian Brown (eds), *Cultures of Confinement: A History of the Prison in Africa, Asia, and Latin America* (Ithaca: Cornell University Press, 2007); Amy Chazkel, "Social Life and Civic Education in the Rio de Janeiro City Jail," *Journal of Social History* 42.3 (2009), 697–731; Ricardo Salvatore and Carlos Aguirre (eds), *The Birth of the Penitentiary in Latin America* (Texas: University of Texas Press, 1996).

Index

.